# NECESSARY VIRTUE

## The Pragmatic Origins of
## Religious Liberty in New England

### CHARLES P. HANSON

UNIVERSITY PRESS OF VIRGINIA

*Charlottesville and London*

THE UNIVERSITY PRESS OF VIRGINIA

Printed in the United States of America

*First published 1998*

The paper used in this publication meets the minimum requirements of the American National Standard for Information Sciences— Permanence of Paper for Printed Library Materials, ANSI Z39.48-1984.

Library of Congress Cataloging-in-Publication Data

Hanson, Charles P., 1960–
    Necessary virtue : the pragmatic origins of religious liberty in
New England / Charles P. Hanson.
        p.   cm.
    Includes bibliographical references and index.
    ISBN 0-8139-1794-8 (cloth : alk. paper)
    1. Freedom of religion—New England—History—18th century.
2. Anti-Catholicism—New England—History—18th century.
3. New England—Church history—18th century.   4. New England—Politics and government.   5. France—Foreign relations—
United States.   6. United States—Foreign relations—France.
7. United States—History—Revolution, 1775–1783—Participation,
French.   I. Title.
BR530.H37   1998
323.44′2′097409033—dc21                                    97-45092
                                                                CIP

*To*

D.R.H.

*

*and to the memory of*

H.P.H.

*Let tyrants shake their iron rods,*
*And Slaver'y clank her galling chains,*
*We fear them not, We trust in God,*
*New England's God forever reigns.*
—WILLIAM BILLINGS, "CHESTER," 1770

The earliest days of a state are
generally the most pure in religion.
The prevailing principles of
individuals at such a season, the
providential interpositions that they
are witnesses to, and are strongly
affected with from the peculiarity of
their situation, and the modes they
are under a necessity of adopting,
lead to it.—WILLIAM GORDON, ELECTION
SERMON, JULY 19, 1775

# Contents

# Acknowledgments

I gratefully acknowledge the many debts incurred in researching and preparing this book. I benefited greatly from the financial assistance and expert guidance made available to me as a Peterson Fellow of the American Antiquarian Society, Mellon Fellow of the Massachusetts Historical Society, Keck Fellow of the Henry E. Huntington Library, and Canadian Studies Research Fellow at the National Archives of Canada. Librarians at Doe Library of the University of California at Berkeley, Houghton Library of Harvard University, Davidson Library of the University of California at Santa Barbara, Love Library of the University of Nebraska at Lincoln, Sawyer Library of Williams College, and Perkins Library of Doane College helped me at every turn. For gracious hospitality to a penurious itinerant, I thank Jackson Galloway, Anita Carlson, Neil Hunter, Paul Grisar, Bruce and Elizabeth Kieffer, John and Karen King, the late William Knight, and Wallace Bird. For helpful advice and suggestions on the manuscript, Robert Middlekauff, James Kettner, Arthur Holden, Jenny Franchot, Matthew Willen, Benjamin Woods Labaree, Stephen Marini, Lisa Rubens, Wendy Nicholson, Ann Fairfax Withington, Frank Cogliano, James German, Carol Lilly, Philip Goff, Richard Holway, Jay Gilbert, and Allen Guelzo. For logistical support beyond the call of professional duty, Kathryn Sand and Sheryl Skala of the Doane Educational Office Personnel Association. For all of the above and considerably more besides, Katharine Cheap.

# Introduction

Posterity is familiar with the benefits the alliance with France provided to the American cause during the Revolution. Once convinced that the rebellious colonies could succeed, the French government found the way open to the alliance and, ultimately, to Yorktown. Events at the close of the 1780s underscored the cost of the alliance to the French monarchy: the aid extended to the Americans helped bankrupt the ancien régime, and financial crisis then provoked the disorderly reform of Bourbon rule. The costs incurred on the American side were of a more subtle nature. To be sure, the dire prophecy of the Loyalists—that the acceptance of French patronage would simply consign America to a new and far worse European prince—was disproved when Rochambeau's army sailed from Boston at the close of 1782, so the price the rebels paid for French help was not as high as their independence. But it did extend to the abandonment of a characteristic trait of American, and especially New England, society. Anti-Catholicism had figured prominently in the settlement of New England, buttressed the social and political power of the Congregationalist clergy, and mobilized popular support for generations of colonial warfare, so it could not be bartered away for a trifle. But it was bartered away for the French Alliance, or at least put in escrow.

This book explores the disruptive effects of the American

Revolution on the religious culture of New England Protestantism. It is a topic that has attracted comment ever since the time of the Revolution itself. Many writers have stressed the apparent continuity between New England's roles as the citadel of American Puritanism and the cradle of American liberty. Even those, unsympathetic to the American cause, who have preferred to trace a connection from the religious pretensions of the Puritans to the presumption of the Patriots have acknowledged a degree of continuity between the two. While there is doubtless some truth in this notion, there is not so much as to allow us to reduce a complex political event to a morality tale of unambiguous import. In that sense, and unhappily perhaps, the immediate aim of this study is to recomplicate our understanding of the role of religion in the Revolution by recovering something of its fluid and contingent quality.

The last few years have seen a revival of interest in this area, and not only among scholars. Indeed, several of those scholars who have written recently on the religious history of the Revolution have done so precisely in order to contribute to a broader debate that is under way on the "original intent" of the Revolutionary generation with regard to the proper role of religion in a democratic society.[1] As is usually the case with historical writing, this renewed interest in the late eighteenth century reflects certain developments in the late twentieth century. Thirty years have passed since Alan Heimert published *Religion and the American Mind*. In that massive and controversial study, Heimert criticized what he took to be an unduly self-congratulatory strain in the then-current religious historiography of the Revolution. Liberal urban sophisticates, he complained, having grown ashamed of their Puritan forebears, had begun peddling a version of events that assigned chief credit for the Revolution to those in the late colonial period who most closely resembled themselves. The victims of this genteel fraud were the Calvinist evangelicals of the time and their descendants. When these Americans opened their history books, they found their religious beliefs treated quite unsympathetically. Calvinism, they read, had been a drag on the Revolution, a backward-looking hindrance to the putatively simultaneous triumph of independence, democracy, and Unitarianism. To these victims Heimert would give a voice.[2]

It may dismay Alan Heimert today to see his work adduced in support of attempts to reintroduce prayer in public schools, but it should not surprise him. In *Religion and the American Mind* he tweaked the conscience of a liberal establishment (*establishment* by then having taken on a strictly secular meaning) that was soon to lose much of the very self-confidence for which he upbraided it. In 1966 Martin Luther King and Robert Kennedy were still alive, and so was a broadly held belief in the legitimacy and liberality of America's political and academic institutions. The existence of such a climate of opinion has become steadily more difficult to imagine for those not old enough to recall it. If Heimert was one of the first to kick at the pillars of this edifice, others were quick to follow. His championing of evangelical underdogs against faux-patriotic liberal snobs in the 1760s and 1770s had a natural appeal for those who challenged the legitimacy and liberality of American elites two centuries later.[3] Their challenge soon found expression in scholarship that pushed well beyond Heimert in its revision of Whiggish historiography.[4] More recently, however, the loudest dissent from conventional thinking about religion and politics has come not from the radical left but from the religious right. As those evangelicals for whom Heimert offered to speak increasingly speak for themselves, there has arisen a new "politics of authenticity" based on open hostility to the secularization of American society.[5] In response, some recent scholarly works have shown a tendency to look over their right rather than left shoulders when defending the present arrangements between church and state.[6]

What follows here is a modest contribution to the long-standing and lately reheated conversation on the religious history of the Revolution. If there is a risk of polemical reductionism on all sides, there are also many studies that have stressed the complexity and incompleteness of any reasonable attempt to excavate our religious past.[7] I have used as my digging tool the peculiar roles of Catholicism and anti-Catholicism in the religious politics of the period. On the one hand, anti-Catholicism was a hallmark of New England society from the first Puritan settlements to the eve of the Revolution and beyond. On the other hand, the aid of Catholic allies was instrumental in securing American independence. This is a paradox left unexamined by nearly all historians of the Revolution. It nevertheless will reward examination, revealing as it does a deep strain of pragmatism in the Glorious Cause.

An appreciation of that pragmatism in turn will allow us, first, to look with a critical eye on the religious content of Revolutionary ideology. Just because Patriots and Tories alike said there was a link between Calvinism and rebellion does not make it so; it may only show how well suited that notion was to serve divergent political interests. Furthermore, to reflect that the rebels reacted in pragmatic ways to the obstacles they encountered is to be reminded of the part that sheer contingency played in these events. Accidents are prosaic material for the historian, and there is always a ready market for explanations that uncover in human affairs the more compelling force of necessity. It is not hard to detect the hand of God—or of the rising bourgeoisie—in the movement for American independence if one first takes its Calvinist character for granted. But it is just here that the facts intrude, for the Revolution was bankrolled not by Dutch burghers but by the king of France. Small wonder, then, that most historians have been willing to pass over this topic with dry remarks about politics making for strange bedfellows.[8]

These same notions of pragmatism and contingency shed light as well on the origins, in the Revolutionary era, of American religious freedom. The resort to Catholic allies, however hasty, had the effect of redrawing the boundaries of religious difference and disabusing at least some Americans of their habitual intolerance. To the extent that this is true, the alliances with the French Canadians and France constitute a neglected chapter in the history of church and state in America. At the same time, the limits of that irenic influence tell another story, this one about the rather blunt relationships of power that underlie the polite language of rights and liberty. If the religious history of the United States turns out to have been intimately bound up from the start with shifting configurations of political power, distaste should not blind us to the fact. Whoever examines the religious politics of the Revolution in detail will exchange a pleasant belief in American moral exceptionalism for a perhaps chastening sense of the moral ordinariness of the participants therein. Any disappointment this may occasion ought to be leavened by the realization that if the men and women of the Revolutionary generation were no better than we are in this respect, we are no worse than they.

# 1

## *The Catholic Question*

I f thy spirit be not with us, carry us not up hence." With these words of Scripture the Reverend Samuel Spring exhorted the Continental soldiers who crowded the Congregationalist church in Newburyport, Massachusetts, on a Sunday in September 1775. A graduate of Princeton and devotee of the late revivalist George Whitefield, Spring was serving as chaplain to a group of soldiers detached from Washington's camp before Boston and sent to drive the British out of Quebec. Their first stop was in Newburyport, where Whitefield was buried. Seizing the opportunity, the chaplain not only "preached over the grave" but proceeded—to his own subsequent chagrin—to open the tomb, remove bits of clothing from Whitefield's skeleton, and hand them out to Benedict Arnold, Aaron Burr, and the other officers.[1]

Spring lived to regret his gesture because the expedition to Quebec went very badly. Arnold's party suffered terrible hardships just to reach Quebec City and rendezvous in December with another American force that had come up from Albany via Montreal. Their joint attack on the fortress city of Quebec on New Year's Eve was a disaster: hundreds were taken prisoner, and the rest were easily routed by the British once the ice in the St. Lawrence River broke and warships could sail up to raise the siege. Spring afterward blamed himself, feeling that he had cursed the venture by "such blasphemous, un-Protestant conduct" as distributing holy relics.[2] In other words, the spirit he invoked in Newburyport had not accompanied the expedition to Quebec. But if Spring thought the most un-Protestant aspect of the ill-fated venture was his own flirtation with idolatry, he was swallowing camels and straining at gnats. He was ignoring the historically bizarre fact that he and his comrades had made common cause with the Catholic French Canadians. This should not have been possible. From the days of John Winthrop, New Englanders had defined their "true" Protestantism in opposition to the "popery" that festered to the northward.

For the Puritans, whether in Old or New England, hostility to the Church of Rome was in the deepest sense a matter of principle. It served as a shibboleth, a test that discriminated between faithful partisans of the Reformation on the one hand and trimmers and compromisers on the other. It expressed fear as well as loathing, the Marian persecutions and later the pan-European violence of the seventeenth century having confirmed the Puritans in their belief that the Catholic Church was a merciless, implacable enemy. Flight to the New World had offered a measure of protection from the internecine strife in Europe, where Catholics and Protestants lived together in a volatile mix. Yet the Catholic colony of New France lay to the north, and hatred and suspicion were easily transplanted to America. It was with alarm that John Winthrop learned in 1632 that the Scottish settlement at Cape Sable had been bought by the French, who renamed it Port Royal. Not only were the new inhabitants in possession of "the fort and all the ammunition," Winthrop noted; they were under the direction of a Catholic cardinal who planned to send "divers priests and Jesuits among them." In response, Governor Winthrop "called the assistants to Boston, and the ministers and captains, . . . to advise what was to be done for our safety, in regard the French were like to prove ill neighbours (being Papists)."[3]

The Puritan colonists decided to build a fort at Natascott to ward off the military threat, but the ultimate source of danger seemed as much spiritual as temporal. In 1647 the General Court cited "the great Wars, Combustions and Divisions which are this day in Europe" and the role of the Jesuits in fomenting them as grounds for an act forbidding any "Jesuite or Spiritual or ecclesiastical person . . . Ordained by the Authority of the Pope" from venturing into the colony of Massachusetts Bay. First-time offenders would be "tryed and proceeded with, by banishment or otherwise. . . . And if any person so Banished, be taken a second time within this Jurisdiction, upon lawful tryal and conviction, he shall be put to Death." A thoughtful exception for cases of shipwreck or other accidental trespassing notwithstanding, it must have seemed an effective means of keeping New England pure.[4]

A long series of frontier wars, waged directly and through Indian proxies, did nothing to smooth the tenor of relations between New England and New France. In 1628 an English-sponsored party of French Huguenot exiles captured Samuel de Champlain's outpost at Quebec City, but it was restored to the kingdom of France after a few years. Intermittently thereafter the two North American colonies played out a local version of Britain's slow and bloody struggle to wrest supremacy from France. When William of Orange confirmed the Protestant succession by defeating Scottish and Irish Catholics in 1690, the governor of Massachusetts tried to rise to the occasion by retaking Quebec. In 1704 the War of the Spanish Succession under Queen Anne took the form in New England of an attack on Deerfield by Indian allies of the French. Two generations later, New Englanders gloried in the capture of Louisbourg while the British put down the Young Pretender's rebellion at Culloden. The climactic event in this sequence was the Great War for Empire, known afterward as the Seven Years' War and at the time, in America, as the French and Indian War. The identification of the French Canadians as spiritual enemies still came naturally. In a sermon in 1754, a Boston clergyman predicted that defeat at their hands would mean "Christianity banished for popery! the bible, for the mass book! . . . Instead of a train of Christ's faithful, laborious ministers, do I behold an herd of lazy Monks, and Jesuits, and cowled and uncowled Impostors!"[5]

Once again the outbreak of war with Canada evoked a whole range of fears and hatreds known as anti-Catholicism. In strictly sectarian terms New England Protestants of all stripes derided as "popery" what they considered a corrupt, heretical, and wholly degenerate perversion of Christianity. The robust strain of millennialism in English Calvinism led many ministers to treat depictions of the Antichrist in the Book of Revelation as prophecies of Satan's temptation of the Church of Rome.[6] According to this view, Catholics were not even Christians, having succumbed to the Prince of Darkness. In a sermon delivered during the French and Indian War, the Calvinist Joseph Lathrop scrutinized the "dragon, beast, and false prophet" in chapter 16 of Revelation and concluded that the dragon symbolized the Holy Roman Empire, the beast the French monarchy, and the false prophet "the papal clergy, or the Hierarchy of the church of Rome." The "general war in Europe," Lathrop declared, signaled the onset of Armageddon. "The battle to which the kings of the earth are gathered," he said, "is the battle of the great day of God Almighty." It was to "nearly precede . . . the fall of a great Babylon, or the Roman church."[7]

Popular accounts of the war echoed this apocalyptic language, casting the French enemy as the Whore of Babylon. A song printed in Boston to mark the fall of Quebec City to Wolfe in 1759 not only gloated over the French defeat— "Behold the bloody Sons of Gaul / Rejoice with trembling at their Fall"—but expressed the hope that Catholicism itself had received a mortal wound.

> *The Time will come when Pope and Fry'r*
> *Shall both be roasted in the Fire;*
> *When the proud Antichristian Whore*
> *Will sink, and never arise more.*[8]

Such abuse of Roman Catholics and their faith was ritualized by New Englanders in Pope Day, the annual commemoration on November 5 of the Catholic "gunpowder plot" to blow up Parliament in 1605. A broadside printed in Boston for the occasion in the 1760s called attention to an effigy of the pope that would be paraded on the Common. His "palsy Knees" were "a proof that He is the Scarlet Whore." The verses included forms of abuse deemed appropriate for the pope's figure:

> *"A Pagan, Jew, Mahometan,*
> *Turk, Strumpet, Wizzard, Witch;"*
> *In short, the number of his Name's*
> *Six Hundred, Sixty-Six.*[9]

An ancestral enemy and degenerate heresy, popery was also, in New England eyes, a political system radically incompatible with civil liberty. The rigid hierarchy of pope, bishops, clergy, and parishioners precluded both the independence and the virtue necessary to sustain republican citizenship. The duty of submission to hierarchy was a mere license for the tyranny by which, as John Lathrop put it, "the church of Rome hath not only usurped authority over the *conscience* of her members, but over their *fortunes.*" The predatory tendencies of the church toward the worldly goods of its helpless subjects—the forging of wills, selling of indulgences, and resort to outright extortion—formed a favorite refrain of anti-Catholic tracts.[10] A church that systematically bilked its members of their property could not produce good citizens, since it would never suffer them to become independent of its control. Furthermore, the argument went, the church's jealous control over knowledge and learning, its vested interest in the ignorance of its charges, made ordinary Catholics unfit to participate in civil society. Kept in the dark from birth, they never learned to see. Given this supposed antagonism between Catholic traits and republican virtues, antipopery contributed to New England's political as well as theological creed. It was routinely asserted, for instance, that a Catholic's loyalty to the pope, by superseding any other allegiance, rendered him ineligible to enter into the compact of rights and responsibilities on which civil society rested. A good Whig, therefore, as John Adams explained, was by definition anti-Catholic. Whig principles "have been invariably applied," he wrote, "in support of the reformation and Protestant religion, against the worst tyranny ever invented, I mean the Romish superstition."[11]

Adams was writing in early 1775, well after the transfer of Quebec from French to British rule in 1763. The shifting balance of imperial power did surprisingly little to soothe New Englanders' anxieties about the French Canadians, who remained an overwhelming majority in the newly acquired British province. On the contrary, Quebec only took on greater prominence as a touchstone of American concern over new departures in British policy. At the same time that disputes over taxation produced the Stamp Act riots and the Sons of Liberty, the threat of an Anglican episcopacy in America revived old Puritan doubts about the quasi-Protestant credentials of the Church of England.[12] The two streams of suspicion about British motives came together in the indignant colonial response to the Quebec Act of June 1774.

On its face, this measure was the British government's tardy but in some respects quite judicious attempt to organize its rule over the new province. Given the large Catholic majority in Quebec and the fact that British Catholics were still subject to the civil disabilities of the Test and Corporation Acts, it is not surprising that Parliament dithered for ten years before taking up the question of ecclesiastical arrangements. The legislation of 1774 finally addressed it by declaring the Church of England the established church in Quebec and at the same time granting official toleration to Catholics, including the right of the clergy to collect tithes. The resulting controversy was in part an accident of timing. From the British government's point of view, its decision had little to do with bringing fractious New Englanders to heel. But Parliament was as quick to respond to the Boston Tea Party of December 1773 as it had been slow to grapple with the problem of Quebec. As a result, the roughly simultaneous passage of the Quebec Act and the Coercive Acts invited the unhappy colonists to view all of them together as forming one great scheme of oppression.[13]

Criticism of the Quebec Act had a distinctly Calvinist tone. Alarmed ministers and others claimed to detect in it a plot to subvert American religious as well as civil liberties. One witness to the times recalled his grandfather's dying admonition, "a little while before the commencement of the Revolutionary war," that King George was scheming to establish Roman Catholicism in the Protestant colonies. The old man charged the youth to "stand fast, and remain sound in the faith." When his regiment marched for Boston in the summer of 1775, the soldier and his fellows "were all ready to swear, that this same George, by granting the Quebec Bill, . . . had thereby become a traitor" and "was secretly a Papist; . . . whose design it was to oblige this country . . . to be given up and destroyed, soul and body, by that frightful image with seven heads and ten horns." The same dread of Catholics "stimulated many timorous pious people to send their sons to join the military ranks," where they rallied in militia companies to cries of "No King, no Popery!"[14] New Lights and Old Lights alike seized on this evidence of Anglican backsliding. Among the former, David Jones denounced the outrageous policy of "establishing popery in near one half of North America" and asked, "Is not this the loudest call to arms?" Speaking for the latter, Ezra Stiles imagined that Anglican support of the Quebec Act had occasioned "a Jubilee in Hell and Thanksgiving throughout the Pontificate."[15]

The British commander in Boston, General Gage, took these complaints seriously and informed his superiors in London that the Quebec Act, by inflaming rural opinion against him, had made his job more difficult. It is certain that rebel agitators were quick to appreciate the political usefulness of this recent turn in religious affairs. The rekindling of anti-Catholic chauvinism well suited the needs of a movement whose chief slogan was the refusal of a free people to be made slaves. "Popery, we see," warned a Massachusetts almanac, "is already established in one colony, and slavery is its never-failing concomitant." If King George was willing to accommodate the pope in Quebec, then perhaps the two were conniving to enslave the other colonies as well. The Canadians, already trapped under the combined weight of king and pope, were an army of serfs ready to be unleashed on the Americans. As one alarmed colonial minister put it, this latest "refinement in politicks" meant that "Papists shall be compelled by law to murder their Protestant neighbours." Tory writers exploited such fears for their own purposes, as when one observed with satisfaction that the Quebec Act had "not only fixed the fidelity of those Canadians to their new king" but "established also an ample and sufficient force to quell the democratic spirits of the American sectaries." [16]

For the colonists this way of depicting the sordid aims of the Quebec Act and the dangerous character of the French Canadians had uses beyond the ability to arouse fear and alarm. It also appealed to the idea of moral exceptionalism, the sense that New England's peculiar religious culture was grounds for a right to self-government. John Adams made this case explicitly in his pamphlet debate with a leading Boston Tory early in 1775. His opponent, Daniel Leonard, approved of the Quebec Act and scoffed at the pious declarations of its critics. Adams not only respected those declarations but joined in them. He singled out anti-Catholicism as precisely that quality which raised New England to a higher moral plane vis-à-vis Britain. In overly sophisticated circles, he supposed, daring ideas about religious toleration and so-called enlightenment might enjoy a certain cachet. Every society had its libertines; the French philosophes were only the most notorious of these, and there were signs that Britain was also in danger. The willingness of the king's ministers to tolerate popery in Quebec was the latest evidence of this regrettable fact.

Fortunately, said Adams, there were still those in Britain and America who could tell enlightenment from decadence. Sound politics, like sound religion, depended on the ability to recognize and insist upon just such distinctions. The Quebec Act was a perfect case in point. Its supporters betrayed an unseemly haste to abandon the very rules that safeguarded their Protestant inheritance. Whereas Leonard had contrasted the British government's support of religious toleration with the outdated fanaticism of New England Congregationalists, Adams positively welcomed the charge of old-fashionedness. He likened the Puritan legacy of anti-Catholicism to the Ten Commandments themselves. Each was a set of rules, and as such would naturally draw criticism from those who chafed at all restraints. A true Patriot was a true Protestant, and unlike an Anglican trimmer, a true Protestant hated Catholics.[17]

This syllogism, however neatly it harmonized the religious and political elements of the Glorious Cause, would disintegrate almost instantly in the face of the war itself. When protest against the excesses of British misrule gave way to open rebellion, few old rules seemed to apply. Antipopery was one of the first to fall by the wayside as diplomacy turned Catholic enemies into much-needed friends. Evidence of the speed and scope of this change can be found in the behavior of Benedict Arnold after his narrow escape and flight to New York in the fall of 1780. It is a revealing document. Casting about for a way to extenuate his treason, Arnold claimed that he was too good a Protestant to stomach an alliance with Catholic powers. As a student of history he was right, of course; but as a politician he was proved quite wrong. Congress had indeed attended mass on more than one occasion, but there had been no riots in Boston to protest the fact. It was no longer possible in 1780 to scandalize American opinion by inveighing against papists. The anti-Catholicism Adams had taken for granted in 1775 had so dissipated by then that it could not provide Arnold even the slimmest of footholds. But if it was easy to see that Arnold was grasping at straws, it was harder to explain why his sudden embrace of Puritan tradition was any less principled than the Patriots' hasty abandonment of it. The question lingered, and remains, how such a drastic transformation could have been so swift.[18]

It is a question that historians have been noticeably slow to take up. Alan Heimert did not address it in his enduringly influential description of the contribution of Calvinist revivalism to the Revolution. Like many writers to follow the path he blazed, Heimert found it easier to account for the intertwining of religious and patriotic zeal during the period leading up to the heady days of 1775 than to explain their subsequent unraveling. When describing "the breakdown of the evangelical synthesis" upon contact with "the necessities of the war against Britain" and the way those necessities "impinged on the Calvinist mind," Heimert passed over the Catholic alliances. Yet surely the swift accommodation to Catholic allies stands out as an example of the Calvinist clergy's resort, under duress, to what Heimert aptly termed "a de facto doctrine of justification by works."[19] While he famously derided the antirevivalist New England liberals for their opportunism, Heimert avoided asking whether the Catholic alliances made opportunists of everyone. This omission in turn allowed him to exaggerate the peculiar moral clarity of Calvinist as against liberal patriotism. In fact, however, just as New Lights and Old Lights joined in proclaiming their anti-Catholic credentials in outrage at the Quebec Act, so they shared the embarrassment of having to explain their conversion to a more tolerant stance when Revolutionary diplomacy headed off in unexpected directions.

For later historians, as for contemporary witnesses, it has proved an awkward task to trace the religious history of the Revolution much past the martyrdom of Lexington and Concord. This proved as true of Heimert's critics as of those who accepted his general thesis. Among the latter, for instance, Patricia Bonomi stopped short of the Revolution itself in her analysis of the connections between religious dissent and the growth of an ideology of independence. While stressing the ease with which religious dissent "flowed in with" political radicalism, she did not examine the compromises and disappointments that would soon cause these two streams once again to diverge. So while she succeeded in establishing colonial religion as "an authentic area of American exceptionalism," by leaping from the outbreak of the Revolution to its successful conclusion she overlooked how unexceptional an undertaking it proved in this very respect. The same may be said of Donald Weber's *Rhetoric and History in Revolutionary New England*, which also pauses at the threshold of the war.[20]

Most prominently among those who have taken issue with Heimert, Nathan Hatch reversed the thesis by emphasizing the political pressure that events exerted on religious beliefs rather than the other way around. Taking Heimert to task for slighting the importance of the Seven Years' War in the secularization of Great Awakening revivalism, Hatch argued for a religious history of late colonial and Revolutionary America that put politics first, or at least made it an important independent force. But even he has been more effective in revising our understanding of events before and after the Revolution than in applying his insight to the murky religious politics of the wartime period itself. Having argued for the emergence of a stridently anti-Catholic "civil millennialism" by 1774, he did not pursue the implications of the sudden reconciliation with the Canadians and the French. Nor did Ruth Bloch, despite distancing herself from both Heimert and Hatch in her detailed treatment of millennialism in late eighteenth-century American thought. The structure of Bloch's exposition in *Visionary Republic* is itself revealing in this regard. Part One repeatedly emphasizes the tendency of New England Calvinists of all types, revivalist and antirevivalist, to identify French Catholicism with the Antichrist. In Part Three, on the 1790s,

Bloch shows how this tradition at first undergirded a millennialist consensus that was well disposed toward the anticlerical zeal of the French Revolution but then caused a split between Federalist and Democratic-Republican notions of just how much anticlericalism was a good thing. What is notable in the present context is what Bloch does not say in Part Two, entitled "The Rise and Decline of Millennialism in the Revolutionary Era." Here her references to France become very scarce; they do not figure at all in her explanation of the "withdrawal from politics" that "apparently stemmed in part from disenchantment" among millennialist thinkers "with the course of the American Revolution." This would seem to beg the question of the Catholic alliances. If, as Bloch writes, it "no longer remained crucial" after 1775 to associate British perfidy with "the influence of Rome" and patriotism with anti-Catholicism, it might be added that such a depiction of affairs was no longer even plausible.[21]

We will fare little better if we look for an exploration of this problem in works that concentrate on the period of the Revolution itself. General treatments of the war grant the military and diplomatic significance of the French Alliance but do so without inquiring into its reverberations in religious and cultural life.[22] This is true even of specifically religious histories of the Revolution.[23] One may read widely in such works without being asked to consider the odd fact that a struggle launched in an atmosphere of Calvinist fervor was fought, even in New England, in a distinctly ecumenical style. A case in point is Charles Royster's *A Revolutionary People at War*. Insofar as Royster set himself the task of contrasting the prosecution of the war with the ideals in whose name it was undertaken, this would seem a promising place to look for a treatment of the Catholic Question. But once again we will be disappointed. Royster devotes more space than most writers to the Quebec Expedition of 1775–76 and includes Reverend Spring's blessing. His interest is not piqued, however, by the camaraderie between the French Canadians and the invading Yankees. He records the anti-Catholic gloating of an American chaplain but not the difficulty such chaplains had in reminding the rank and file of their duties as good Protestants.[24]

The story of the wartime accommodation to Catholicism has thus been allowed to fall between the cracks of religious and more general histories of the Revolution. All the same, such a catalog of omissions still obliges its compiler to argue for the importance of what others have been content to leave aside. What can that story tell us that we do not already know? There is, first of all, the matter of perspective. While it is surely a mistake to read the mores of our comparatively secular age back into the late eighteenth century, the aim of understanding late colonial American religion "on its own terms" is problematic in itself.[25] Taking the religious content of the Revolution seriously means taking the religious ideas of the participants seriously, but it does not mean taking them at face value. Sometimes they meant what they said to the point of putting faith before self-interest, and sometimes they did not. A shift of perspective that brings Canadian and French Catholics into the picture will allow us to test the accuracy of some of our notions about Protestants as we watch the different groups come into contact with one another. Calvinist theology and anti-Catholic ritual, however instructive as starting points, can serve as little more in explaining the effects of the unprecedented and unexpected intimacy of the encounter. The Quebecois peasants and priests and the French soldiers, sailors, and chaplains who took part in this cultural exchange were at least as well situated as the New Englanders to ponder what it revealed about the faith of "les Bostonois." We have often heard the Congregationalist version of Revolutionary history, but there are other voices to be heard.

Nor is it only a question of contrasting Protestant and Catholic, native and foreign, interpretations of the same events. Within the New England community itself, the Catholic alliances provided new grist for a whole variety of controversies, presenting difficulties for some parties while handing new ammunition to others. The gleeful charges of hypocrisy leveled by Tory Anglicans are only the most obvious case in point. More generally, the resort to Catholic aid severely taxed the rhetorical skills of those Patriots who sought to narrate the course of the Revolution along providential lines. Like historians after them, these men and women found it easier to construct such narratives for the long prehistory of the Revolution, from the Reformation to 1775, than to extend them much beyond.

Alan Heimert, for his part, explained "the fragmentation of evangelical religion generally" as "a consequence of the variety of responses of Americans, people and pastors alike, to the moral and political phenomena of the middle years of the war." But rather than look to the middle years for the disillusioning effects of the war, we can detect them at its very outset. Nor was it simply "economic pressure and temptation" that brought "the true character of the people" to the fore. War profiteering aside, the Catholic alliances provided early and irrefutable evidence that "the nature and purpose of the Revolution were hardly definable by Calvinism alone."[26] And Samuel Spring was hardly alone among his contemporaries in responding to this difficulty with a discreet silence. David Avery, his fellow revivalist and chaplain in Quebec in 1776, struggled with the implications of the expedition while trying to persuade an audience of Continental soldiers that every twist of the war to date revealed the work of "the Lord's hand." He preached this sermon in March 1778, when the adventure in Quebec was old news (and the French Alliance, just signed, had not yet been announced). In it Avery referred elliptically to the invasion of the province as a "concurrence of very unexpected, surprising incidents." As for the French Canadians, his brief account of their role in the fighting did not include any mention of their religion. Such subterfuge would be impossible when the time came to explain the alliance with France, an open secret which Avery acknowledged only in an aside about "the propitious winds" bringing "war-like stores . . . from foreign ports." The arrival of French fleets and armies in New England would place almost unbearable strain on the providential narrative, thereby creating an opening for alternative ways of construing events.[27]

This is not to say that the adjustment to diplomatic real-politik was the sole cause of the much-noted disillusionment of the more religious-minded as the war dragged on, only that it contributed in ways that merit a closer look. The Catholic alliances exposed the relative rather than absolute status of anti-popery in the New England cosmology. After a century and a half during which no important social interest had come into conflict with that principle (or prejudice), the sudden failure of New Englanders to hate Catholics made it clear that the privileged position of Calvinist values was at risk. It was one thing for Benjamin Franklin to endorse the alliance; he was a New Englander only by birth. The enthusiastic support of men like John Adams, who had entered the fray with Puritan banners flying, was something else. Three years after his comparison of antipopery to Mosaic law, Adams was living in Paris and reading letters in which Mercy Warren described for him the glorious spectacle of a French fleet riding at anchor in Boston Harbor. And two years after that, Benedict Arnold discovered for himself just how far the cultural devaluation of anti-Catholicism had progressed.

This cannot have been a merely temporary and cosmetic change, for it did not reverse itself when the French army and fleet left Boston for home in 1782. Instead, a bitter struggle ensued between Congregationalist conservatives and liberals over the meaning of recent events. One side saw the French Alliance as a Faustian bargain full of risk to the survival of true religion. The other rejoiced at the demise of a prejudice they considered a relic of unenlightened primitivism. The argument is itself proof that a decisive shift had taken place. If one group denounced the opening to Catholics as the beginning of the end of New England's religion while another held it up as the dawn of a new age, then we may be sure they agreed it had not been a mere freak of politics.[28]

The opening to Catholics had put the New England clergy in the uncomfortable position of following rather than leading public opinion. While it is not easy to assess the extent of the resulting erosion of ministerial authority, the evidence does suggest two things. First, the alliances constitute a hitherto missing chapter in the history of American religious liberty. The existential fact of Protestant-Catholic cooperation against the British strengthened the hand of those who sought to restrict the public role of religious authorities as part of the overall Revolutionary settlement. Even where this did not directly concern the rights of Catholics (of whom there were extremely few in New England throughout the eighteenth century), the boost that the alliances gave to the idea of religious toleration in general proved a useful tool in dismantling the claim to primacy of the Congregationalist Standing Order.

The contributions of Enlightenment philosophy and Baptist separatism to this movement, while important, were not exhaustive. The social as well as intellectual history of church and state in America is incomplete if it ignores the experiences of the Yankees who found themselves in Quebec and the Frenchmen who found themselves in Connecticut during the Revolution. At the same time it should be said that the story here told is not a secular version of the providential one that foundered on the inconvenient facts of the war. By embarrassing the Black Regiment and undermining its rhetorical authority, the shock of the Catholic alliances created a space in which previously marginalized ideas about religious toleration could circulate, thereby attracting adherents and respect. But if events during the Revolution dealt a blow to Old Calvinists and New Light evangelicals alike in favor of their latitudinarian rivals, that blow did not prove fatal. Rather, the growth of Unitarianism in Boston was the exception rather than the rule in New England by 1800. For many New Englanders the Revolution was less a turning point in the rise of liberal religion than a temporary disturbance in a long and durable evangelical tradition.

Martin Luther compared man to a horse ridden by either God or the Devil. If evangelical Christianity was knocked out of the saddle during the Revolution, it nevertheless managed to clamber back in again in most parts of New England. Oddly enough, France and French Catholicism were as central to the restoration of Calvinist influence in the 1790s as they had earlier been in its weakening. Of all the hotly contested ways of making sense of the French Revolution, the one that predominated in New England by 1800 was one that endorsed the legitimacy of the Congregationalist establishments. The Antichrist was back in recognizable form and spoke in a familiar tongue. So recognized, it could also be kept at arm's length, or so it seemed for a while. For no sooner was the Catholic "other" safely reconstituted as wholly external to New England than Irish immigration brought it once again within the walls. Recent scholarship has illuminated the mixture of fascination and dread with which a self-consciously Protestant United States regarded the expanding Catholic presence in its midst. But "the Protestant encounter with Catholicism," in Jenny Franchot's phrase, did not leap in one bound from colonial frontier warfare to the burning of the Charlestown convent in 1834. What first brought Catholicism home to Boston and Cambridge, Hartford and New Haven, was the Revolution.[29]

# 2

# The Encounter in Quebec

In May 1775 the Roman Catholic bishop of Quebec, Jean-Olivier Briand, circulated a letter to be read aloud in all the parish churches. In it he announced his plans to undertake a tour of the diocese. As he had on the last such occasion, the bishop would visit a different parish each day.

> Arriving on the previous day in the parish, we will go to the church around 4 o'clock, we will read the pastoral letter on which we will then speak, as well as on the particular failings [*abus*] of the parish, which the priest will take care to put in writing and remit to us on our arrival. After the exhortation, . . . confessors will hear those who present themselves. . . . On the day of the visit services will begin around 9 o'clock with the sermon, then I will perform confirmations, say the high mass, give absolution for the dead, after which I will give general absolution and grant indulgences.[1]

Despite this detailed planning, the bishop's tour never took place, superseded as it was by more urgent matters. The summer of 1775 saw the rebellion in the British colonies of New England spill north into Quebec and wreak havoc with civil and ecclesiastical authority alike.

The American invasion of Quebec was not a success, which may explain the scant attention it receives in most accounts of the Revolution.[2] It began almost by default on May 9, 1775, when a loosely coordinated American force under Benedict Arnold of Connecticut and Ethan Allen of the New Hampshire Grants took possession of Fort Ticonderoga from the startled and unresisting British garrison. Seth Warner and a squad of Green Mountain Boys took Crown Point the next day. Intended partly to embarrass the Tory government of New York (the Boys' opponents in the range war over what became Vermont), these easy exploits presented the rebels with control over Lake George and the southern reaches of Lake Champlain. The way north to Canada lay open, and debate began in Patriot councils over the advisability of an incursion there. Whether or not Quebec could or should be won over to the Glorious Cause, any diversion that tied up British troops there would relieve some of the pressure on Boston and prevent New England's being cut off from the other colonies.

To this end, spies were sent to Montreal and Quebec City and small raids mounted in the countryside. On June 9, 1775, the British governor and commander in chief, Guy Carleton, declared martial law in the province and ordered the reestablishment of the militia, suspended since 1763. This was not much of a success: the English colonists in Montreal balked at enlisting, as did many of the French Canadian farmers; and French city dwellers were put off by gross favoritism in the handing out of commissions in the reconstituted officer corps. Such lukewarm attachment to the crown encouraged the Americans, who saw an opportunity in Quebec. At the end of June, after the battle of Bunker Hill had penned the British in behind their fortifications at Boston, the Continental Congress formally voted to invade Canada.[3]

General Philip Schuyler assembled a force at Albany, assisted by Richard Montgomery. While these officers readied their collection of New England militia and New York and Pennsylvania regiments, Ethan Allen and his associates continued to probe the British positions farther north, building barges to maneuver along Lake Champlain. Captain Remember Baker of the Green Mountain Boys was killed in a skirmish near the British fort at St. Johns in late August; his head was cut off and carried back to the fort by Mohawks allied with the British. A diary found on his body revealed that Baker had been in correspondence with Thomas Walker, a merchant formerly of Boston and now an ardent promoter of the American interest in Montreal. Walker had told Baker that he could count on fifteen hundred armed Canadians to join him, as well as the Mohawks of Sault-Saint-Louis.[4]

On August 28 the force under Schuyler began to move north to Crown Point and onto the lake. Montgomery went ahead with fourteen hundred men, including the 1st New York Regiment and Connecticut infantry and artillery, and Schuyler followed with the rest. After meeting British and Indian resistance, they took Isle-aux-Noix and early in September appeared before St. Johns. After Schuyler fell sick and returned to Albany, Montgomery assumed the command and laid siege to St. Johns with perhaps a thousand men. Although Ethan Allen was captured in an abortive attempt on Montreal in late September, the British fort at Chambly surrendered without a shot on October 18, providing Montgomery with much-needed military stores. On the twenty-sixth Carleton tried to land a party at Longueuil on the south side of the St. Lawrence in hopes of relieving St. Johns, eighteen miles away; but Seth Warner and his Boys turned them back from the shore. On November 3 Montgomery received the surrender of St. Johns, and on the thirteenth he entered Montreal.

While Montgomery prepared to chase Carleton to Quebec City, Benedict Arnold was on the point of arriving there before either of them. Detached by Washington from the army at Cambridge in late September, Arnold's eleven hundred riflemen and musketmen had marched to Newburyport and sailed to the mouth of the Kennebec River. The miseries of their expedition overland to Quebec City are notorious.[5] From the first days of October, when they passed through Norridgewalk, until the first days of November, when an advance party made contact with the French Canadians, the Americans saw no settlement other than a wigwam. Three hundred men under Colonel Roger Enos turned back late in October with more than their share of the remaining provisions, and those who pushed on were reduced to boiling their moccasins and cartridge pouches for nourishment. When they reached the French Canadian settlers along the Chaudière River, they were well received. The inhabitants charged for their provisions but offered no resistance as the Americans advanced to Pointe Levy, across the St. Lawrence from Quebec City. Of the original force of eleven hundred, two hundred had been sent back sick, three hundred had returned with Enos, and seventy or eighty had been lost in the wilderness. A little over five hundred remained. The British burned all the French Canadians' boats on the Pointe Levy side once they learned of Arnold's approach, and it took until November 10 for the Americans to build new ones and cross over by night. They paraded before the walls but, too few to lay a siege, retreated twenty miles upriver to Pointe-aux-Trembles (now Neuville) to await reinforcement by Montgomery.

The news that an American force had already reached Quebec City from another direction was an unpleasant surprise for Carleton as he made his way downriver from Montreal to the capital. He narrowly escaped capture by the American battery at Sorel and arrived at Trois-Rivières, between Montreal and Quebec City, on November 17. Here he received the bad news about Arnold, which he at first refused to believe. Convinced of the fact by the local seigneur, the chevalier Godefroy de Tonnancour, Carleton decided to march his 130 men and their officers through the night to Quebec City, where Arnold's force was too weak to keep them from entering.[6]

Once inside, Carleton found himself in command of British regulars, sailors, marines, and British and French Canadian volunteers numbering about eighteen hundred altogether, up from eleven hundred when Arnold had first appeared outside. Aware that both the militia within the city and the suburbs without contained partisans of the invasion, Carleton set about doing what he could to purge his ranks. He announced that all those in the city who declined militia duty would be expelled; if they refused to leave, they would be treated as spies. Residents of the suburbs of Saint-Roch and Saint-Jean were told to enter the gates or be considered rebels. A few entered, many joined the besiegers, and the British bombarded the towns to deprive their opponents of cover.[7]

On December 1, the day Carleton's ultimatum to the malingerers expired, Montgomery joined Arnold at Pointe-aux-Trembles. He had left Montreal on November 28, posting garrisons there and at St. Johns and Chambly under General David Wooster. Montgomery advanced from Pointe-aux-Trembles and set up headquarters at Holland House, two miles from the city walls in the town of Sainte-Foy. The soldiers were quartered there and in other suburbs. The total American force before Quebec was about fifteen hundred, with another five hundred friendly French Canadians also under arms. The Americans were now strong enough to blockade the city, and their chances of taking it seemed good. Carleton's second in command, Lieutenant Governor Hector Cramahé, told Howe in Boston that "there was little reason to believe that the Capital would be able to withstand the expected attack." But many of the New York and New England militia enlistments were due to expire on the last day of 1775, and Montgomery's hand was about to be forced.[8]

The attack came before dawn on December 31, in a heavy snowstorm. It quickly proved a disaster for the Americans when Montgomery was killed at a barricade and the men he was leading turned and fled. Arnold, leading a second attack on the Lower Town from another direction, was wounded in the leg; his men fought on but were soon surrounded and nearly all killed or captured. The plan was doubtful from the start. Its only chance of success probably rested on a mass uprising of the city's residents in favor of the attackers, and this did not occur. Instead, the Americans suffered hundreds of casualties and were never again able to threaten the city.

Although they maintained the blockade until the arrival of British ships in the spring, provisions never ran low inside the city before then. Nor were the Americans, despite the artillery pieces they had taken at Chambly and St. Johns, capable of effective bombardment. "They see plainly that they can make no kind of impression upon the Town," wrote one diarist, a British customs official and militia officer. "Hitherto they have killed a boy, wounded a Sailor, and broke the leg of a turkey." [9]

Arnold, recovering from his wound, had two hundred Canadians still with him and between five and six hundred Americans. About as many Americans were prisoners of war, reasonably treated in the city but exposed there to smallpox, which killed perhaps fifty of them during the winter. Those prisoners born in Britain—the Old Countrymen, as they were called—were told that they could avoid trial for treason by joining Colonel Allen MacLean's Royal Highland Emigrants. Ninety-four of them accepted the offer, swearing to serve the king until June. Once made soldiers, they quickly set about trying to desert; and after ten had made off, the remaining eighty-four were put back in prison. [10]

Arnold meanwhile tried to muster a force for a second attack. When he asked Congress for "eight or ten thousand men to secure and form a lasting connection with this country," he was told to expect no more than two hundred and by mid-February had received only 175. Even with this reinforcement, smallpox and desertion kept his number of effectives at about eight hundred. On his own authority he raised a Canadian regiment of three hundred on the same terms as the Continental troops, including commissions for the officers, and then asked Congress to approve it. Congress did so, sending the Anglo-Canadian refugees Moses Hazen and Edward Antill back to Quebec at the end of February with commissions to raise a second regiment. [11]

Recruitment was slow. The French Canadians by now were becoming openly disaffected to the invaders, beginning with those who chafed under Wooster's authority in Montreal. Wooster commanded there until the end of March, when he left Moses Hazen in charge and went to Quebec City to switch places with Arnold; Arnold left Quebec on April 10 and in turn relieved Hazen in Montreal on the nineteenth. Arnold tried to undo some of the damage Wooster had caused to relations with the Canadians but quickly decided that their hostility was implacable. In the countryside things were not as bad. In late March sixty French Canadian farmers (or habitants) rallied on Arnold's command to defend Pointe Levy against a group of Canadian loyalists, surprising them at their headquarters on the estate of Michel Blais. They killed five, shot and wounded a priest, and took thirty-four prisoners. But by now there were risings against the Americans in some parishes, something that had been very rare before Montgomery's defeat. Hazen's regiment had not been paid, and the Americans were also defaulting on payments for supplies and transport.[12]

In order to salvage the American position in Canada, Congress dispatched a commission composed of Benjamin Franklin, Samuel Chase, and Charles Carroll of Carrolltown. They sought to shore up Congress's credit in Montreal so that Arnold could continue to buy supplies with paper money. This proved impossible, however, as their stay in Montreal—from late April to late May—coincided with the collapse of the American military effort. Reinforcements were constantly hoped for, and a few did trickle up through Montreal and Trois-Rivières to Quebec City in the course of the spring. There were rumors that General Charles Lee had been on his way north with a large party before being ordered to join Washington on Long Island. General John Thomas of Massachusetts arrived at Quebec City on May 3 and relieved Wooster. He had nineteen hundred men with him, of whom nine hundred were unfit for duty and another three hundred were clamoring to be discharged. Thomas knew little about the situation; and Wooster, disgruntled at having been replaced, did little to help him. The result was that neither paid much attention to reports from downriver that a British fleet was approaching.[13]

Two frigates and an armed sloop, with two hundred marines among them, reached Quebec City on the morning of May 6 and easily raised the siege. Carleton sallied out with three hundred regulars and nine hundred militiamen and put the Americans to a complete and humiliating rout. Abandoning their baggage, they ran forty-five miles before even trying to make a stand at Pointe Deschambeault and immediately had to resume the retreat. Reinforcements were sent from Crown Point, and Washington ordered Thomas to try to hold Sorel, forty miles below Montreal, with the eight hundred men he had left. By May 16 the reinforcements had not come, and Thomas had contracted a fatal case of smallpox.[14]

At the end of May, Brigadier General John Sullivan arrived at Sorel with five thousand men and took command. By now American efforts had been reduced to rearguard actions under Wooster at Montreal, Hazen at La Prairie, and Arnold at Chambly. Sullivan tried a counterattack at Trois-Rivières on June 8 that resulted in another crushing defeat. On the fourteenth he evacuated Sorel, and on the fifteenth and sixteenth Montreal was abandoned after a seven-month occupation. On the seventeenth Sullivan and Arnold met at St. Johns and decided against making a stand there. They embarked their troops on Lake Champlain on the eighteenth and left Canada, Arnold insisting on shoving off the last boat himself. On June 20 Carleton entered Montreal.[15]

This is not the kind of exploit one expects to find recounted to schoolchildren along with the Boston Tea Party and Paul Revere's ride. On its face, the American invasion of Quebec was an ignominious failure. Poor planning, discipline, and morale resulted in defeat at the hands of a British force that was weak, scattered, and unpopular with the Canadians. Yet it was a very near thing. Remarks abound to the effect that the weather in late 1775 and early 1776 was unusually foul, a fact that favored the British defenders. Heavy rains caused dysentery among Montgomery's men at St. Johns, and on May Day,

1776, heavy snow fell in Trois-Rivières. As late as July it was reported that "the weather is so cold that the Canadians do not expect a good crop of corn."[16] Had Montgomery carried Quebec City he would have commanded the entire province and perhaps rallied its residents permanently to the American cause. As it turned out, his troops succeeded at least in harassing Carleton and alarming his superiors in London. The British could no longer count on Canada's loyalty, and a year would pass before they made any move to pursue the retreating Americans. That attempt, when it came, ended at Saratoga.

Furthermore, the expedition warrants closer examination for what it reveals of the different religious cultures from which it arose and on which its effects were to prove so unsettling. Consider, on the Canadian side, the joint effort of the British governor, Guy Carleton, and Bishop Briand to restore order in the wake of the American retreat. In the summer of 1776 Carleton dispatched three leading Quebec City officials to investigate loyal and disloyal behavior among the habitants during the occupation. François Baby and Gabriel Taschereau, both French Canadian seigneurs, and Jenkin Williams, a Welsh-born judge, traveled from village to village interviewing residents, taking testimony, and meting out rewards and punishments. Their method bore a number of similarities to the one Briand had envisioned for his own tour. As Briand had planned, they visited a parish a day. Their routine, recorded in the report they compiled, included conferral with the parish priest, assembly of the militia, reading aloud of the investigators' commissions from Carleton, nomination of new officers, denunciation of "bad subjects" and dismissal of disgraced officers, an address exhorting the new officers to do their duty, and a general shout of "Vive le Roy." Undertaken at the governor's command rather than the bishop's, it was a secular version of the canceled pastoral visit.

The similarities extended beyond the merely formal as well. Like Briand, who called on sinners to confess, Baby and his partners required the public humiliation of those who had strayed from loyalty to the crown. They directed five remorseful habitants to "ask the king's pardon next Sunday in the presence of the entire militia, and also for the forgiveness of the few loyal subjects" in the parish "for having scandalized them with indecent talk." [17] The commissioners also saw to the ritual degradation of militia officers who had accepted commissions from the Americans. In the parish of Saint-Antoine they noted that Louis Rousseau had accepted a captain's commission from Benedict Arnold on March 27. After ordering him to turn it over, they had it "read in a loud and ironic voice" and "told him before the whole militia that, since all papers from the hands of the rebels . . . were to be burned at the hands of an executioner, and since it would take too long to have one come here," they would oblige him "to serve instead by burning the said commission himself, which was done on the spot." Bazil Buché was forced to burn his American commission in a lantern provided by his inquisitors after it, too, had been read "in a loud voice and ironically." Like Rousseau he had to play the part of executioner in a ceremony that "seemed to make a great impression on the assembly." [18]

The imagery here is not just of confession but of exorcism, the extermination of the contaminating spirit of rebellion. What accounts for the otherworldly quality of this inquiry into the political allegiances of the French Canadian farmers? The bishop and the governor each confronted what he saw as gross misbehavior calling for punishment and redress. Each, furthermore, saw the other as a natural ally. Modern readers may be accustomed to distinguishing between the religious and civil aspects of authority, power, and subversion. To the participants in the events of 1775–76, on the other hand, it was the idea of separating the sacred and the secular that would have seemed odd. Nor was this the case only in Quebec, where British rule over the Catholic majority made the relationship especially problematic. In New England as well, the invasion of Quebec raised uncomfortable questions about the proper role of religious considerations in practical matters of politics and war.

For those on either side of the frontier, the traditional way of understanding conflicts between New England and Quebec was through the rhetoric, and on several occasions the practice, of religious warfare.[19] Patriot leaders accordingly presented the Quebec Act of 1774 as an immoral pact whereby the British would tolerate popery in return for French Canadian help in disciplining the New Englanders. Nevertheless, the notion of making common cause with the French Canadians in order to eject the British from Quebec quickly persuaded Congress to abandon such sectarian rhetoric.[20] And the unexpected success of American overtures to the habitants then prompted Jean-Olivier Briand to remind his parishioners just what sort of people the Congregationalist invaders were. The bishop did not mince words. "No other sect," he charged, "has persecuted Romans as have the Bostonians; no other has insulted priests, and profaned churches and relics of the saints as they have." The Bostonians were "apostates, schismatics, and pure heretics, Protestants of the Protestantism furthest removed from the Roman religion and its cruelest enemy." In Montreal a French Canadian royal official shared Briand's despair as he contemplated the approach of the bigots from the south. "The fanaticism of the Bostonians is known everywhere," Simon Sanguinet wrote in his diary. "It did not spare the Quaker; will it spare the Roman Catholics?"[21]

Would it, indeed? The question was apposite. In pursuit of their goal of expelling the British, the Americans could not afford to antagonize the French Canadians by indulging in the trappings of a Protestant crusade. However clear this was to the rebel leaders, there was no way to know before the fact how easily the rank and file would accept Congress's new policy of finding allies among old Catholic enemies. Just as uncertain was the amenability of the habitants to the idea. Their bishop exhorted them to remember the same ancestral hatreds that the Bostonois urged them to forget. Any successful collaboration would therefore ask much of both parties. Quite apart from the risk involved in defying the British government, Yankees and Quebecois alike would have to confront within themselves the challenges such an alliance would pose to familiar notions of religious identity, difference, and duty.

If there was some doubt as to how the French Canadians would respond to instructions from their betters, there was no ambiguity in the instructions themselves. As he had done repeatedly since the Peace of 1763, Bishop Briand made it clear that he staked all his spiritual authority on the side of loyalty to the British government. It helped that he had always enjoyed excellent relations with Governor Carleton. Far from admitting any nostalgia for the days of French rule, Briand insisted that Canadian allegiance had properly passed from King Louis to King George. He instructed his parishioners to be tolerant of the Protestants who were beginning to settle among them. "Any other conduct would only alienate their hearts," he advised. It "would not make any converts, and might encourage the government to withdraw the protection and the freedom that it is pleased to accord our holy religion."[22] Chief among Briand's rewards for his conciliatory policy was the Quebec Act, which the governor interpreted to the bishop's advantage. The two connived at a private understanding that the clause in the act qualifying "the free exercise of the Religion of the Church of Rome" as "subject to the King's Supremacy" did not imply any diminished role for the pope.[23] Writing to a superior in Paris, Briand positively gloated over his modus vivendi with the governor. "I exercise my ministry without restraint," he explained. "The governor loves and esteems me; the English honor me." He had even convinced the British Parliament to amend the proposed oath so that "every Canadian can take it: in the Quebec Act there appears the word 'supremacy'; but we don't swear on the act. I spoke of it to . . . our governor, who responded, 'What do you care about the act? The king will make no use of this power . . . but the act would not have passed without this word. . . . Say the word and then believe what you will.'"[24]

In keeping with his belief that accommodation to British power best served the church, Briand inveighed against the American rebels in the strongest terms. In May 1775 he issued a mandamus calling on all Canadian Catholics to remain loyal. At first he thought it needed circulating only in Trois-Rivières and farther south, around Montreal. By June he recognized the need in the district of Quebec City as well.[25] In October, faced with widespread defections among the habitants, he resorted to the excommunication of all those of his "blind, restless, but ever-cherished children" who "knowingly incite rebellion, or even only aid and favor it without being personally compelled to." Priests were not to perform marriages for such parishioners or post the banns. Briand stressed that to administer any of the sacraments to a rebel would be a mortal sin. Those who died without repenting were not to have funerals inside a church, a ban still in effect in 1778.[26]

Briand also called upon his priests to campaign actively against the Americans. He asked Etienne Montgolfier, superior of the Sulpicians and vicar general of Montreal, to draw up and distribute notes for a model sermon on the subject. Its four main points were the Canadians' patriotic duty to resist the invasion, their obligations under the oath of loyalty to King George, their religious duty as Catholics to obey their rulers, and their debt of gratitude to Carleton and the king for generous treatment since 1763.[27] The priests needed little prodding; by all accounts they were overwhelmingly hostile to the Americans. Arnold's reference to "the clergy, our bitter enemies" and a British officer's praise for "the steady and distinguish'd loyalty of the Canadian Clergy" are typical of the prevailing mood.[28]

In their pastoral roles the priests explicitly encouraged the association of the church with British fortunes. Montgolfier had a Te Deum sung "in all the churches of the province in thanks to the Supreme Being" for the failure of Montgomery's first attempt on St. Johns. At Easter 1776 the vicar general of Trois-Rivières had the *Domine, salvum fac Regem* sung for three days in the Ursuline church "to ask heaven's blessing for our arms." Some priests gave even more to the cause. Father Bailly de Messein was shot twice in the abdomen during a skirmish between loyalist and rebel French Canadians in March 1776. At the battle of the Cedars in May, the Americans took the precaution of placing Father Denault under a guard of six Canadian sentries and a Continental sergeant. After their defeat the captured rebel officers were in turn put under the guard of two Sulpician missionaries at the Lake of Two Mountains.[29]

Their conduct brought the priests little honor in their own parishes. Despite Briand's best efforts and the cooperation of most of the clergy, many habitants proved resistant to sectarian appeals and threats of excommunication alike. This struck Briand as evidence of declining religious faith. Denouncing the trend, he singled out a peasant who, faced with the local priest's disapproval of his choice of godparents for a baptism, had "had the audacity and impiety to take his child back instead of finding other godparents." Many others had "spoken insolently in church," often to express their displeasure at the loyalist behavior of their priests.[30] Thus, after hearing Father Bonaventure preach on the obedience due a prince, Denis Frichet asked in a loud voice on the way out of church, "What is our curé saying now, what's he on about? Has he turned English, too?" Father Lefranc was expounding a similar theme when a listener interrupted him, shouting that "that was enough preaching for the English." When the curé of Saint-Thomas tried to muster the village's militia companies, recalcitrant parishioners told him, "You are an Englishman and you want to make us English." In Cap la Madelaine the rumor went about that Bishop Briand and his vicar general at Trois-Rivières were taking money in return for preaching royalist doctrines.[31]

In their report to Governor Carleton, François Baby and his two colleagues recorded several instances in which peasants had desecrated their churches by using the occasion of the mass to organize collaboration with the Americans. In one parish the commissioners dismissed a militia officer for having "shouted at the church door that those who disobeyed the orders of the Congress would be pillaged." When Joseph Langlois and Gabriel Langlais saw the local militia officers meeting in the presbytery with Monseigneur Desgly and the whole parish assembled outside, they chose the moment to call for "strong hands to carry off the said officers so that they could not receive any orders."[32] The hesitant behavior of one group of rebel habitants suggests that the symbolic importance of such acts was clear to all sides. Uneasy about the propriety of agitating on holy ground, they read out American manifestos "before and after the mass in houses next to the church."[33]

Briand himself was under few illusions as to either the extent of popular disaffection or his own ability to win back his parishioners. "I write and I punish . . . ," he sighed, "but what is said? That my priests and I are afraid. What is needed are troops; they would persuade better than the word of God." Nor did he shrink from naming the specific grievances of the peasants against their curés. As he wrote to the parish priest of Saint-Thomas in the dark days of October 1775, "It is said of me as of you that I am English. . . . I am English in fact: you should be, and they should be as well because they have sworn an oath."[34] As the foregoing examples attest, many French Canadians rejected this assessment and moved easily from disenchantment with their priests to open support of the Americans. Hundreds took up arms under Arnold and Montgomery, and many more served them as scouts, spies, and suppliers.

The ambience of shifting loyalties is captured in Baby's description of an obstreperous butcher named Beaudouin. This resident of Champlain had "always held bad opinions" and had "spoken impertinently" to the seigneur. When he became embroiled in a dispute with the residents of the local presbytery, the latter suggested that they all agree "to abide by the decision of the vicar general or Monseigneur the bishop when it would be possible to see him." Beaudouin retorted "that he recognized neither the bishop's authority nor that of the vicar general and that he would take his complaint to the Bostonian commander at Trois-Rivières." In a single gesture of defiance, a mere butcher had insulted his superiors, his church, and his government. But what mortified the loyalist French Canadian nobility struck the Americans as a most encouraging sign.[35]

As soon as the invasion got under way, George Washington had put aside any religious scruples of his Massachusetts hosts in favor of a more expedient spirit of toleration. In September he gave Schuyler strict instructions on "the absolute necessity of preserving the friendship of the Canadians." He enjoined Arnold "to protect and support the free exercise of the religion of the country and the undisturbed enjoyment of the rights of conscience in religious matters." He published a letter to the people of Canada and later had David Wooster, then in command at Montreal, distribute three hundred copies around the province. In it Washington declared that "the cause of America and of liberty is the cause of every virtuous American Citizen Whatever may be his Religion or his descent." The United Colonies, he wrote, "know no distinction, but such as Slavery, Corruption, and Arbitrary Domination may create." By November he had become even more emphatic, suppressing the annual Pope Day (or Guy Fawkes) celebration in Boston out of consideration for the offense this anti-Catholic ritual was likely to give his Canadian allies.[36]

It was thus from a rather broad range of opinions that American soldiers could take their cue as they sought to understand the greater meaning of their march to Quebec. Some New Englanders had enlisted under the rallying cry of "No King! No Popery!" Others, from Pennsylvania and New York, were less likely to view their enterprise in the apocalyptic terms of Calvinist sermonizing. In Boston, Washington hoped for the best while in Quebec City, Briand and Sanguinet predicted the worst; but none could control the individual events that would make up the encounter between their respective peoples. Unsurprisingly, the record was uneven from the start. Sent forward by Montgomery to sniff out local opinion near Montreal, Ethan Allen reported cheerfully that he had made his way down the Sorel River and up the St. Lawrence to Longueuil "preaching Politicks . . . with good success" and giving assurances that the Americans would not molest anyone in their religion. The members of Arnold's expedition felt less sure of themselves as they struggled through the desolate backcountry of northern Maine. When they finally reached the first Canadian settlements at Sartigan (now St.-Georges), Arnold's men were in desperate straits. Those who survived knew that their lives depended on Canadian hospitality, but they were far from counting on a friendly reception. As one put it, "After having been lately our enemies, at war with us, we did not expect to experience from them too much friendship." And yet, he added, "had we been in New England among people of our own nation, we should not, I think, have been treated with more kindness."[37]

The suggestion that less might have been expected from the Canadians recurs in several veterans' accounts. In their diaries they described the Canadians as "exceedingly kind" and "exceedingly rejoiced with our company," one old woman "singing and dancing 'Yankee Doodle' with the greatest air of good humour." At Sainte-Marie the "amiable people" provided a "warm and comfortable" house for John Henry when he was sick and "very good entertainment" for Isaac Senter.[38] The Americans continued to feel welcome as they descended the Chaudière River from Sartigan. When they reached the St. Lawrence and stopped to collect their straggling forces, they spent two weeks in Pointe Levy and found the residents "generally to be friendly to both officers and soldiers, and to wish to do what they could" to make them "comfortable." The same was true at Pointe-aux-Trembles, where the Americans entered winter quarters after Arnold decided that they could not take Quebec City without reinforcements from Montgomery.[39]

The fall of 1775 was the high-water mark of good feeling between the invaders and the French Canadians. Even before Arnold arrived at Pointe Levy, pro-American habitants held a large meeting to rally support and resist the reconstitution of the militia. Clement Gosselin of the Ile d'Orléans and Pierre Ayot of Kamouraska organized many such meetings, accepted officers' commissions from Congress, and in the spring of 1776 oversaw a system of signal fires to provide warning of British ships sailing up the St. Lawrence.[40] The Canadians gave Montgomery a similar reception to the west. When Carleton sailed upriver on September 7 to oversee the defense of Montreal, he found the habitants more and more hostile the closer he got to the city. Residents of the parishes along the Chambly River convinced Colonel Allen MacLean of their eagerness to serve the crown, only to take the arms he gave them and promptly desert to the Americans. Feeling unsafe anywhere on shore, MacLean then broke camp, loaded his cannon onto boats, destroyed the rest of his stores, and proceeded to the defense of St. Johns by water.[41] He was chased back down again to the mouth of the Chambly by a combined force of the 2d New York Regiment, the Green Mountain Boys, and a thousand Canadians who had enlisted under the local merchant James Livingston.[42] From Lake Champlain to Montreal the Quebecois farmers were almost universally in favor of the Americans, at least while Montgomery swept all before him. They provided pickets for the American camps, turned out in militia companies for review, and brought wagons and provisions. Holed up in the fortress of Quebec City, Colonel MacLean complained of "the treachery and Villainy of the Canadians," without whose connivance "it is a certain fact" that the Americans "never could have done us any mischief." At the same time that they hauled food to sell to the besiegers, the Canadians helped block relief supplies from reaching the garrison by land or water. MacLean did not dare reduce the number of mouths to feed by expelling anyone for fear "of having the Canadian Militia mutiny."[43]

Yet relations between the Americans and the Canadians were never completely smooth. The question of payment for supplies in specie or paper money was one area of unease, exemplifying as it did the delicate balance of goodwill and self-interest. While always preferring coin, the Canadians were at first willing to accept Continental paper despite having suffered severe depreciations under the old French regime. Mindful of this fairly recent experience, Arnold held out as long as he could before resorting to paper.[44] Taking advantage of both the language barrier and the currency problem, the royalist notary of Trois-Rivières, Jean-Baptiste Badeaux, dabbled in psychological warfare while on his way to Montreal to discuss capitulation terms with Montgomery. Fluent in English and accompanied by an Anglo-Canadian, he was able to pass for an American and found himself receiving "many compliments and thanks" along the way "for having (they said) come to give them their liberty." When he and his companion stopped to eat, Badeaux saw his chance to drive a wedge between the Americans and what he considered the disloyal habitants. "When we had finished eating, I took out a piastre and said to the hostess: pay yourself what we owe you. She took the piastre; holding it between two fingers she showed it to everyone in the house, saying: 'Look how these Bostonians are out of money! They wanted us to believe they had nothing but paper money left. Here's proof, you just watch: they talk about paper money, but they'll pay in good coin.'"[45]

Relations could only become more strained in the wake of the crushing American defeat on New Year's Eve. When Arnold tried to rally the Canadian militia in the first days of 1776, the response was cautiously muted. "The peasants," one American wrote, "however friendly disposed, thought it too precarious a juncture to show themselves in that capacity, and those nigh rather retreated back into the country, than give any assistance." Military considerations dictated that Arnold withdraw his powder and stores to a less exposed place farther from the city walls, but he told Congress he dared not, "lest it should make unfavourable impressions on the Canadians, and induce them to withdraw their assistance." He resolved "to put the best face on matters, and betray no marks of fear." [46]

Wooster, after taking command from Arnold on April 1, took a similar view of the psychological dimensions of the situation. It was a frustrating problem: imprudent to trust the Canadians, impolitic not to. Restless habitants near Quebec City had begun threatening to switch sides if a second attempt on the fortress was not made. Without in fact intending a second attack, Wooster ordered the construction of a large number of scaling ladders and fascines in the surrounding towns so as to give the opposite impression. Not surprisingly, when he gave the command for three hundred men from Charlebourg to carry the ladders up to the walls, the residents declined to risk their lives for the sake of making a show with some props. Wooster then stopped using Canadian sentries and posted only his own. The Canadians continued to withdraw into neutrality as the spring—and the threat of British warships in the river—drew closer. [47]

Quite apart from the shifting calculus of military and political self-interest, great cultural differences lay in the way of mutual comprehension and sympathy between the parties to the hastily arranged Canadian-American alliance. It was first of all a meeting of strangers, with the absence of a common language the chief obstacle to friendly relations. Frequent references to the need for interpreters suggest that few on either side could speak the other's tongue. [48] But one way and another, they managed. A Connecticut militia officer with Montgomery reported with satisfaction that friendly Indians and French Canadians were learning to say "liberty," "Bostonian," and "me Yankee." [49] A feeling of mutual strangeness nevertheless predominated. In one ironic case this ignorance of the other caused the destitute condition of Arnold's men to inspire not just pity but a certain mystified respect. When the French Canadians saw the light clothing the Americans were wearing in the harsh fall weather, "the report spread that these people were insensitive of cold and wore nothing but linen in the most severe seasons—the French word *toile* (linen) was changed into *tolle* (iron plate) and the rumor then ran that the Bostonois were musket-proof, being all covered with sheet iron."[50]

At a deeper level still than the difference of languages was that of religious faiths. Yet here too the Americans were often explicit in their gratitude to, and sympathy for, their Catholic hosts. When John Henry's friend and fellow Pennsylvanian fell sick and died near Sartigan, the villagers buried him with "due respect." "This real catholicism towards the remains of one we loved," Henry recalled, "made a deep and wide breach upon my early prejudices." Henry wrote his recollections in old age, by which time he was a Pennsylvania politician with perhaps a vested interest in a reputation for tolerance. Even so, other contemporary accounts show outbursts of anti-Catholic feeling on the part of the Americans to have been the exception rather than the rule, as when David Wooster ordered all the "mass houses" in Montreal, as he called them, closed on Christmas Eve.[51] In another instance, the soldiers who stole a silver cross from the church at Sainte-Geneviève gave it back when a parishioner chased after them to ask for it. A court of inquiry held after their departure nevertheless judged this one of the more noteworthy cases of looting.[52]

The treatment of the Catholic clergy revealed much about American attitudes toward the Canadians' religion. In an effort to cultivate the Jesuits, the invaders restored to them a Montreal residence that the British had confiscated for use as a prison. When Benjamin Franklin and Charles Carroll visited Montreal on behalf of Congress in April 1776, they brought with them Carroll's brother John, a Jesuit priest. He said mass at the church of Pierre-René Floquet, the Jesuit superior. This indiscretion earned Father Floquet an angry letter from Briand and the threat of an interdict. In reply, Floquet admitted to having offered confession and communion to rebel Catholics and explained that he thought it best to remain on good terms with the Americans and their friends.[53]

While Father Floquet was one of several priests who walked

a careful line between sympathy for the rebels and obedience to his bishop, as a rule there was little love lost between priests and Continentals. Sanguinet applauded the clergy's loyalty and observed that it had "brought upon them much persecution on the part of the Bostonians," for "many were sent for with guards, taken to the Bostonians' camp, and very nearly sent as prisoners to the colonies." Indeed, the Americans arrested and detained priests in several parishes. In December 1775 the aide-de-camp of the local American commander wrote a letter containing "reprimands and threats" to the priest of Saint-Pierre-les-Becquets after his parishioners had denounced him for withholding the sacraments from them. An armed party of Continentals set out from Lachine the next month to seize Father Besson at his church in Sainte-Geneviève. Around the same time the Americans arrested two priests in Lavaltrie, imprisoned them at Sorel, and told them they would be deported to the colonies.[54]

All the same, the Catholic clergy appear to have suffered abuse from the Americans not so much qua Catholics as qua political opponents. A blacksmith who made cannonballs for the Americans near Trois-Rivières advised Congress to tolerate "the novenas and prayers" being offered in Quebec for God's help against the invaders. The priests were irritating, he granted, "but policy requires in the circumstances that they be kept on, and not eliminated." A similar willingness to discriminate between Catholic friends and enemies was demonstrated during the American troops' celebration of St. Patrick's Day in Trois-Rivières. In the course of parading around the town, they stopped to give three cheers outside the Ursuline convent before moving on to strictly political affairs. Reaching the house of the seigneur, Godefroy de Tonnancour, they shouted "Goddam that house and all that is in it!," to which Tonnancour's son replied, "May God forever damn you all!"[55]

Far from any principled hostility, what runs through contemporary accounts of the soldiers' reactions to Canadian Catholicism is simple curiosity. They might have heard dire descriptions from their ministers at home, but few could have met a Catholic person before. William Goforth, in command at Trois-Rivières, was more curious than hostile in his own demeanor. On his way to supervise a militia election, he passed through a village whose priest had just died. In a gesture difficult to imagine in David Wooster, he paused at the church to watch the funeral through the open door. It was a scene repeated many times that winter and spring: as one would expect, death and dying were especially compelling topics for the soldier diarists. Abner Stocking's description of the old ruined church at Norridgewalk captured the eerie quality of the spot, "a place formerly inhabited by the French and Indians. The former had erected a mass house for their devotions, but had deserted it at the time the New England forces made great slaughter among them in the French war." He noted that "the temple of worship contained some curiosities, such as crosses &c." The same church caught the attention of Simeon Thayer, who knew that its "Curate, or Friar, named Francisco," had been killed "about 40 years ago, at the time when the provincials drove back the Indians. His remains lie buried here with a cross over them, as is customary in France, Spain, Italy, and all Roman Catholic countries, when their clergy Die." [56]

James Melvin of Hubbardston, Massachusetts, recorded two more intimate encounters. The first was in January 1776, after Melvin had contracted smallpox and been moved from the monastery to a hospital. There he was able to observe a performance of the last rites.

> A Frenchman being at the point of death the nuns came and read over him, afterwards a priest came in; then they fetched in a table covered with a white cloth, and lighted two wax candles, about three feet long, and set them on the table. The priest put on a white robe over his other garments, and the nuns kneeled down, and the priest stood and read a sentence, and then the nuns a sentence, and so they went on for some time; then the priest prayed by himself; then the nuns, and then the priest again; then they read altogether a spell, and finally the

priest alone; then the priest stroked the man's face, and then they took away their candles, and tables, &c., and the man died.[57]

The following July, while held in the jail, Melvin saw a priest leading a procession to visit another sick person. Ahead of the curé walked a man ringing a bell, then two boys carrying candles on long poles. The priest himself walked under a canopy held up by two more attendants, and wore "things as heavy as board . . . tied to his knees, and dangling and knocking against his shins. They have crosses on those two things." The "great cross" on the priest's chest caught Melvin's unaccustomed eye, as did the "thing of wooden beads hanging by his side. The people all have these beads when they go to church, to help them remember their prayers. They also use the same ceremony when they go to a burying, and have choristers singing before the corpse."[58]

Whatever his minister in Hubbardston may have hoped, James Melvin did not have much of the Puritan crusader about him. Nor did this mildness distinguish him from his fellow diarists. Simon Fobes, though a devout Congregationalist from Canterbury, Connecticut, recorded no objection when Arnold "circulated manifestoes among the inhabitants, assuring them that they should . . . enjoy their religion."[59] On St. Patrick's Day, 1776, Caleb Haskell "had the curiosity to go to Mass in Bonpoir." Return Meigs of Middletown, Connecticut, was "entertained with hospitality and elegance" while billeted "at the house of the curate of the parish of St. Augustine." At Pointe-aux-Trembles Henry Dearborn wrote that "the Curate of the Parish Dines at Head-quarters To-day." Simeon Thayer felt "well-treated" at Sartigan. The troops were well provisioned, and "even the minister was generous eno' to let us have all that he could spare."[60]

The contest for Quebec does not seem to have had any similarly broadening effect on British sensibilities. If anything, what they saw as the treacherous behavior of the Canadians tended only to reinforce anti-Catholic feeling among the Regulars. Compare the tone of Melvin's funeral descriptions to another by Alexander Colquhoun of the Royal Navy: "There came a burial which the way of their Burying was Strange to us we Staid the Space of tou hours there to See there ways. . . . The Priests begun aspeach But it being in french I Could understand nothing they Said. . . . The Priests nield' Doun to our Saviour on the Cros and to agreat many more images all there transactions is tou tidious to mintion I Staid there neigh the Space of tow hours and I was obliged to live them as I found them." [61] The experience does not seem to have worked any change on the narrator: the classic accusations of Catholic obscurantism and idolatry are intact. In a similar vein, Simon Fobes attributed the only case of outright anti-Catholic behavior that appears in the various journals to another British sailor, this time aboard the ship where Fobes was being held prisoner in July 1776. A member of the crew died, and Fobes was among the party ordered ashore under the command of a boatswain to bury the body. "When we had set the coffin down by the grass, the steward, a papist friar, pulled a book out of his pocket, and began to read something, which I could not understand. The boatswain, however, soon got out of patience with the friar, d——d him off, and told him he would hear no more of his 'Paternoster,' and immediately ordered the corpse to be buried." [62]

Whether from conviction or necessity, the Americans tended even in the privacy of their writings to be considerably more polite. A final observation on this score is the more convincing for coming from a member of the loyal French Canadian elite. Jean-Baptiste Badeaux recorded the rumor current in April 1776 that American reinforcements would soon arrive accompanied by five hundred Catholic priests. The Bostonians, far from having earned a reputation for Protestant fanaticism, were seen by the rebel habitants as possible suppliers of the spiritual guidance their own priests continued to withhold from them. [63]

Where, then, were the bigots whose "fanaticism," Sanguinet had said, was "everywhere known"? [64] Their own words cannot be used to convict the Americans of intolerance toward the Catholic Church or its members. What is more, their enemies largely declined to charge them with that particular offense. Even Sanguinet, while berating the citizens of Montreal for their shameful acquiescence in the occupation then drawing to a close, did not accuse them of having tolerated the desecration of their religion. Yet this is just the charge one would expect him to have leveled had he felt it was warranted. In the course of a long and harsh harangue, he listed many abuses of the Montrealers' docility—low prices paid for food, deportations without trial, dishonor to French ancestors who had fought the New Englanders in their own day—but nowhere did he mention any insult or injury to religion.[65]

As the invasion itself had shown, the Protestant-Catholic divide was far from the most important criterion of difference in Quebec. The French Canadians found themselves in the unaccustomed position of having to choose between two potential allies, English Protestants and American ones. When Bishop Briand cast his lot with the former, his decision reflected both gratitude for the crown's protection of Catholic privileges and a belief that New England Congregationalism was a more virulent strain of heresy than Anglicanism. His attempts to enforce that decision, however, brought him face to face with the limits of his own influence. Contrary to his hopes, the fact that the invaders were members of a Calvinist sect did not make them repugnant to the habitants. Nor did his status as their bishop compel lay Quebecois to obey him. Briand's immediate reaction to these unpleasant discoveries was to construe them as proof that his countrymen were poor Catholics, lacking in faith.

Impiety, however, was only one way to construe the habitants' behavior. In more secular terms, other members of the French Canadian elite sensed with alarm that the arrival of the Americans had shaken the foundations of Quebecois society, humiliating legitimate authority and loosening the undisciplined passions of the lower orders. It was the French-speaking leadership of Montreal who organized the reconstitution of the militia, an act of public-spiritedness (as they thought) little appreciated in the poorer quarters of the city.[66] The militia was an obvious bone of contention, involving as it did the coerced enlistment of those who resented the exemption from service of members of the governor's council, judges and other civil officers, seigneurs, retired military officers, members of the clergy, "students at the seminaries of Quebec City and Montreal, and private persons employed in the public service."[67] When ordered to form their companies in the summer of 1775, those whose status did not excuse them offered a lukewarm response in some places and active resistance in several. In Nicolet, Colonel MacLean found no one but women and children in sight, the men having hidden in the woods. Three gentlemen sent by Cramahé from Quebec City to the Ile d'Orléans to take command of militia companies thought it wise to take along ten heavily armed sailors. Despite this precaution they were dissuaded from their errand by 250 habitants wielding sticks.[68]

The tensions between French Canadians distressed many of those who felt their lead no longer being followed. Several of them dwelt at length on the incident in March 1776 during which Father Bailly de Messein was shot. A band of 150 loyalist French Canadians under Louis Liénard de Beaujeu de Villemonde, seigneur of Ile-aux-Grues and Ile-aux-Oies, had attempted to dislodge the Americans and their friends from Pointe Levy and then relieve Quebec City, just across the river. An advance party of Beaujeu's force took for its headquarters the house of Michel Blais, a militia captain and minor seigneur. Betrayed by one of their own number, they were attacked and the house pillaged by 80 Americans and 150 habitants. It was only with some difficulty that the Americans dissuaded their allies from slaughtering the 20 loyalists they took prisoner.[69] This instance of civil war greatly disturbed those members of the French Canadian elite who wrote about it. After seeing the loyalist prisoners frog-marched into Trois-

Rivières, Badeaux remarked in his journal that nothing was "more execrable and repugnant to nature than to see such unfortunates led by their compatriots without the latter seeming affected in the slightest; on the contrary, they displayed great joy, as if they were leading men they had never heard of, or their worst enemies." For his part, the bishop of Quebec singled out the affair as an "action accompanied by circumstances that will forever disgrace the Canadian nation, and paint it as a nation of more than savage cruelty and barbarity." It had even "caused the indignant Bostonians to say that if they ever needed to roast a Canadian they would find a hundred others to turn the spit." [70]

Distressed though they were by the spectacle of farmers killing farmers, Badeaux and his peers were even more fearful of farmers attacking them. When a delegation from Trois-Rivières met with Montgomery to discuss the town's surrender, Montgomery told them that he was "quite mortified" to think they felt it necessary to seek protection from his troops. The delegates replied that they were not afraid of the Americans, "but of the Canadians who would descend . . . with them." When the residents of Machiche threatened to take Tonnancour and another seigneur hostage, Badeaux felt his own sort of people to be "between life and death since these beggars of Canadians have risen up; they are rabid and seek only to pillage and murder." [71] Although rarely bent on pillage, murder, and revenge, many of the habitants were quite self-consciously out to challenge existing authority. Their attitude was exemplified by Beaudouin, the butcher from Champlain. By appealing to the Americans as an alternative locus of authority, he showed how slippery status relationships had become. The Americans—to paraphrase John Adams—had put the pot to boil, and the scum was beginning to rise.

Elite French Canadians saw a link between social status and loyalty to the British crown. Considering themselves both worthy and loyal, they understood disrespectful and disruptive behavior as the natural province of lowly habitants and

Americans. The report of Baby, Taschereau, and Williams, exuding as it does a grave concern for the disregard of social distinctions, provides instance after instance of the kind of behavior that violated proper forms. One evocative case was that of Pierre Bérubé of Rivière-Ouelle, who, along with Jean Levesque and two of Levesque's children, "struck sergeant-major Pierre Boucher last fall while he was serving as a guard to Sieur Saint-Aubin, the notary, for having read aloud an order of General Carleton on the way out of mass." [72] Like Pierre Beaudouin in Champlain, Bérubé and his friends combined many sins in one offense. They assaulted a militia officer, they did so before the whole parish and at the church, and they openly declared their opposition to Carleton. Lastly, Jean Levesque had failed to control his children. Things were evidently out of joint in Rivière-Ouelle. Yet all these infractions recur again and again in the commissioners' village-by-village account of their eight-week tour. They were assiduous in noting instances of insufficiently deferential behavior, including but not limited to lack of regard for social station, age and gender differences, and the sanctity of holy places. [73]

The contagion of insubordination seemed to know no bounds. Even the pinnacle of French Canadian society came under assault, its aristocrats accosted by peasants. When Lanaudière the Younger and Tonnancour the Elder left Trois-Rivières in October 1775 to help defend Montreal, the villagers of Paroisse-au-Chicot stopped them in the woods between Berthier and Le Chicot, disarmed them, and detained them for three days. As their captors led them back to Le Chicot, "all the women along the road cried to their husbands in derision, 'You've had good hunting today for sure!'" When the same Godefroy de Tonnancour, in his capacity as colonel of the militia, sent Badeaux to speak for him, the people of Nicolet told the notary to go to the devil. Badeaux persisted, telling them he had come "only out of friendship for them" and "not with the design of giving them commands." Even so, he reminded them that Carleton had "declared anyone who refused orders to be rebels and punishable as such, and that the punishment for rebels was the gallows." By then, however, the threat was visibly empty. Carleton could be safely ignored in the fall of 1775, and Godefroy de Tonnancour along with him. One could even, as happened in Saint-Thomas, help oneself to the vicar's wine by the hogshead.[74]

Within the higher strata of Canadian society, French- and English-speaking subjects shared a sense of indignation at the threat from below. Nor was this the only inducement to smooth relations at the rarefied level of generals, bishops, and seigneurs. The Quebec Act had opened public offices to Roman Catholics for the first time. Mindful of the chance for advancement, members of the French Canadian elite passed from accommodation to the British presence to active assimilation. At the level of polite society, the British establishment set the standard for French Canadian aspirations. Thus Mme DuMuy-DeLisle was anything but sorry when the British retook Montreal in 1776. "Although we have a garrison here, we are very tranquil," she wrote to a relative. "The officers are very well-bred, the soldiers well disciplined." There had been "two balls this winter, a magnificent one given by General Fraser, another at Varennes." Her daughter had made an excellent impression: "General Fraser thinks she has the air of a duchess . . . ; the English consider her a grand dancer."[75] The Americans in Quebec, on the other hand, were conspicuously lacking in well-bred officers and disciplined troops. Disdain for their low social status united upper-class Canadians of both nationalities. The Continentals lacked a proper officer class: Montgomery was "now styled General" but in British eyes retained his former rank of captain. Moses Hazen, once a captain in the British Rangers, had "dwindled down to a Colonel in the Rebel army"—a formulation that captures nicely the perceived debasement of rank itself by the Americans.[76] "With respect to the better sort of people, both French and English," wrote an American officer, "seven-eighths wish to see the throats of the continentals cut."[77]

What the upper strata of French Canadian society saw as a dangerous disturbance looked rather different from below. The habitants' disdain for their British rulers was matched by a keen appreciation of the new possibilities that arose when the initial success of the Americans caused established forms of authority to collapse. To them, the vacuum at the top of the social pyramid was an exciting and not altogether unattractive prospect. One area in which this became apparent was the struggle over the composition and legitimate powers of the local militia under the new state of affairs. Given the choice for once, the residents of Rivière Basticant reelected all their militia officers. The same men held the same powers, but those were now vested by the habitants, not the king. In Lobinière the villagers went one better, declining to elect militia officers at all and simply sticking with bailiffs, "since as they were changed every year they would not dare to commit injustice, and it was not the same with a captain who was fixed" in his post.[78]

Seen from above, this vacuum was an invitation to "usurpers," as Baby and his colleagues called the Americans and their collaborators. But the habitants were reluctant to move in and fill the void themselves. Nicholas Maillot received a militia commission from the British in 1775, but "neglected or rather did not wish to have himself recognized as captain in the parish," and acted only as a bailiff, the post he had previously held. Such diffidence would cost him his commission in 1776, but it was a popular evasion at the time. Joseph Duquet played it similarly cool in Sainte-Croix. He was "cashiered primarily for having neglected to have himself recognized as captain last summer when he received his commission" from Carleton.[79]

Rather than appropriate to themselves the power they saw draining away from their putative superiors, the habitants consented to let it devolve upon the Americans. The parishioners of Sainte-Marie were unmoved when their bailiff announced orders for the clearing of roads during the winter of the invasion, perhaps because he somewhat indelicately did so in the name of the king. "He was called names by several inhabitants over this order and notably by Jean Bilodeau the Younger, who asked him in indecent terms, 'Where is your king? He is in the city, hiding in the muzzle of a cannon.'" From this, one Campanais of Sainte-Anne drew the logical conclusion. Accosting the loyal militia captain Louis Goin on the way out of mass, he said, "You are no longer under the British government. It's the Bostonians you are dealing with now." [80]

This was in fact the rule. The habitants denounced royalists and handed them over to the Americans rather than imprisoning or otherwise punishing them on their own authority. The band that pillaged Taschereau's farm and mill in February claimed to have orders from Benedict Arnold to justify the public auction they held of the booty. It was Richard Montgomery's name that nine habitants invoked when they held Louis Goin hostage in his own home, "offered him several insults, threatened to burn down his house, and obliged him to give them ninety-six silver shillings of the province, several possessions, and his arms." [81]

With the powers of both the British and French Canadian elites denuded of legitimacy, Americans became the arbitrators of disputes among the habitants. William Goforth was clearly sensitive to this role while in command at Trois-Rivières. Accompanied by Badeaux, who served as interpreter and recorded the scene, Goforth went to Saint-Pierre-les-Becquets in February to supervise the election of militia officers. First he had to settle an argument over whether to hold the election in the presbytery or in a house. He chose the former, which was the customary location. Once the assembly began, voices were raised against the incumbent captain. Etienne Chandonnet protested to Goforth, "Sir, the reason . . . is that his heart is English, and he received commissions from General Carleton, when the rest of us refused them." Goforth made what Badeaux termed "a judicious reply. He told them, 'Although this man . . . served the

king, that is not sufficient grounds; he could be as good a subject of Congress as he was loyal to General Carleton; but to
avoid all difficulties I will proceed to a new election.'" The
captain lost.[82]

Several things about the incident are notable. The American commander had decreed the election and would look
upon the officer chosen as "a subject of Congress." Second,
Goforth would accept a notorious royalist in the post if he had
to. Similar flexibility in view of past behavior was a hallmark
of the efforts of Baby, Taschereau, and Williams to replenish
the corps of militia officers in 1776. Their main task was to
gauge and if possible improve the political and martial relia-
bility of the habitants. This was not merely a retrospective
concern of Carleton's, since new invasions threatened in 1778
and 1780. It was difficult to be sanguine about the future conduct of the French Canadians in view of the fact that their
desertion to the American side had been so general. In Saint-
Augustin the commissioners threw up their hands. Some of
the villagers had rebelled, some had stayed neutral, but none
had declared for the king and all had supplied the Americans
"without objecting. For this reason, having been unable to
obtain any information in order to recognize the most faithful subjects," the commissioners decided to "put off the nomination of parish officers until another time."[83] Such evasion
could not work everywhere, or none of the villages would have
officers and there would be no system of command in the
countryside. In most cases where royalist candidates with
clean records were lacking, the investigators had to settle for
compromise.

The fundamental tension was between justice and order,
that is, between the strictly equitable punishment of all officers in dereliction of their duty and the maintenance of an
effective militia even in the short run. The first would have
meant returning virtually every officer in Quebec to the ranks
and thus rendered the second impossible; yet the second was
crucial not just to the military but to the civil security of the

province. Carleton presumably had already written off the military value of the militia in a second invasion, although he might at least hope not to have to fight his own subjects again. The militia, however, was not only a military body. It was the police as well, the basic instrument of legal force in Quebec. The judgments handed out by Baby and the other commissioners reveal this dual role of the militia and the compromises it dictated for the treatment of offending officers.

Not every officer who had agreed to take and transmit orders from the Americans was demoted to the ranks, much less barred from holding office again. As long as he had not served the rebels with too much "zeal and affection," he might keep his rank.[84] The infamous Pierre Ayot had bullied Captain Michel Blais into making an announcement for rebel recruits at the church door, but only "so as to avoid a greater evil and, as he explained, in such an ironic tone of voice" that he found no takers. Blais was continued in his post. Captain François Bourassa and two of his lieutenants also had shown the requisite bad faith. They had carried out the Americans' orders until replaced by popular election but were judged not to have "served the usurpers of this parish with affection." Nor were they cashiered.[85]

Captain Chorel Dorvilier, on the other hand, was dismissed for having "served as a captain for the rebels last winter" and then having tendered his commission to them when asked for it. Still, Baby and his colleagues made it clear that Dorvilier had "always held the sentiments of a zealous subject." They cashiered him because they decided he "had only engaged in such conduct out of fear and weakness." His loss of face, in other words, was the greater offense: he was dismissed as an officer not because he had collaborated with the enemy but because he could no longer inspire confidence and respect. The commissioners made the same point in the opposite way when dealing with Augustin Gingras, who had held captain's commissions from Carleton and from Governor Murray before him. He refused a new commission from the British at the time of the invasion and then "served the rebels in that capacity by his punctual execution of their orders without any objection on his part." But he apparently had contrived to carry out those orders without encouraging rebellion or abusing those who remained loyal. Noting that Gingras had taken sole responsibility for these actions, having appointed no subalterns or sergeants during the period of his collaboration, Baby and his colleagues declined to demote him to the ranks. They preferred, however grudgingly, a leader who had switched sides to a coward like Dorvilier who had not: a keeper of order to a loyal but ineffective partisan. Officers who had served the rebels could stay on because they were too difficult to replace. As a result, not all the damage done in 1775–76 would be made good.[86]

In the event, neither the Yankees nor the French Canadians made use of religious categories to understand what took place between them. From the habitants' point of view, the essential distinctions were those of class and ethnicity. It was a sense of betrayal by their Anglophile priests and seigneurs that caused them to welcome the American invaders.[87] No longer convinced of the legitimacy of their leaders, the habitants were amenable to the American offers of alliance and even political union. As the conduct of the militia officers shows, they greeted the Bostonois as secular instruments of justice and revenge.[88]

The idea of a widening split in French Canadian society was most useful for American propaganda. The accent on what divided Canadians from one another had the further advantage of obscuring what separated them from the Americans. Eager to finesse the religious issue, the invaders based their appeals on distinctions of power instead. Washington took this tack in his letter of September 1775. The British, he wrote, had "persuaded themselves . . . that the Canadians were not capable of distinguishing between the Blessings of Liberty and the Wretchedness of Slavery; that gratifying the Vanity of a little

Circle of Nobility would blind the Eyes of the people of Canada . . . ; but they have been deceived." [89] This appeal to republican sentiment, the direct challenge to the habitants to separate their own interests from those of their social superiors, was a new departure in American exhortation. In place of religious categories that united all Quebecois against virtually all Americans, it substituted social categories that detached the Canadian farmers from their nobles and placed them alongside the embattled yeomen of New England and New York.

At the same time it was a strategy that involved certain risks. Just as Bishop Briand had been unable to marshal his forces in defense of the faith, Montgomery and Arnold could not be sure their men would prove willing to fight under the banner of enlightenment and toleration. It was conceivable, beforehand, that they would behave in Quebec like the Puritans they had claimed to be when they marched from home. In the end they did not. Collaboration with the French Canadians did not plague the consciences of the New Englanders who went to Quebec. Perhaps it is just that, like atheists in foxholes, bigots were scarce in the Maine woods. Isaac Senter, a Rhode Island doctor who accompanied Arnold's party from Cambridge to Quebec City, related the depths to which the men had been reduced by near starvation. Captain Dearborn's "poor dog" had "hitherto lived through all the tribulations," but now "became a prey for the sustenance of the assassinators. This poor animal was instantly devoured, without leaving any vestige of the sacrifice." [90] The choice of word is suggestive. By describing the event as a sacrifice and thus extenuating the normally repugnant act, Senter provided a metaphor for the theological elasticity displayed by the Americans in the desperate circumstances of their adventure in Quebec. "The voracious disposition many of us had now arrived at, rendered almost any thing admissible. Clean and unclean were forms now little in use." [91]

Impatience with such distinctions is characteristic of any

situation, like battle, in which one's life is at stake. The problem for Senter and his comrades was not whether it was right
or wrong by the standards of their ordinary lives to eat dogs or
befriend Catholics but simply whether it was possible. Others
might object to such new practices, but it is the province—
some would say the luxury—of those who are still leading ordinary lives to continue to apply familiar standards. To the extent that American propaganda had to justify the awkward
novelty of the expedition to Quebec, it was not the participants who needed convincing but distant observers. It was in
this second sphere that the final accounting would be made
for the ill-fated expedition to Quebec. Sullivan and Arnold
could escape with their surviving men and burn the forts they
abandoned, but they could no more restore the Puritan character of their enterprise than revive the dead. Far from the
walls of Quebec City—in Boston, London, and Versailles—
the ashes of the American defeat would be sifted for clues as
to the true nature of this young and as yet somewhat ungainly
rebellion.

# 3

## *Conquered into Liberty*

Whoever sought to explain what had happened in Quebec needed to account for the Americans' reversal of their position on the Catholic Question. He or she could argue, for instance, that the New Englanders had grown in understanding, putting aside the crabbed strictures of the past to embrace the more modern mood of reason and toleration. In this they could be seen as following the lead of their compatriots in Pennsylvania, Virginia, and other places where the European Enlightenment had managed to take root in America. Whether crediting New Englanders with achieving enlightenment or Virginians with bestowing it upon them, such explanations asserted that the ideological novelty of the Quebec Expedition was to the credit of the American cause.

Others saw it differently. To opponents of the Revolution, the embrace of the habitants was merely the latest proof of the rebels' crass opportunism and moral bankruptcy. For this reason the military struggle that ended with Carleton's rout of the Americans gave rise to a polemical struggle that lasted much longer. The same facts could support widely divergent conclusions, and not just in disputes over the question of American independence. Within the Patriot camp itself, the decision to carry the war into Quebec met with bitter objections, on the grounds both that Catholics were unacceptable allies and that the invasion of a neighboring province was unjustified. The fact that the invasion ended in disaster only emboldened its critics, putting pressure on those who had endorsed it. To respond to these critics was to stake out a position on the relevance (or otherwise) of religious belief to political conduct. With Calvinists in their own ranks charging that they had fallen away from their faith and Tories sneering that they had never had any to begin with, Patriot apologists faced a complicated task. Since they had not paused to construct a rationale for their actions before undertaking them, they were obliged to improvise as they went along. Consequently, what their explanations lacked in coherence they made up for in what they revealed of the difficult process of reconciling moral and political imperatives. This problem received its earliest illustration in the American colonists' deeply ambivalent response to the Quebec Act.

For most Americans the first event to link Canada with the struggle against Britain was Parliament's passage of the Quebec Act in August 1774. Letters, newspaper items, and Congregationalist sermons denounced the measure as a latter-day Popish Plot. The analogy was a potent one, since the Whig idea of a right of revolution was descended from the opposition to the Catholic James II. From this point of view the most offensive and threatening feature of the act was its regularization of the status of the Catholic Church in Quebec. The statute stipulated that "His Majesty's Subjects, professing the Religion of the Church of Rome may have, hold, and enjoy, the free Exercise of the Religion of the Church of Rome, subject to the King's Supremacy," and that "the Clergy of the said Church may hold, receive, and enjoy, their accustomed Dues and Rights, with respect to such Persons only as shall profess the said Religion."[1]

American protests tended to interpret the reference to the king's supremacy as a sign of creeping Romanism at court and to overlook the restriction of tithes to Catholic subjects. They expressed amazement that the Church of Rome, still subject to severe disabilities in Britain itself and unwelcome in nearly every American colony, should be, as they saw it, established in Quebec. Nor was this their only qualm. The act stipulated an appointed Legislative Council ("whereas it is at present inexpedient to call an Assembly"), restricted the powers of the council and local bodies in matters of public finance, and extended the boundaries of the province to include the territory between the Great Lakes and the Ohio River.[2] Here were more secular signs of the conspiracy of a corrupt royal ministry against American liberties.

Yet for American propagandists trying to link the Quebec Act to the Patriot cause, there quickly arose a snag. On the one hand, the overwhelming majority of Canadians were Catholic and therefore prima facie enemies of liberty in the New England view of things. They were born and bred to slavery, ripe for use as mercenaries by Governor Carleton. On the other hand, if the Canadians could be convinced that their own best interest lay in an alliance with America against British rule, then America's hand would be strengthened as it sought to negotiate a new imperial relationship. There was also a small but influential English-speaking Protestant minority in Quebec, mostly fur traders in Montreal. They could be cultivated, their poor treatment under the Quebec Act pointed out. They might serve in turn as a conduit to the French Canadians, helping to convince them to rise against their recent conquerors and avenge the defeat of Montcalm. At the outset, then, the Americans sought to have it both ways on the issue of Quebec. To British and domestic audiences they waved the bloody shirt of the Jacobite rebellions of '15 and '45, while at the same time they sent feelers to Anglo-Canadians and the Quebecois alike.

The Quebec Act quickly appeared on the agenda of the First Continental Congress when it met in Philadelphia in September 1774. An address drafted on the fifth informed the British public of the delegates' indignant opinion that Parliament was "not authorized by the constitution to establish a religion, fraught with sanguinary and impious tenets." Yet there it was: Parliament had consented in the Quebec Act "to establish in that country a religion that has long deluged your island in blood, and dispersed impiety, bigotry, persecution, murder and rebellion through every part of the world." Congress managed to portray even the civil provisions of the act as evidence of questionable Protestant credentials. "Such declarations we consider as heresies in English politics, and which can no more operate to deprive us of our property, than the interdicts of the Pope can divest Kings of sceptres which the laws of the land and the voice of the people have placed in their hands."[3]

Toward the end of the same session, however, Congress sent another address, this one "to the Inhabitants of the Province of Quebec." Rather than merely ignore the religious question, the delegates preferred to assert their own broad-mindedness and generously impute the same to the French Canadians. "We are too well acquainted with the liberality of sentiment distinguishing your nation," they assured their readers, "to imagine, that difference of religion will prejudice you against a hearty amity with us. You know, that . . . freedom elevates those, who unite in her cause, above all such low-minded infirmities." The religion of the French Canadians, far from being the mother's milk of slavery or any sort of barrier to "hearty amity," was part of a heritage that made them the natural friends of liberty. Bringing to bear "the natural sagacity of Frenchmen" on "the specious device" of the Quebec Act, they would "find it, to use an expression of holy writ, 'a whited sepulchre,' for burying your lives, liberty and property." The delegates even had the audacity to deny that the Quebec Act served the interests of that religion. It did not grant liberty of conscience, since "God gave it to you," but only made its temporal security depend on the pleasure of the king. "Such is the precarious tenure of mere *will* by which you hold your lives and religion."[4]

The new party line on Quebec found expression in many

places other than the address to the French Canadians. The articles of the Continental Association included the Quebec Act together with the "late cruel and oppressive acts . . . respecting the town of Boston and the Massachusetts Bay" as justifications for the retaliatory boycott of trade. While complaining of the absorption of western lands and the denial of an elected assembly under that legislation, the association's authors showed unwonted restraint on religious matters. They declined to repeat the anti-Catholic strains of their address to the British public; rather, they accused the royal government of stooping to stir up "ancient prejudices" so as to "dispose the inhabitants to act with hostility against the free protestant colonies, whenever a wicked ministry shall choose so to direct them." The shoe was now on the other foot, or so Congress affected to believe.[5]

The New York Provincial Congress followed suit, doing its best to calm Canadian anxieties and promote good feelings across the frontier. In its resolution of May 25, 1775, printed in French for public distribution, it denounced rumors of an impending American invasion as a plot by "the enemies of liberty" and promised to condemn any attack on Canada. Another broadside a week later was even more forthcoming. Addressed in French to "our very dear brothers and compatriots," it promised "that we look upon you as our friends and love you as our brothers." New York had no aggressive designs on Quebec but sought only to defend itself against the British forces there. The provincial congress apologized for those who had shown "the impudence to attack St. John's." Religious intolerance was not to be feared from the New Yorkers; they were dedicated to liberty, property, and "the right to render to the Supreme Being the worship we believe most agreeable to him."[6]

When the delegates to the Second Continental Congress decided in late June 1775 to raise an army for the invasion of Canada, they also decided to make a virtue of necessity and parade their abandonment of anti-Catholicism. They reminded "the oppressed inhabitants of Canada" that ever since 1763 they had "perceived the fate of the protestant and catholic colonies to be strongly linked together." They solemnly advised the Canadians to "be not impressed upon by those who may endeavour to create animosities" between them. The address repeated the charge that the Quebec Act only pretended to safeguard Catholic worship, as it left priests "exposed to expulsion, banishment, and ruin, whenever their wealth and possessions furnish sufficient temptation." Congress was now undertaking to protect the riches, so recently presented as ill-gotten, of the Church of Rome.[7] It was therefore impolitic for Thomas Jefferson to refer to the religious provisions of the Quebec Act when calling for its repeal in his response to Lord North's conciliatory resolution of February 20, 1775. Congress rewrote Jefferson's draft and on July 31 adopted a version that omitted any mention of religion. The same editorial policy was applied to the second petition to the king, the second address to the British public, and the "Address to the People of Ireland," all of July 1775. In their statement of July 6 "setting forth the causes and necessity of their taking up Arms," the delegates passed over the Catholic Question and objected to the Quebec Act simply for "erecting, in a neighbouring province . . . a despotism dangerous to our very existence."[8]

The sudden and wholesale conversion from Catholic baiting to the airy dismissal of "all such low-minded infirmities" brought hoots of derision from supporters of the British government. Sir John Dalrymple belabored the issue in a pamphlet published in February 1775, soon after Congress's overtures to the French Canadians became public. He began by noting that he had seen Congress's addresses to the people of Great Britain, the people of America, and the king. "And we wish we could add that we had not seen their address to the

French Inhabitants of Quebec, because it flatters them . . . with the protection of a religion, which the Congress in their Address to us, say, is fraught with 'Impiety, Bigotry, Persecution, Murder, and Rebellion,' and therefore complain of Parliament for protecting." The rebels had also been so absurd as to propose political union with the French Canadians, "a people, whose genius and government" the members of Congress, in their addresses to the American and British people, "represent as incompatible with freedom." What could account for such behavior? Dalrymple could only bring himself, he told his American audience, to "impute" the "insidious views or insidious arts" of the address to the Canadians "to those who framed it, and not to you." [9]

American Tories expressed similar views. Thomas Chandler called the address "undoubtedly the most unpardonable" of Congress's petitions. It revealed "the deepest and most inveterate malignity against the mother country" and made use of "every mean, cajoling art." Unable to resist the opportunity for irony, Daniel Leonard referred to "the truly jesuitical address to the Canadians." Like Dalrymple, Peter Oliver was taken aback by the sheer audacity of the Patriots' change of tune. They had "interlarded" their letters to the British and Irish, "as artfull Cooks do some Species of Fowls, with Dissertations upon Popery." They presumed to warn England "of its approaching Martyrdom," pretending that Parliament was bent on making "the Realm and its Dominions . . . a Smithfield of Fire and Faggots." In "their Address to the popish Inhabitants of Canada," on the other hand, Oliver could find not "a Word about the Rags of Popery, about a Smithfield Fire, or an Inquisition Coach." "Will Posterity believe," he asked, "that such a Compound of Absurdity, Weakness of Head, and infernal Wickedness of Heart, could be mixt by 52 Men, in whom was consolidated the sense of the thirteen united colonies?" Even "an Hottentot," if he read the "different Addresses," would have to put them down to "errant Folly or knight Errant Villainy." [10]

Dalrymple, Chandler, Leonard, and Oliver at least were willing to distinguish between the perfidious Congress and an American public that might yet see through its devious tricks. In this sense they held out some hope for a reconciliation between "reasonable Americans" and the crown.[11] Dr. Samuel Johnson, on the other hand, offered no such benefit of the doubt in his caustic pamphlet *Hypocrisy Unmasked*. Dismissing absurdity, weakness of head, and folly as explanations for congressional maneuvering, Johnson declared firmly for infernal wickedness of heart and knight-errant villainy. Far from representing a betrayal by Congress of its constituents, this duplicity struck Johnson as a fair reflection of the weak moral fiber of Americans in general.

The rebels, according to Johnson, were guilty of the most craven opportunism. After recounting the contents of the various addresses of 1774 and 1775, he stepped back to marvel at the crassness of the technique. Unlikely though it might seem, Congress was at the same time "so lost to all shame, as to write . . . a panegyric to the popish religion" to the Canadians and "so lost to all sense, as to publish it with the same letter which reprobates popery to the people of Great Britain." This had in fact been done in a compilation from which Johnson proceeded to quote with relish. "The religion which in page 38th the parliament had NO AUTHORITY to grant, belongs in page 72 by right *divine* to the Canadians. . . . The Congress in page 38th are afflicted because administration has been *too* favourable to the religion of Canada. In page 72, they are afflicted because administration has not been favourable *enough*." [12]

Johnson professed himself unable "in this place to decide, whether our indignation at the Colonies should be most excited by the baseness of their hypocrisy, or the insolence of their presumption." With pungent eloquence, he summed up the contradictions and prevarications of the American position. The Canadians were "blood-thirsty bigots" and a grave danger to New England, but Congress had set about "meanly flattering these bigots as they call them, into rebellion." Although it was a wicked abuse of power for Parliament to protect the Catholic Church in Canada,

> the Delegates, however, may grant them all the rights of Protestant subjects within the realm. . . . When the legislature of Great Britain thinks of arming the Canadians, then the difference of their communion instantly threatens the total overthrow of our glorious constitution. But when the Delegates want to arm them, "then the *exalted nature of freedom* lifts the French above all *low minded infirmities* arising from a dissimilarity of faith;" and it becomes perfectly justifiable in the Colonies to cut our throats with popish swords, though it is horrible in us, to think of employing Papists against the Colonies.[13]

This double standard was all too characteristic, Johnson thought, of an assortment of "preachers from the turf, and reformers from the gambling table." Those who had "suddenly started up into champions of the orthodox faith" were in fact "men whose lives are a scandal to all religion." Far from acting on honest (if fanatical) religious principles, the Americans had "played off their spiritual artillery upon the British nation" in the calculated hope of arousing anti-Catholic passions there. The outcry against the Quebec Act presumed upon British Protestant faith, seeking as it did "to build the most desperate views of ambition, upon the mistaken pity of mankind." But it did not follow that the Americans shared the faith they stooped to exploit. Furthermore, their simultaneous advances to the French Canadians demonstrated not a sudden change of heart but simply the lack of any principled grounds for rebellion in the first place.[14]

Even among believers in the moral character of the American cause, support for the Quebec campaign was lukewarm from the start. By some accounts the motion to raise a force for the invasion passed in the Continental Congress by a single vote.[15] The colonies rarely met their own agreed-upon levies of troops and money for the expedition.[16] This lack of enthusiasm both resulted from and contributed to the indifferent news that came back from the front. When Fort Chambly fell in October, providing Montgomery with 124 desperately needed barrels of powder, Samuel Adams expressed his relief at the "happy Turn to our Affairs in that Quarter the Success of which I almost began to despair of." The following May, John Adams blamed "this scandalous Flight from Quebec" on "those who ought to be the Contempt and Detestation of all America for their indefatigable Obstruction to every Measure which has been meditated for the Support" of efforts there.[17]

More to the point, there were widespread doubts as to the moral right of the Americans to carry the war into another country. To do so was to detract from the purely defensive stance the Patriots had thus far maintained. Worse, the alliance with the French Canadians invited the epithet of "praying hypocrites." A realist at Ticonderoga resorted to the old excuse when trying to reconcile a friend to the venture. "Your countrymen with united voices cry aloud for your utmost exertion in this time of need," he wrote. "Inter arma silent leges. Pray to arms, to arms, my friend!"[18]

The assertion here was that extraordinary circumstances justified an otherwise dubious course of action. Less flexible minds preferred to stress the dubiousness rather than the justification. The very failure of the invasion could be taken, after the fact, as a sign that God did not favor flirtation with the Romish Canadians. Judah Champion reasoned this way in his Connecticut election sermon of May 1776, when the outlines if not the scale of the debacle were already apparent. "Repeated successes" like those of the previous fall, he warned, tended to have "a far different effect upon mankind, in this fallen state, from what they ought." The early triumphs at St. Johns and Montreal, by tempting the victors to "carnal confidence," had made them "forsake the alliance of Heaven" and "fetch all our hope and spirit from such feeble things as ourselves." God felt "the highest resentment" at "such an horrid affront. . . . He sends such offenders to the Gods they have chosen and served, saying, let these deliver you in the time of your tribulation. Cursed be the man that believeth in man." Here was a view clearly at odds with the expansive humanism of Congress's letters to the Canadians. To accommodate the Canadian Catholics was to stray from the truth, and God would not pity any who came to grief as a result. "Whether we have been guilty in these respects," Champion added, "should certainly be considered." His ensuing account of the siege of Quebec City left his audience of Connecticut politicians in little doubt as to the minister's opinion.[19]

Even more straightforward was the analysis offered several years later by another conservative Congregationalist minister. In his version of the beginnings of the Revolution, the author recalled that "Heaven smiled on our undertakings, in America so far as self-defense was their object." Far from being disproved, this observation had only been borne out by the "distressful issue of our expedition against Quebec." However it might have been "justified in policy, as providing against a probable danger to come," the invasion of Canada "was not strictly within the line of self-defence: and as that is the limit of lawful war, it was the kindness of Heaven to hedge our way so as to confine us to it, by the force of his providence, as well as the authority of his word."[20] This was at once a gentler and firmer picture than Champion's of divine displeasure with the Quebec adventure. Defeat reflected an act of kindness to keep the Americans on the straight path, not the exasperated abandonment of wayward children. Either way, however, God had not smiled on Montgomery, Arnold, and the French Canadians. Nor had he looked kindly on so-called "enlightened" ideas about the unimportance of religious differences.

In defending their policy in Quebec, apologists for the Patriot party had to counter the objections from among their own. The Congregationalist clergy, after all, were for the most part firmly within their camp. How might their various misgivings be defused? Not surprisingly, rebel propagandists made use of more than one device in this effort. Anticipating objections of the sort voiced by the ministers, they promoted the advantages of political union with Quebec—letting Quebec become one of the United Colonies—and passed over the risks of consorting with Catholics. Thaddeus Maccarty was a Congregationalist minister who did not balk at the argument from self-defense as applied to Canada. In a Thanksgiving sermon in Worcester in November 1775 (when the outlook was still bright), he termed it "a favorable event in divine providence, that part of our forces have been led to penetrate the country of Canada . . . and that there is so promising a prospect of their becoming masters of the whole country." This was an "important affair," Maccarty said, in view of the plan that had been concocted ("it appears from various circumstances") to "let loose the Canadians and Indians" to reenact "the same bloody tragedy that they were wont formerly to do." But this dangerous British plot "bids fair . . . to be defeated," foiled by "our operations in the country of Canada" and by the Canadians themselves. They had defied Carleton's orders and "very generally" shown "a friendly disposition towards our people."[21]

The appeal to self-defense was only a particularly compelling version of the argument from necessity. Its proponents granted that there was something fishy about the invasion of Canada, but they insisted that given the consequences of inaction, the situation called for the suspension of ordinary standards. This was an amoral position—*inter arma silent leges*—but an enduringly popular one.[22] Congress resorted to it in its second address to the people of Great Britain. Citing "the Powers vested in the Governor of Canada" and "frequent Intimations, that a cruel and savage Enemy was to be let loose," the authors said they had taken "such Measures as Prudence dictated, and Necessity will justify." Never mind that Carleton's instructions were identical to those of all the other colonial governors: the greater the apparent danger, the easier it was to excuse whatever actions were taken to avert it.[23]

While not quite willing to assert as a matter of fact that it was necessary to preempt an attack from the northward, John Adams still claimed that the invasion of Quebec was a defensive act. The "unanimous voice of the Continent" that "Canada must be ours" was a response to the prohibitive danger of letting it remain British. "In the hands of our Enemies it would enable them to inflame all the Indians upon the Continent, and perhaps induce them to take up the Hatchet and commit their Robberies and Murders upon the Frontiers of all the southern Colonies, as well as to pour down Regulars, Canadians, and Indians, together upon the Borders of the Northern."[24] If the Americans had a right to self-defense, then they had the right to stage a preemptive attack: they were not obliged to show the patience of martyrs while waiting for Carleton to move first. In a corollary way this approach made it easy for the Americans to overlook the French Canadians. By framing the problem simply in terms of the occupation of certain territory by either British or Continental forces, the apologists were able to "see" only the British in Canada and ignore the habitants. These people entered the picture only as mercenaries doing Carleton's bidding, not as men and women who had lived along the St. Lawrence for two centuries and might have ideas of their own about who ought to rule there.

The Americans soon discovered, however, that while it might be convenient to overlook the French Canadians when talking about the invasion, it would be necessary to engage them directly when actually undertaking it. This engagement went beyond the promise of protection for their religion to include the offer of political union. Not content to stand its former theological opposition to the Quebec Act on its head, Congress said it would not only tolerate the French Canadians as neighbors but welcome them as fellow citizens. The first address "To the Inhabitants of the Province of Quebec," in the fall of 1774, reported that the Continental Congress had "re-solved . . . that you should be invited to accede to our confed-eration." To further this "highly desirable" end, it invited the Canadians "to meet together in your several towns and dis-tricts, and elect Deputies, who afterwards meeting in a provin-cial Congress, may chuse Delegates, to represent your prov-ince in the continental Congress to be held at Philadelphia on the tenth of May, 1775." Happily for all concerned, there was precedent to ensure that religious differences would not im-pede the proposed union. Rather than the sectarian blood-baths of the Thirty Years' War, Congress had in mind the secure harmony of the Protestant and Catholic cantons of Switzerland. These "States, living in the utmost concord and peace with one another," had been "thereby enabled, ever since they bravely vindicated their freedom, to defy and defeat every tyrant that had invaded them." [25]

This was not merely a sop to Canadian aspirations. Al-though the French Canadians were not agitating for inclusion among the United Colonies, the Americans persisted in the offer and took it seriously themselves. John Adams observed that "a momentous political Question" would arise if the Americans "should be successful in that Province. What is to be done with it? . . . This appears to me as serious a Prob-lem as any We shall have to solve." The president of the Con-tinental Congress, John Hancock, was clear about that body's wishes in instructions he sent to Schuyler in October 1775. The members, he said, expected that the Canadians would be "induced to accede to an Union with these Colonies" and to "form from their several Parishes, a Provincial Convention, and send Delegates to this Congress." A year after it was first made, the offer was still on the table. [26]

Unbeknownst to Hancock, Schuyler had already handed over command of the expedition to Montgomery and returned to Albany in poor health. Montgomery was happy to adopt the policy Congress had recommended. Writing to Schuyler, he described his "pleasure" upon learning that his own "politicks . . . squared with the views of Congress." He would "lose no time in calling a Convention, when my intended expedition is finished." When Montgomery was killed, Benedict Arnold carried on in the same spirit. He went through Montgomery's papers and came across instructions from Congress "to endeavour to form, on a lasting basis, a firm union" between the Canadians and the colonies, "by forming a provincial Congress, and, from that body, giving them full representation in the Grand Continental Congress." Arnold promised to continue to pursue what Montgomery "had labored for with the greatest assiduity, and with as great a degree of success as could be expected."[27]

By then even less could be expected: hundreds of Americans had been taken prisoner, and Arnold was exerting himself to convince the Canadians that there remained a chance of expelling the British. Montgomery had not lived to organize elections and see the idea of political union given serious consideration, and Arnold now doubted whether circumstances in Quebec would ever permit it. But Congress still lent its support. In late January 1776, when the Canadians might have begun reassessing their chances and perhaps distancing themselves from their newfound friends, Congress repeated its invitation. On their return from Philadelphia with commissions for raising a Canadian regiment, Moses Hazen and Edward Antill carried a declaration signed by John Hancock. It repeated the formula of local elections to a provincial assembly and a delegation from the assembly "to represent them in this Congress."[28]

Although never put to the test, this vision of union showed considerable staying power. In February 1775 Congress had dispatched agents to Montreal and Quebec City to gauge reaction to its overtures. Under the pretext of shopping for horses, they met with Anglo-Canadian merchants and arranged a larger meeting to be held in secret in Montreal. Although they invited French Canadians to attend, none did.[29] The latter were for the most part cool to the idea, perceiving that the Americans were not in a position to deliver any of the supposed benefits. Once the Americans invaded in force, however, the peasantry and some of the townspeople came out in their favor. Valentin Jautard, a journalist whose taste for Voltaire had already brought him into disfavor with polite society, published a message of welcome to Montgomery "from the inhabitants of three neighborhoods of Montreal." "We look upon and receive the troops . . . as our own," he declared. "In two words, we accept the union offered us by our brother colonies."[30] That was in November, near the high tide of American fortunes. In December, when Montgomery approached a blacksmith from Trois-Rivières with his plan for elections and a Canadian delegation to Congress, the project proved impracticable. After failing to drum up interest in the elections, the two men conferred at Montgomery's camp and decided that "such a convocation could not take place until after the taking of Quebec."[31]

Since the fortress never fell, the question of Canadian enthusiasm for membership in the United Colonies remained moot. Nevertheless, the persistence with which it was bruited about in later years points to the sincerity of interest on the American side. It reappeared, for instance, in the eleventh Article of Confederation, drafted in the fall of 1776. And once France had formally allied itself with the Revolutionaries, it was easier than ever to appeal to anti-British feeling among the French Canadians. Forswearing any desire to reclaim the province for France, the comte d'Estaing in a declaration of October 1778 tried to rekindle the memories of "those Canadians who saw the brave Montcalm fall in their defense." Through its support of the Americans, France would avenge the fallen hero. Could the French Canadians now "be the enemies of his nephews, fight their former leaders and arm themselves against their relatives?" The Bostonois would return, he promised, and it would be easier than ever for the Canadians to be their comrades.[32]

The Reverend Samuel Cooper, d'Estaing's friend and collaborator in propaganda, meanwhile went to work on American opinion. He prepared a detailed memorandum on the question of American policy toward Canada. In what amounted to a brief in favor of a second invasion, Cooper considered and refuted some possible objections: that the Canadians were hostile to the Americans, that the necessary funds could not be raised, and that the removal of the British from Quebec might cause New England morale to become lax. He pooh-poohed the second and third and said experience in 1775–76 had disproved the first. Union with Canada, according to Cooper, was both desirable and attainable.[33]

Observers in Europe were distinctly cool to Canada's absorption into the newly declared United States, and they did not simply dismiss the proposal as folly. Just a week after d'Estaing's declaration, a French diplomat reporting to his superior on talk of a second expedition to Quebec doubted whether it would be "in the interest of the king to support it."[34] Similar cold water had been thrown on the idea by the French chargé d'affaires in London in the summer of 1776. He advised Vergennes that French interests lay in British possession of Canada, since it would preserve American dependence on France.[35] For their part, the British also took the American designs on Canada seriously. Lord North advised the members of the Carlisle Commission to be particularly on their guard, during the impending peace negotiations with the Americans, against proposals to revise the Quebec Act. "The eagerness shown by the revolted Provinces for such an alteration is very suspicious," he observed. "They certainly consider it as a step favourable to the uniting Canada to themselves as a fourteenth State." The unhappy prospect continued to exercise British and Loyalist councils for several years thereafter.[36]

The espousal of political union with Quebec had two salient implications for the larger project of accounting for the invasion itself. First, it recast the invasion as something less aggressive and thus more easily excused—in short, as the liberation of an oppressed people. If the Canadians yearned to be free and the British forbade it, then Montgomery and Arnold were removing an obstruction to their will, not imposing a foreign one. Second, this way of framing the expedition entailed a new way of looking at the French Canadians themselves. In order to see themselves as harbingers of freedom and self-government, the Americans had to see the French Canadians as not only eager for such blessings but fit for them as well. Yet this was hardly what Americans were used to doing. One task, then, was to dismantle the received idea—which the Patriots had done their best to stir up in 1774—that the Canadians were papist slaves, sure to follow every whim of their corrupt and tyrannical bishop. A new identity for the French Canadians would go a long way toward excusing the new American attitude toward them.

A way of constructing a new identity was to point out the divergence of interests between ordinary habitants and their priests and seigneurs. By expressing one's displeasure with the Quebec Act in constitutional rather than religious terms, for instance, one brought attention to the love of liberty that united the new allies. Thus John Adams, in March 1775, put aside his diatribes against popery to condemn the Quebec Act as dangerous in the way the Coercive Acts had been dangerous, as a usurpation of power. "There never was an American constitution attempted by parliament," he wrote, "before the Quebec bill and Massachusetts bill. These are such samples of what they may, and possibly will be, that few Americans are in love with them." Reflecting on the same events many years later, Adams recalled that "the People said, if Parliament can do this in Canada, they can do the same in all the other colonies: and they began to see, that Parliament had no authority over them in any case whatsoever." The Quebec Act received the same treatment in the Declaration of Independence, where it was termed a piece of "pretended legislation" designed to abolish "the free system of English laws in a neighbouring province, establishing therein an arbitrary government, and enlarging its boundaries, so as to render it at once an example and fit instrument for introducing the same arbitrary rule into these colonies."[37]

Although the abuse of power in question involved religious establishments, it was no longer politic to dwell on the fact.

The point, rather, was that if the habitants disliked their priests and resented the Quebec Act, then they were not all bad. Patriot writers hurried to underline the implications. Even as he railed against the favors recently afforded their priests, John Lathrop carefully used the past tense to refer to the French Canadians as "those who we used to consider as natural Enemies." For his part John Adams could foresee at worst a future state of things, for which the Quebec Act had "laid a foundation," in which the Canadians might pose a threat to American liberty. He distinguished it, though, from the present, when "we hold the power of the Canadians at nothing" and "know their dispositions are not unfriendly to us."[38]

The "power of the Canadians" was negligible; in that belief lay an important ingredient of the ease with which Americans would entertain the notion of a Catholic fourteenth state. It certainly helped that the Canadians were friendly, and that their numbers were so small relative to the thirteen United States: ninety thousand to more than two million.[39] Transcending these more or less objective factors was the belief that the habitants were essentially childlike and therefore tractable. It was one the Americans shared with the British and the assimilationist French Canadian elite. When the time came to contemplate Canadian partnership in the Republic, American propaganda preferred to leave this stereotype intact, since it could be made to serve a useful purpose. In their comments on the French Canadians, the British and Americans alike compared them to that other group whose territory became the scene of war, the Iroquois. They tended to look on both as less sophisticated than themselves, less intelligent—in a word, as children. The habitants were good children: benighted but well-intentioned, susceptible to instruction, and likely to behave well if given time and encouragement. The Indians, on the other hand, were incorrigible, untrustworthy, and certain to misbehave unless closely watched. Like adolescents, they were physically mature and therefore dangerous if not restrained either by their consciences (in which the whites had little faith) or their betters. The difference, as Ethan Allen put it, was that while a show of military force might be enough "to overawe the Canadians," it would still be necessary to "inveigle the Indians," who were more shrewd.[40]

The Canadians were thus seen not as dangerous but merely as fit objects of condescension. Carleton ascribed the habitants' disloyalty to their having "been governed with too loose a Rein for many years" and having "imbibed too much of the American Spirit of Licentiousness and Independence administered by a numerous and turbulent Faction here." This corruption of the simple Canadians was already too far advanced for them "to be suddenly restored to a proper and desirable Subordination." Jean-Baptiste Badeaux and Simon Sanguinet were likewise more eager to blame the Anglo-Canadian merchants like Walker and Price for their bad influence on the habitants than the latter for listening to them.[41]

The Revolutionaries largely concurred. The Canadians were incapable, they thought, of forming a modern civil society. Even their "noblesse or gentry" had "not the least notion . . . of liberty or law."[42] As for the habitants, they were "very Ignorant," "extremely Ignorant," "too ignorant to put a just estimate on the value of freedom." This was not necessarily to be construed as their fault. Like Carleton and Badeaux, the Americans were willing to view the Canadians as empty vessels rather than responsible actors. Benedict Arnold thought it was due to their "having been so long habituated to slavery" that they were "naturally timorous and diffident" and were possessed of "but a faint sense of the value of liberty."[43] Montgomery told the Canadians so to their faces. Attempting to coax the residents of Quebec City into surrendering, he explained that Carleton had craftily concealed from them the knowledge that would have opened their eyes to their true interests.[44] Once again, in other words, their resistance was not their fault.

The demands of survival caused many of the Americans

who fought in Quebec to put aside their religious prejudices against the French Canadians. While John Henry of Pennsylvania was one of the most eloquent of the diarists on this point, his comments on the habitants' character were less high-minded. At first he was pleasantly surprised. Where he had "expected there could be little other than barbarity," he and his comrades "found civilized men, in a comfortable state." Such generous feelings did not last. Six weeks later, waiting anxiously for the order to attack the fortress, Henry decided the Canadians were getting on his nerves. They now struck him as "vociferous and vile," given to "noisy jabber," and "as cowardly as noisy." [45]

The less charitable view was the more common. The attitude of superiority from which the invaders contemplated the Canadians throughout 1775–76 appears unvarnished in an ode to Washington composed by one of his officers. The anonymous author, who published his poem in Massachusetts, depicts Washington addressing a council of war to propose the expedition to Quebec:

> *Our armed legions well secure the coasts,*
> *And terror awes the western Pagan hosts;*
> *But in the north th'unpolished race reside,*
> *Who basely yield to Britain's lawless pride.*

Timely intervention, Washington suggests, might make it possible to save the Canadians from themselves.

> *Should forces now be rais'd without delay,*
> *And to that northern clime direct their way,*
> *A calm serene might sooth the Peasant's mind,*
> *From harm secure, and to his toil resign'd.*
> *Could we but once persuade that rueful land,*
> *We might redeem the virtuous by our hand.*[46]

This is one of the more frank expressions of the American opinion of the junior partners to the alliance. It would not be enough to remove the British yoke from their necks; America would also have to "redeem the virtuous" among the Canadians by educating them. Try as they might, even those Americans who were most disposed to flatter and entice the French Canadians could not conceal their lack of respect for them. The letter to the Quebecois of October 1774, for instance, devoted considerable space to what amounted to a primer on Whig political theory. In the tone of a patient teacher, the authors explained the concepts of republican government and the power of the purse, trial by jury, habeas corpus, freehold land tenure, and freedom of the press.[47] The assumption in each case was that the Canadians were wholly unfamiliar with and perhaps unable to grasp such sophisticated ideas. "Is there Knowledge or Understanding enough among them," John Adams wondered, "to elect an Assembly, which will be capable of ruling them and then to be governed by it? Who shall constitute their Judges and civil Officers?"[48] His colleagues in Philadelphia did not bother to shade this concern even when addressing the Canadians. "You have been conquered into liberty," Congress informed them, "if you act as you ought."[49]

Properly instructed, they might indeed so act. D'Estaing was only being disingenuous in his declaration of October 1778 when he pretended to refuse to "urge an entire people . . . that to join the United States would secure their happiness." He would not do so, he said, "since an entire people, when they acquire the right to think and act for themselves, must know their own interest."[50] The common opinion of d'Estaing, Cooper, and other supporters of union with Quebec was in fact that the Canadians, while not yet ready to think and act for themselves, could be made ready.[51] In his memorandum on a second invasion, Cooper anticipated the objection "that the Canadians can never comprehend a republican form of government and that therefore the proposed union with these States is Chimerical." He argued in response that although the Canadians were indeed "almost universally

Destitute of every kind of Erudition and of course enveloped in a Cloud of Ignorance," several mitigating factors obtained. First, this parlous condition pointed "to the Dishonour of their Governours" and not to any racial defect in the oppressed Canadians. God had been "Equally Bountifull to them in the gifts of Nature," and they could "readily distinguish Benefits from Injuries" as well as "the rest of mankind." They might not know much, but they knew their "present Despot" well enough to prefer republican government. Second, they were not all of them hopelessly ignorant. Cooper was confident there were "men of understanding sufficient in Canada to organize a government," even if they might "chuse a Constitution entirely New suited to their Circumstances and Ideas." Such innovation would still "afford no argument why they should not be Embraced in the Federal union with the rest of the States."[52]

Not all discussion of the fate of Canada took place on the lofty planes of religion, republicanism, or even politics. More practical considerations counted as well. Quite apart from the question of union, the advantages of open trade with that province were enough to attract support for its emancipation. The Quebec Act, after all, had left legislative affairs in the hands of an appointed council. Surely, the authors of a New York petition argued, Americans would stand a fairer chance of sharing in the northern Indian trade if the Canadians could elect their own assembly. In whatever guise and however presented, a Canada rid of British control was attractive as a means to American ends rather than as an end in itself.[53]

The pragmatic approach to relations with Catholics was an easy case for the Revolutionaries to make when it came to Quebec. True, the habitants were Catholic, but they hated their priests. They were ignorant, but they might be taught. Above all, they were weak. They were no longer the horde of mercenaries originally conjured up in New England minds to arouse resistance to the Quebec Act. In their new guise they appeared as republicans, or at least as promising apprentices to the noble craft of self-government. The fact that they remained French-speaking Catholics receded gently into the background.

The picture thus constructed could soothe the eye and salve the conscience of a Patriot, but two dangers still lurked within it. First, the assertion that a shared republican ideology transcended—and ought to transcend—religious and ethnic differences was too daring for many to accept.[54] It was one thing to congratulate oneself for bringing light to the benighted Canadians; but to assume that all New England would applaud was another. Judah Champion had given notice that some Congregationalists would resist the vogue for enlightenment and toleration precisely in order to defend traditional forms of religious faith and authority. Subsequent events would only deepen this divide within the Revolutionary movement.

The second cloud on the horizon was the insistence on the tractability of the Canadians. Such assurances would prove useless when what needed explaining was an alliance with France, although that does not mean they would not be tried. During a controversy in Massachusetts politics fifteen years earlier involving the power of the purse, James Otis had teased his Tory rivals by observing that "it would be of little consequence to the people, whether they were subject to George or Louis . . . if both were arbitrary, as both would be, if both could levy taxes without Parliament." Otis went on to assure his readers that in fact "the French king is an arbitrary, despotic prince" and "in the present situation . . . the king of Great Britain is not," but the qualification did nothing to dilute the outrageousness of the comparison.[55]

In 1778 the French Alliance called this bluff. Were New Englanders capable of preferring French patronage and protection to British? Was it possible? Here the stakes were clearly higher than in the rapprochement with the French Canadians. Although "a sink of men's lives," the Quebec debacle had never threatened America's independence. France was another question. That country's aid, were it to be effective, would have to be massive. Fleets and armies meant sailors and soldiers: not blank slates like the French Canadians, clay for American hands, but frog-eating Frenchmen with their accompanying officers and chaplains. Such forces as came to fight in America in turn would be only a fraction of what Louis commanded. This time the weight of numbers worked against the Americans, and the Catholic Question proved correspondingly difficult to explain away.

# 4

## *Astride the Tiger*

The formal alliance concluded by the United States and the kingdom of France in February 1778 made it plain that the foray into Quebec had not been an aberration in American diplomacy. The Revolutionaries had decided to pursue rather than abandon the policy of accepting Catholic aid in the war against Britain. This placed the Patriots and their British enemies in the oddly symmetrical position of having to disavow their respective positions on Catholic toleration in general and the Quebec Act in particular. The Americans claimed that they had emerged from the era of tribal hatreds into a new age of tolerant humanism. The partisans of the king, meanwhile, were moving in the opposite direction, forgetting their recent enthusiasm for liberality as they hurled invective at the Catholic-loving rebels.

More was at stake here than a neat exchange of platforms on the Catholic Question. Beyond the issue of the relative merits of Canadian and French Catholics lay that of whether or not religious toleration was a good thing in itself. If so, was it an absolute good? This was one possible approach, to claim that toleration was part and parcel of enlightenment and inherently progressive. But to say so was to invite attack. Not a few people believed that taken to an extreme, religious freedom would degenerate into mere license and indifference. New Englanders could no more repudiate Calvin than Londoners could pretend to be scandalized by Voltaire. For polemical purposes, each had to cobble together a structure that would house the useful aspects of enlightenment while excluding, or at least concealing, the rest.

As one would expect, the resulting briefs on political morality displayed little elegance of design. Worsening the confusion was the belief, found on both sides, that the masses were less tolerant and more hostile to enlightened thinking than their betters. Members of the elite, despite privately approving of religious toleration, were therefore willing to appeal to the supposedly backward passion of the common people in order to advance their own political interests. This was just as true of the Patriots who feigned pious distress over the Quebec Act as of Tories who called the French Alliance a dagger aimed at the heart of Protestantism. Each spoke the language of traditional Calvinism without remotely believing it. It was a calculated subversion of meaning and one that would not go unpunished, although the repercussions were sometimes long in coming.

At the outset the British stood for toleration. In the controversy over the Quebec Act, the crown's supporters contrasted their own mild acquiescence in religious freedom for the Canadians to the bigoted fanaticism of the New England dissenters. While taking the Congregationalists to task for the sectarian fervor of their opposition to the act, one English pamphleteer termed religious toleration "that fairest flower of cultivated humanity." He hoped its extension to the French Canadians "pleased our God, though it pleased not your Congress." [1] Samuel Johnson, in a pamphlet written for the British general election of 1774, sought to dismiss the "clamorous complaints, that the Protestant religion is in danger, because Popery is established in the extensive province of Quebec." He ridiculed the idea as "a falsehood so open and shameless, that it can need no confutation" except for "the most unenlightened zealot." "Persecution," he pointed out, "is not more virtuous in a Protestant than a Papist." Catholics had as good a right to liberty of conscience as anyone else: because they were men, if it was a natural right, and because other sects enjoyed it, if was an indulgence from the government. It was certainly unreasonable of the New Englanders to raise such a cry against toleration for the Canadians when their own dissent from the Church of England was so well protected.[2]

Johnson took satirical pleasure in the sight of Congress's sudden agreement with him at the time of its appeals to the French Canadians. In addition to skewering the rebels on this score, Johnson took time in *Hypocrisy Unmasked* to repeat his approval of the policy of Catholic toleration. He denounced as absurd the idea of "representing the grant of the Popish religion to the Canadians as a measure highly alarming to every Protestant of the empire." After all, the toleration of Catholics in Maryland had not led to disaster. "The Maryland Charter," he pointed out, "was granted by Charles the First to Lord Baltimore in the year 1632, just 143 years previous to the act for regulating the constitution of Canada; yet the disaffected Provinces did not discover till the year 1774, that popery had ever been established in any part of British America." This was a bit disingenuous, since the rights of Catholics had not enjoyed smooth sailing in Maryland throughout that period. Still, it was fair to point out that Pennsylvania, "the very Province where the Congress is at this moment deliberating," thought it fit to allow its Catholic minority "the free exercise of the Romish communion."[3] British Catholics did not enjoy such freedom, but Johnson certainly thought they should. He went on to argue on practical grounds that the emancipation of the Irish Catholics would take "fifty thousand gallant fellows now groaning under the weight of religious disabilities" and make them available for use against the revolted colonies. "Since Protestants can take up arms against the constitution," he asked, "why should not Papists be employed to preserve it?" Once such pointless distinctions were done away with, Ireland "might be converted into a constant nursery for the armies of

Great Britain." In this view the only differences between Catholics and Protestants were archaic and therefore meaningless. Johnson wrote as if from a vantage point well above sectarian quarrels.[4]

Another royal pensioner and essayist preferred to rub salt in New England wounds by championing toleration on the very grounds he knew would irritate them most: his positive preference for Catholics over dissenters. In a pamphlet defending the Quebec Act, John Shebbeare joined Johnson in making light of the pretense "that his majesty is an errant Jacobite and is now actually preparing to surrender his crowns, kingdoms, and dominions, to the pretender: that in order to facilitate this wonderful revolution, he is now, by all possible means, endeavouring to bring popery dingdong into this realm." Far from ceding supremacy in Quebec to the pope, Shebbeare argued, the Quebec Act established that of the king over any Canadian bishop. As such, it marked the beginning of "a reformation of the catholic church in Canada." This was a truly bold suggestion: that the Quebec Act was an advance rather than a retreat in the long struggle for independence of the Church of England from Rome. Just because one indulged Catholics, Shebbeare dared to suggest, one was not therefore abetting the pope. Although "the malignity, the falsehood, the ignorance, or a combination of all these qualities" had prevented "the intellects of patriots and presbyterians" from discerning the fact, "popery and the Roman Catholic religion are not necessarily conjoined." Henry VIII, after all, had left Catholic worship intact while assuming the supremacy of the Church of England from the pope, and George III had simply done the same in Quebec. As reformations went, the Quebec Act was for that matter a distinct improvement on the brutal policies of the Tudors. The ban on further immigration of priests to Canada would make "the monastic orders . . . imperceptibly decay without the cruelty of turning numbers of inoffensive men from their abodes to starve, as it had been so inhumanly done in England."[5]

Here, as elsewhere, Shebbeare showed a partiality toward Catholics and a notable sympathy for the Stuart kings. The dissenters, he said, pretended "that popery has, at all times, been attended with slavery in this kingdom," and that they themselves were, "and ever have been, the fast friends of freedom and the constitution" and "advocates for universal toleration and liberty of conscience." But this was not evident "from facts alone." Rather, the dissenters were far more vigorous persecutors than the Catholics of those who differed from them. Puritanism was deeply at odds with reason, Shebbeare said. Calvinism, "mixed with fanaticism," made for an "irresistible" conviction of one's own righteousness. "Zeal is the sharpened edge, and predestination that tremendous weight which drives through all opposition." Defending the government's Canadian policy, Shebbeare asked his "fellow countrymen" to "decide then, . . . whether, from the hands of Roman Catholics, or of presbyterians, your destruction be most likely to proceed." The implication, however unorthodox, was understood.[6]

It was one thing for Englishmen to sympathize with Charles I, or to observe after the fact that the Catholic priests of Quebec had proved loyal during 1775–76 and perhaps deserved some credit for it.[7] It was another to voice such sentiments in America, where anti-Catholicism had greater currency. Nevertheless, "Bob Jingle" mocked the intolerance of the Patriots in his parody of the text of the Continental Association:

> If Gallic *Papists have a Right*,
> *To worship their own way*,
> *Then farewell to the Liberties*
> *Of poor* America.[8]

Even in New England there were Tories who approved of the Quebec Act. Daniel Leonard endorsed the "Quebec bill" during his pamphlet debate with John Adams, dismissing opposition to it as "prostituting our holy religion to the accursed purposes of treason and rebellion." He favored religious toleration in principle and called it "a strange kind of reasoning to argue" that the enjoyment by the French Canadians of the religion "in which alone they repose their hopes of eternal salvation" somehow implied that New Englanders would be deprived of their own.[9] In keeping with this movement beyond the traditional New England view of Catholics, Leonard discreetly avoided papist absolutism when he sought a metaphor for despotic rebel tendencies. He wrote instead of "the enormous monarchies of the East" and the "thick mist that hovers over the land, and involves it in more than Egyptian darkness." For the moment, at least, it seemed that the Tories had left the ritual abuse of Catholics behind.[10]

Further evidence that Tory thinking had undergone a sea change was the chorus of complaint from those who preferred that Catholics continue to receive the old treatment. British Whigs, for instance, drew attention to the movement for toleration by loudly opposing it. Joseph Towers, a dissenting minister and professional agitator, replied to *The Patriot* with a pamphlet lambasting the Quebec Act and denouncing Samuel Johnson as a corrupt placeman. What annoyed him most was the contrast between the toleration of Canadian Catholics on the one hand and the continued legal discrimination against English dissenters on the other. A friend of the government had said that to deny the Canadian priests the right to collect tithes would effectively deprive the Canadians of their religion.[11] "But why so?" asked Towers. "Are the Protestant Dissenters in England deprived of their clergy? And yet it is well known, that no legal provision is made for their maintenance. They are supported only by the voluntary contributions of the dissenting laity. Would it not have been sufficient, if the Popish clergy had been put upon the same footing?"[12]

Having pointed out this unfair treatment, Towers went on to suggest that acquiescence in the Quebec Act was a telling sign of weak Protestant credentials. It was "impossible" that "a truly Protestant Parliament" should have wanted to shore up the Catholic Church in Canada with the prop of a legal establishment. As for the defenders of this policy, Johnson was the only Protestant writer Towers could think of "who ever thought that the Protestant Dissenters and the Papists were to be considered as on an equal footing under this government." By supposing that religious distinctions were irrelevant to civil rights, Johnson had revealed his "known Jacobitical principles." And while Johnson might be "generally considered as one of the most bigotted Jacobites in the kingdom," he paled in comparison to Shebbeare. The latter, a man only "pretending to be a Protestant," actually had "given Papists the preference." In an appendix devoted entirely to Shebbeare's outrageous statements, Towers accused him of trying to "degrade the characters of King William and Queen Mary," rehabilitate the memory of Charles I, and "traduce the revolution." His support for the Quebec Act was thus only part of a larger revisionist scheme.[13]

Shebbeare also drew fire of this sort from the Presbyterians of Scotland, a group with a slightly more disinterested view of the Quebec Act than either the American Congregationalists or the dissenting Whigs in England. Many of them disliked both the Quebec Act and the American rebellion. They did not feel, as most Englishmen and colonists seemed to, that one ought to embrace either one or the other. Thus John Erskine, a Presbyterian minister and close friend of Joseph Bellamy, warned that it was foolish of the English Tories to flirt with popery while soliciting help against a lesser danger, as when they recommended arming the Irish Catholics. The Scots, he noted, were still clearheaded about such things and not "infected with the fashionable notion, that right opinion in religion is of little importance, and wrong opinion not dangerous." He could not say the same for the overeager English. After reciting the familiar anti-Catholic litany, Erskine quoted at length from Jonathan Mayhew's bloodcurdling election sermon of 1754. He then commented, "I seriously recommend it to the Britons who lean upon native Papists, or to Americans who confide in French Canadians, for the support of their respective claims. . . . When Dr. Mayhew gave this warning, it was a day of darkness with North America. It is so now with Great Britain. Let us not render it darker still." [14]

While perhaps unduly anxious about the need for Protestant vigilance in North America, Erskine did show a certain prescience in his warning that should the English alienate the colonists by unforgiving treatment, they would only invite an attack by their "artful and ambitious neighbour," France. Once the rebellion had drained England of its strength, the old enemy would be quick to pounce. Catholic-coddlers like Shebbeare, "who dislike the Colonists for their attachment to revolution principles" and "wish the crown of Britain on the head of a Popish pretender," might find such an event "not an evil to be deprecated, but a consummation devoutly to be wished for." True patriots did not pretend that popery was "politically innocent" but remained on their guard. [15]

These sentiments did not fall on deaf ears, at least in the colonies. Bob Jingle, Daniel Leonard, and Peter Oliver notwithstanding, there were Tories in America who balked at the abandonment of official anti-Catholicism. Along with Erskine in Scotland, they disliked the lumping together of imperial politics and religious principle. Insisting that one could love the king and still hate Catholics, they resisted the progressive ideas of their metropolitan counterparts. If they were out of step in expressing doubts about the Quebec Act, they came into their own when later events seemed to vindicate their reservations.

Joseph Galloway, for one, feared that victory in the Seven Years' War had caused Americans to forget "the danger, and all the horrors of French slavery." Like Erskine, he thought the flirtation with independence risked exciting French ambitions to the peril of "our rights both civil and religious, and our inestimable religion itself," which would "be changed for the arbitrary customs, the slavery and superstition of Rome."

By opposing the Quebec Act on these grounds, Americans like Galloway preserved a link between traditional anti-Catholicism and the revival thereof that would dominate Tory attacks on the French Alliance. These keepers of the anti-Catholic flame made a point of couching their opposition to the Patriots in terms that compared the rebels to papists.[16]

Well before 1778, for example, the Anglican minister Thomas Chandler of New York accused the Revolutionaries of persecuting their enemies just as the Catholics persecuted theirs. "One of their ways of confuting pamphlets," he charged, "like the old popish way of confuting heretics, is by fire and faggot. This proceeds from the same bigotry, and is dictated by the same spirit, which commonly disgraced the dark ages preceding the Reformation." Rebels and Catholics, that is, were equally intolerant. If the Whigs achieved power, "there would be no peace in the colonies, till we all submitted to the republican zealots and bigots of New-England," who would brook no dissent. The Church of England was grateful for its deliverance from all fanatics, "whether Papists or Protestants."[17] Another loyalist writer lumped rebel and papist primitives together by arguing that the Continental Association was an obstacle to trade. Trade was in turn "the foundation of learning," and learning the basis of "true rational religion." Lest this linking of the rebels with ignorance and superstition, the classic emblems of popery, appear too subtle, the writer went on to call the perpetrators of the Boston Tea Party a set of "casuistical . . . , not to say jesuitical gentlemen."[18]

With the coming of the French Alliance, these traditionalist American Tories were well prepared to advance on the religious front. In America as in Britain, those who had argued in favor of the Quebec Act slipped nimbly back into line. Few opponents of the colonial cause on either side of the Atlantic wasted much ink being subtle about their view of the American resort to French aid. Congress, they said, had revealed its true colors by selling out its constituents to France.

A Loyalist song from New York expressed indignation at such shamelessness:

> *Tho' knaves do combine,*
> *With Beelzebub join,*
> *To aim our downfall and undo us;*
> *By GEORGE's fam'd shield,*
> *We never will yield,*
> *To the pimps or the armies of Louis.*[19]

The rebels would get from the arrangement only what they deserved. Unless "blinded by passion," Edward Gibbon predicted, they must see that "their new allies would soon become their tyrants," and their so-called independence would be the plaything of "the despotic will of a foreign court." "Were the Congress now to declare Louis XVI. sovereign and liege Lord of North-America, it would not shock or surprise me," claimed Charles Inglis, an Anglican priest.[20] How could the "language of Mr. Locke, and of all his Disciples, more especially the Americans," an English writer asked, be made to harmonize with the Bourbon monarchy? It might not matter "what political Opinions the *French* Nation shall imbibe in *Theory*, provided there are 200,000 Bayonets ready pointed at their Breasts to make them renounce them all in *Practice*"; but Americans had always claimed to know better. How could the self-styled champions of constitutional government have stooped so low?[21]

As they piled on the invective, the Tories quickly disavowed any interest in religious toleration. In addition to retrograde ideas about government, the Americans (they said) had embraced the old Whore of Babylon, the Catholic Church. The Tories thought they detected certain affinities between the two parties to this sordid pact. Not only did they try to scare the Americans with tales of Catholic treachery and cruelty, they insulted them at the same time by suggesting that they had come to resemble the dreaded papists. With the inconvenient matter of the Quebec Act no longer a consideration, the old themes of Chandler and Galloway returned to the fore. Thus, in 1780 it once more made sense to print a satirical poem that used Catholic imagery to ridicule the rebels' infatuation with the false goddess of Democracy:

> *She calls the nations—Lo! in crouds they sup*
> *Intoxication from her golden cup.*

Her acolytes among the Protestant clergy sported "the splendor of pontific dress"; their alliance with France was a "masterpiece of madness" with "the head of glory" and "a serpent's tail."[22] The Reverend Mr. Inglis thought "the Inquisitors of Spain, Portugal and Rome . . . not more diligent" than Congress "to keep their deluded vassals in profound ignorance." Anyone who believed the rebel lies, he added, "would believe in transubstantiation." The machinations of Congress reminded him of Caesar Borgia, "the natural son of Pope Alexander VI." And Borgia, everyone knew, had come out of his own French Alliance rather badly.[23]

The Americans had not merely betrayed their religion, the Tories said, but had recklessly endangered it as well. "The French alliance," Inglis wrote, "looks with no less malignant an aspect on the Protestant religion, than on the liberties of America." The lesson of the past was that "severe laws and penalties, and the vigilance of civil magistrates, were indispensably necessary . . . to prevent Popish priests from perverting Protestants to their superstition." With the alliance, "the door is thrown wide open to receive Popery," and the signs of its encroachments were everywhere. There had been "large importations of Popish priests, beads, and other such trumpery . . . into the Colonies," including the case of "several thousand Popish beads" discovered on a prize ship taken en route to Philadelphia. In New York, at least, good Protestants still knew their enemy. Father de La Motte had been brought in aboard a captured ship in 1778 and, once paroled, had tried to offer a mass. For this offense he had been arrested, returned to prison, and kept there "till exchanged and sent to Boston, where I presume," Inglis could not resist adding, "he exercised his function without any interruption."[24]

The Carlisle Commission, sent from London to try to nip the French threat in the bud by treating with the Americans, used similar fear mongering to try to sow disenchantment with the alliance. In their "Manifesto and Proclamation" of October 1778, its members professed their desire to revive "that union of interests and force on which our mutual prosperity and the safety of our common religion and liberties depend." The great obstacle to this happy vision was France, "our late mutual and natural enemy." After piously denying that they would seek to promote their aims "by fomenting popular divisions and partial cabals," the commissioners made a blatant appeal to anti-Catholic feeling. They reminded "those whose profession it is to exercise the functions of religion on this continent" that France "has ever been averse to toleration and inveterately opposed to the interests and freedom of the places of worship which they serve." Tory propaganda often returned to this theme, prompting a Boston newspaper to complain about the most recent of such "low productions." This was a letter, purportedly written in New York, claiming that the French had "deprived the Americans of their principal conventicles" in Boston and Philadelphia "and converted them into Mass houses." This outrage supposedly had been quietly "submitted to by them for the convenience of their great and good Ally."[25]

The rebels stood accused of selling their birthright for arms and gunpowder. "America," Simeon Baxter charged, "once the asylum of Protestants, persecuted beyond the seas, is sold to the mother of harlots." Like Inglis, his fellow Anglican minister, Baxter claimed to believe that the alliance condemned the colonies to "Romish bondage." Whether or not they actually thought it would come to that, they clearly saw the Catholic Question as one on which the supporters of the alliance were vulnerable. The inconsistency with previous positions was simply too glaring. An article in the *Pennsylvania Ledger* shortly after the announcement of the alliance laid out the basic Tory case. Congress had "wonderfully altered their tone of late." Whereas the rebels had recently condemned "the bare *toleration* of the Roman Catholic religion in Canada" as "a wicked attempt to establish a sanguinary faith," they were now "willing to make us the instruments of weakening the best friends, and strengthening the most powerful enemies of the Reformation to such a degree as must do more than all the world besides could do, towards the universal re-establishment of Popery throughout all Christendom." When Congress went so far as to attend mass, they only presented an easier target. As Inglis pointed out, Charles the First had been "called a Papist" just for allowing his queen to do the same.[26]

The summit of the Tories' return to anti-Catholicism was Benedict Arnold's claim that what had compelled him to for-swear the American cause was his Protestant faith. When his accomplice, Major John André, was arrested in late September 1780, Arnold managed to escape to New York. The printers in that city were forbidden to publish any news of the events until Arnold presented his own account on October 7.[27] In it Arnold called France "the enemy of the protes-tant faith" and "a proud, ancient and crafty foe . . . aiming at the destruction both of the mother country and the prov-inces." In a second address, this time to the officers and sol-diers of the Continental army, he asked what hope could re-main under the alliance "for the enjoyment of the consolations of that religion for which your fathers braved the ocean, the heathen and the wilderness." Referring to the funeral in Phila-delphia the previous May of Juan de Miralles, the Spanish agent, Arnold told his readers that "the eye which guides this pen lately saw your mean and profligate Congress at mass for the soul of a Roman Catholic in Purgatory and participating in the rites of a Church, whose anti-Christian corruptions your pious ancestors would have witnessed with their blood."[28]

The comparison of Patriot politicians kneeling at mass to Puritan martyrs dying for their faith was a potent one. Yet there was also something Faustian about Arnold's gambit, stooping as he did to manipulate anti-Catholic feelings that he could only pretend to share. In the matter of flexible thinking on the Catholic Question, it was not because they were without sin that the Tories cast the first stone. On the other hand, it was the American rebels who had made such a boast of the purity of their own motives. Having more at stake in this regard, the Revolutionaries were even more loath to be caught in a lie. Further, the challenge to Patriot spokesmen was more daunting as well as more urgent than the one their Tory counterparts faced. For the king's friends to revert from patronizing Canadian Catholics to demonizing French ones did not require a great deal of soul-searching. Anti-Catholicism might be a musty suit of clothes, but for many it remained a comfortable one. Supporters of the American cause, in contrast, had to argue for religious toleration and friendship with France in the face of what they took to be strong popular reservations about both. The obstacles to such an act of persuasion were formidable, and the means of circumventing them occasionally ingenious.

The sheer improbability of the French Alliance was one hindrance to its easy reception in New England. As Mercy Otis Warren put it, "The squadrons of the House of Bourbon, fortifying the Harbour, Riding in the port of Boston, and Displaying the Ensigns of Harmony, are Events which . . . have outrun the Expectations of America." Elbridge Gerry commented on the several ironies involved in this "marvellous Change in the System of the political World." The British government had abandoned its constitution to become "advocates for Despotism" and was "endeavouring to enslave the once most loyal subjects of their King." The arbitrary and Catholic French regime, meanwhile, had become "advocates for Liberty, espousing the Cause of Lutherans and Calvinists, and risking a War to establish their Independence." Everything about the situation was bizarre, what with "the King of England branded by every Whig in the Nation as a Tyrant; the King of France by every Whig in America, applauded as the great protector of the Rights of Mankind, the King of Britain establishing Popery, the King of France endeavouring to free his people from this Ecclesiastical Tyranny, Britain at War, and France in Alliance with America." All in all, it was enough to make one's head spin.[29]

In the first place the alliance brought together two cultures that found each other extremely strange. Americans were being asked by their leaders to embrace and trust a people of whom they knew nothing good, and almost nothing at all. The vast majority of them had had no actual experience of the French. Their sense of their new allies was based on such unflattering descriptions as this one, in a Boston almanac, of "The Character of the French Nation": "The French in general are vain, trifling, changeable, and insincere: Too vain to approve of any but themselves: Too trifling to think deeply or act nobly: Too changeable to be capable of true esteem: Incapable of true friendship, and therefore insincere."[30] Such preconceptions did not augur well for easy cooperation between the two peoples or for compatibility when they met.

They first met in New England, because the objective of the first joint Franco-American venture was the British stronghold of Newport, Rhode Island.[31] The comte d'Estaing left Toulon in April 1778 and reached New England waters that summer. The projected land and sea attack on Newport was not a success. When the British sailed out of the harbor to engage the French, a storm came up and did so much damage that d'Estaing limped back to Boston without offering any help to the besieging Americans, who were in turn repulsed. From Boston he then sailed for the West Indies to look after France's more compelling strategic interest in the sugar islands. Though the French contribution to American finances was of immediate importance, it would be a long while before the alliance produced exciting results on the battlefield. The bad feelings caused by d'Estaing's conduct at Newport were mended somewhat a year later when he returned from the West Indies to contribute ships and men to the attempt on Savannah. This too failed, but not because the allies did not cooperate. Indeed, the specter of effective French action in North America provoked the British into evacuating their isolated force from Newport in alarm.

British fears were realized the following spring, when General Rochambeau assembled a force of more than five thousand troops at Brest, together with warships and transports. Leaving another fifteen hundred men behind as reinforcements, he sailed for Rhode Island and arrived there in July 1780. George Washington sent the marquis de Lafayette, one of several French volunteers already under his command, to arrange a meeting with Rochambeau. This took place in Hartford on September 20 and 21. The two generals quickly agreed to apply to Versailles for additional men and money. Before they could do anything more, such as plan a campaign against New York, Washington learned the awful news of Arnold's plot to betray West Point. Through the fall, winter, and spring, while Rochambeau waited for reinforcements and Washington assessed the condition of his army, the alliance lay in a dormant state.

The situation changed in May 1781 when the French admiral Barras reached Newport to replace Ternay, who had died there after escorting Rochambeau's army. Barras brought with him six million gold livres in new aid but also the word that there would be no more men for Rochambeau's force. The good news, aside from the gold, was that another French fleet was gathering at Brest and would soon head to the West Indies under Admiral de Grasse. He was under orders to sail north during the summer and render assistance to Washington and Rochambeau either in New York or Virginia. The two generals, meeting on May 20 in Weathersfield, Connecticut, decided they preferred an attack on New York if de Grasse could be convinced to venture that far. To that end they also decided that the French expeditionary force, which by then had spent eleven comfortable but idle months in Newport, should take up positions closer to their intended target. In June they marched 220 miles in eleven days, from Newport across the length of Connecticut to White Plains, New York.

As it turned out, de Grasse preferred the deep water of Chesapeake Bay to the shoals of Long Island Sound. In August a French ship reached Newport with word that de Grasse, with three thousand men and four million livres, was headed for the Virginia coast. Washington and Rochambeau hurried to meet him before the fall, when he would again be needed in the West Indies. On August 29 the two armies headed south from White Plains, skirting New York, while Barras assisted by ferrying the siege train. They had already managed to fool Sir Henry Clinton into believing that the main attack would be on New York, so thoroughly in fact that Clinton had prevailed on Cornwallis to send three thousand men up from Virginia to help defend the city. It was Cornwallis's thus weakened force that Washington, Rochambeau, and de Grasse were able to trap at Yorktown after the French fleet had won control of Chesapeake Bay. The loss of Cornwallis's army so demoralized public opinion in Britain that the government was forced to concede American independence and sue for peace.

The French Alliance proved decisive in the end, but it was slow in bringing its weight to bear. During the long hiatus from 1778 to 1781, one did not have to be a Tory to entertain doubts about the wisdom of the venture. For most New Englanders the first opportunity to encounter a Frenchman came with the arrival of French warships in Boston in the summer of 1778.[32] It came as a surprise to most residents that the French sailors, whom they knew to subsist on nothing but "salad and frogs," actually looked healthy. They were "surprised to find that the French were not such weak, diminutive and deformed little mortals, as their prejudices had painted them," but solved the problem by deciding that "the Count and the people in his fleet, had been picked out on purpose, in order to give them a more advantageous idea of the nation." The seamen were also the first Catholics a Bostonian was likely to have laid eyes on, unless he or she had been to Canada. They would take some getting used to, for instance in their habit of profaning the Sabbath. When Prudhomme de Boré had arrived the year before to serve as an officer under Wash-

ington, "his comeing on a Sunday" had prevented his embarrassed hosts from receiving him with the ceremony they had
planned. Conrad Gérard committed the same gaffe, entering
Philadelphia on the Lord's Day in July 1778. The delegates
from Massachusetts could not bring themselves to call on him
until Monday.[33]

These awkward incidents struck the French as evidence
of the inscrutability of American manners. When d'Estaing's
fleet came to Boston in August to recover from the violent
storm off Newport, it needed special permission to do repair
work on Sundays.[34] Claude Robin, a chaplain with the French
forces in Boston in 1781, was taken aback by the enduring
strength of such taboos. The Sabbath, he noted, was "observed with the utmost strictness; all business, how important
soever, is then totally at a stand, and the most innocent recrea-
tions and pleasures prohibited. Boston, that populous town,
where at other times there is such a hurry of business, is on this
day a mere desert; you may walk the streets without meeting a
single person, and if by chance you meet one, you scarcely
dare stop and talk with him." One of Robin's compatriots had
discovered the risks involved in less discreet comportment on
Sunday. "A Frenchman that lodged with me took it into his
head to play on the flute on Sundays for his amusement;
the people upon hearing it were greatly enraged, collected in
crowds round the house and would have carried matters to ex-
tremity in a short time with the musician, had not the landlord
given him warning of his danger, and forced him to desist."[35]

It was thus across a sizable chasm that the parties to the alliance first took each other's measure. One's idea of relaxation
was the other's picture of blasphemy. There were other such
misunderstandings as well, as when Rochambeau landed his
army at Newport. One of his officers, the comte Guillaume de
Deux-Ponts, remarked with disappointment that "we did not
experience on our arrival the welcome we had expected and
ought to have expected."[36] This does not appear to have reflected any desire on the part of the Newporters to give the

French the cold shoulder. General William Heath told Washington that the townspeople were "disposed to treat our allies with much respect" and had voted to decorate the town with lights in their honor.[37] The problem in this case lay less in the sentiments of the Americans than in the difficulty of communicating them to the French. "Coldness and reserve," wrote Deux-Ponts, "strike me to this point as the distinctive characteristics of the American nation." It would take time and effort to make the two peoples comfortable with one another.[38]

In some respects there was reason to be optimistic about this process, chiefly because so many Americans were so grateful for French assistance. It might be unexpected and difficult to get used to, but France's intervention in the Revolution was clearly good news. It was hinted at and hankered after well before it became public knowledge. The *Essex Journal* reported approvingly (though inaccurately) in January 1776 that seven thousand French troops and nine ships of the line were at Hispaniola and suggested that they might be used to help Congress, which "was in high esteem there." Privately, James Warren kept prodding John Adams to stop worrying about self-reliance and think seriously about an alliance with France. "I want to see some French Men of War on the coast," he wrote in July 1776. Adams's reply has not been preserved, but it must have been encouraging. "If the news you have from France be true," Warren wrote back, "the ball must wind up soon. God grant a confirmation. I long to be a farmer again." He was still harping on this point the following winter, complaining to Adams, "You say nothing of any expectations we are to entertain from foreign aid. I long to see French and Spanish Men of War on our Coast, and our harbours full of their Merchantmen."[39]

Warren eventually got his wish, and not all the reports were of impious flute players. In many cases the French managed to exceed the rather low expectations people had of them. Warren's wife Mercy thought that while the older French officers had bitter memories of the Seven Years' War and looked "as if they Wished, Rather than believed ancient prejudices Obliterated," the younger ones, "unconscious of injuries, Discover an Honest Joy Dancing in their Eye, and . . . Extend their arms to Embrace their New allies." Abigail Adams found all the French gentlemen very well behaved, so much so as "to make Europe[ans] and American[s] too blush at their own degeneracy of manners." Not one of them had "been seen the least disguised with Liquor since their arrival." They were, she noted, "gentlemen of family and Education." [40]

Writing as she was to her husband in Passy, Abigail Adams may have been inclined to put the best face on things; but it is clear that the French did occasionally meet with a warm welcome in New England. Their arrival in Newport gave rise to a cottage industry in language lessons: M. Jastram offered instruction in English for the French officers, M. Lemonier in French for the townspeople.[41] Wherever they went, the French created a sensation, among other things with the entertaining spectacle of their military bands. As the chaplain Robin reported during the march through Connecticut, "The Americans, whom curiosity brings by the thousands to our camp, are constantly received with good humour and festivity; and our military music, of which they are extravagantly fond, is then played for their diversion. At such times officers, sailors, Americans, of both sexes, all intermingle and dance together." This practice struck Robin as "the feast of equality," "the first fruits of the alliance," and an important means of acquainting the mutually unfamiliar peoples. "The fathers of the families melt at the sight of these affecting scenes; even those, who when they first heard of our marching, viewing us through the medium of prejudice and misrepresentation, had trembled for their possessions, and for their lives." The vicomte de Noailles saw similar benefits in the personal contacts he and his men enjoyed in Connecticut. He wrote back from Hartford to Newport to say that they had been "received everywhere with the signs of the greatest friendship," and had "danced every day." [42]

Not everyone thought that intermingling the sexes and

dancing with Frenchmen marked any clear improvement in New England mores. William Gordon made a point of noting that during the French stay at Newport, "the cows grazing in the adjoining fields were not injured, or so much as milked." One can only surmise that he was trying to head off less seemly reports. Part of the challenge of making Americans comfortable with the alliance was the need to overcome ethnic stereotypes and the social friction they tended to produce. Robin was treated with politeness by "several of the best families" in Boston despite "being known for a Frenchman and Roman Priest," but he still found that "the people in general retain their old prejudices." As a "remarkable proof" of this, he recounted the time a fire broke out in the house where he was lodging, a building whose owner was also French. At first a concerned crowd collected, "but after they were told whose house it was, they remained idle spectators of the scene."[43]

In Newport the problem struck Robin as even worse. News of the arrival of Rochambeau and his army "spread a general terror through that place: the fields became mere deserts, and those whom curiosity led to visit Newport could scarcely perceive a human form in the street." Confronted with such skepticism, the French "saw the necessity there was for obliterating these prejudices." The preconception they had to overcome was of themselves as a "fickle, presumptuous, blustering, haughty people." At another point, commenting on the views of the Bostonians, Robin expanded on this picture. "It is difficult to imagine," he complained, "what a strange idea the Americans had of the inhabitants of France, prior to the war." They thought of them "as a people bowed down beneath the yoke of despotism, given up to superstition, slavery, and prejudice, mere idolaters in their public worship, and, in short, a kind of light, nimble machines, deformed to the last degree, incapable of any thing solid or consistent." French people were seen as "entirely taken up with the dressing of their hair, and painting their faces; without delicacy or fidelity, and paying no respect even to the most sacred obligations."[44]

By "sacred obligations" Robin meant marriage, "the most

sacred of all connexions" but one "the French have in general been upbraided a long time for paying no regard to. . . . Perhaps Newport may have afforded some examples." Still, for the most part the French were judged not on their actual conduct but according to preconceived notions. "The English," Robin thought, "were pleased to disseminate these prejudices amongst them, and confirm them therein." Nor were English beliefs alone the problem. "Presbyterianism, a most bitter enemy to the Catholic Faith, had likewise rendered the Bostonians, among whom this sect is predominant, more ready to listen to and believe them." [45] Such prejudices proved durable and deep-seated. Several years later a Frenchman in Boston was not surprised to be casually disparaged as a "frog-eater." In sum, as one recipient of this treatment put it, the New Englanders might feel themselves Americans when dealing with the English, but they were Englishmen when they beheld the French. [46]

The startled reactions of the comte de Deux-Ponts and Père Robin are one way of gauging the depth of New Englanders' wariness in the face of the alliance. Another is to examine the private impressions of one who was in a position to inspect the same cultural frontier from the opposite side. William Greene, a Bostonian of no pronounced Patriot or Tory beliefs, found himself moving among the French just as the French were beginning to move among his own people. During the spring and summer of 1778, he traveled from Dieppe to Paris and on to Nantes, where he found passage back to America. No convert to the French way of life, as he sailed for home he recorded in his diary that he had "bid adieu to France never to return to it, as I can never love the Constitution, the manners and customs of this country." [47] His often disdainful comments on French religion offer an interior view of the ingrained anti-Catholicism that Robin and his colleagues observed from without.

Like the American soldiers in Quebec, Greene felt drawn by curiosity to observe masses, festivals, and religious parades.

Unlike them, he constantly poked fun at these rituals. Witnessing a procession of the host, he explained facetiously that the "cloth, leather, or silk, supported by two sticks carried by two priests," was a contraption "to keep God from the rain." At a service on Maundy Thursday, the priests washed the feet of several beggars, then "chanted Mass all kneeling," after which they "carried their God about the church as sanctification of what they had said, continually throwing incense on it." When Greene and his companions went to see the procession on the feast of Corpus Christi, they set out "like children to see a Poppet Shew." From a vantage point "close to one of the resting places for the God (which is exposed this day)," the visitors were able to "see numbers of *useless beings*" march past. "Some of the fri[a]rs look'd droll enough," Greene recalled, "and would have excited much laughter, had I dared." [48]

The use of Latin in French churches was so much mumbo jumbo as far as Greene was concerned. "All their prayers and singing is in Latin, so that there is not one in a thousand understands what they say." What they did understand did not make sense anyway, Greene thought; Catholicism was not a rational religion, and a rational man would struggle in vain to be reconciled to it. In the meantime the French people suffered for it, "governed by their priests." Watching four hundred clerics pass by in the Corpus Christi parade and hearing of three thousand more doing the same sixty miles away at Angers, Greene was struck by the display of mass idleness. "How much better if seven eights of these priests served the King in the Army, or Navy, that wou'd be doing good to their country, but at present all they do is to endeavour to deceive, and to keep in error their fellow creatures and to be examples of the greatest debauchery and most licentious lives." [49]

French government, like French religion, was something William Greene had been raised to dislike. Once again, his diary furnishes stock examples of the New England view of life in that country. It did not occur to him to doubt the story of a ten-year-old Protestant girl who had been kidnapped "by order of the King" and put into a convent. "It is very common," he observed blandly, "for Protestant people to have their children taken from them and bro't up in the Romish religion." Even secular political power was "altogether arbitrary and govern'd by the Army." The king was a despot whom no one dared disobey. The terror of royal power made for an outwardly happy scene in which "not the least noise, discontent or uneasiness is heard, but all pleased, calm, and quiet." The dark underside of this smooth exterior, however, was the squalor of "those miserable beings called Galley Slaves, chained two and two together," of whom the king had more than five thousand in Brest alone.[50]

After pausing in that port city on his way from Nantes, William Greene sailed back to America, hoping never to return and pondering the poor odds for the successful operation of the alliance. The "great inveteracy and hatred" he observed aboard the *Providence* "between our sailors and the French" struck him as a harbinger of things to come. France and America could never make a truly common cause, being "so different . . . in every thing, manners, customs, behaviour, constitution, government." This was something "impossible for a person who has not been in this country" to understand. But Greene had been, and he knew.[51]

In light of such attitudes, the French Alliance was bound to have a certain aura of the Trojan horse about it. To anyone who disliked and distrusted the French on principle, the attempt to create a general euphoria over the French entry into the war overlooked a number of dangerous possibilities. French morals, notoriously loose, might somehow rub off on the simpler, impressionable Americans. Catholic chaplains would accompany the soldiers and sailors, bringing peril to American religion. Not least of the worries was that the political and military strengths of the two allies were so unbalanced that Americans might be swept along in the wake of French policies over which they had no control. A series of unhappy incidents in the early months of the alliance made it more urgent to confront these concerns. Hearty friendship between the two peoples was not going to prove an easy sell.

In the first place there was the moral danger of relying on foreign aid of any kind, whether from a nation of luxurious dissipators or anyone else. A foreign alliance was a crutch, and if Americans leaned on it too heavily, they might not make full use of their own resources.[52] There was something unseemly about the idea. "It is a Cowardly Spirit in our Countrymen," John Adams admonished, "which makes them pant with so much longing Expectation, after a French War." America ought to stand alone. The alliance seemed an inauspicious way to secure the independence of a republic whose survival, Americans agreed, would depend on the superior virtue of its citizens. "Under a well regulated Commonwealth," Adams had written in 1776, "the People must be wise virtuous and cannot be otherwise. Under a Monarchy they may be as vicious and foolish as they please, nay, they cannot but be vicious and foolish." Once allied with France, until then the classic example in American writing of this connection between despotism and moral vice, America would be exposed to transatlantic infection.[53]

Arthur Lee thought he detected signs of just that among the members of Philadelphia society who fawned on the French minister. Writing in a sour mood to James Warren, he responded to the other's "wish to have some observations on the manners of this place." Lee found them "as little worthy of panygeric as an awkward imitation of the French can make them. Broke suddenly loose from the simplicity of quaker manners, dress and fashions and affecting the vanity, and nonsense, if nothing worse, of French parade, you may conceive they are more fit subjects of ridicule than of admiration." The fear that America would not prove immune also exercised Samuel Adams, who prayed that his country would "never be addicted to levity and the folly of parade." Such "pomp and show" might suit "the purposes of European and Asiatic grandeur" by making people "believe that they are born to be subservient to the capricious will of a single great man," but they had no place in a republic. If America's leaders were not careful, they might succumb to a taste for "vanity and foppery," and "the body of the people would be in danger of catching the distemper." Likewise, John Adams thought it important even after the war had been won to "guard as much as Prudence will permit against the Contagion of European Manners." James Warren concluded that some ground had already been lost. Compared with other countries, he thought, "none ever ran with more rapid strides or was more distinguished by its virtue and public spirit" than America, and "no Country ever Catched the Vices of others and degenerated so fast." [54]

Anxieties of this sort were common enough to tempt John Hancock to exploit them for his own ends. He conspicuously boycotted "an Elegant Entertainment made at Marston's House by our Council" for the officers of the first French frigate to arrive at Boston in May 1778. According to James Warren, Hancock also put it about "for the sake of Establishing his own popularity" that "this Connection will ruin America." The Tories were making hay with "the danger of Popery," and it seemed scandalous to Warren that a member of Congress would stoop to their tactics. Hancock was almost certainly acting opportunistically rather than on anti-Catholic principle: a year and a half later, a French observer accused him of playing the opposite game, feigning affection for France in order to undermine Adams and Bowdoin. The fact remains that the former tactic appealed to an ambitious politician in Boston in the month the alliance was announced. [55]

Moral infection, religious friction, and general cultural incompatibility all hindered full-blown American enthusiasm for the alliance. In the highest Patriot circles, moreover, there were serious qualms about the simple asymmetry of power between the two parties. This was the most obvious risk involved and the one that caused George Washington the most concern. Although his worst fears were far from being borne out by events, he did not enter into collaboration with the French without reservations or dismiss his doubts all at once. They lingered, as when he weighed the pros and cons of a second invasion of Canada. At first glance it might have seemed an ideal joint effort by the new allies. American soldiers would move north again, this time supported by French ships in the St. Lawrence and with Catholic, French-speaking comrades to display. D'Estaing's declaration of October 1778 was intended to help set the stage for such an expedition. The way was largely open, since the British had reacted to the disaster at Saratoga by burning all the forts south of Isle-aux-Noix. In addition, Moses Hazen and the Canadians who had retreated south with him in 1776 had been put to work building the Hazen Road, a path designed to carry a force up from Vermont toward Montreal.[56]

Still, Washington demurred. He told Lafayette that his decision against a second invasion in late 1778 stemmed from the unlikelihood of a British evacuation of Rhode Island or New York, the immmediate danger posed by those troops, and his inability to spare any of his own men for the northern front.[57] Writing privately to a member of Congress, however, Washington gave as his main reason his unwillingness to trust French designs in Canada. There was, he said, "one objection" which he had left "untouched" in his public letter to Congress on the subject but which seemed to him "insurmountable." This was the prospect of "the introduction of a large body of French troops into Canada," a place still "attached to them by all the ties of blood, habits, manners, religion and former connexions of government." Washington feared "this would be too great a temptation, to be resisted by any power actuated by the common maxims of national policy." D'Estaing had explicitly renounced French claims to Canada two weeks before, but Washington evidently had not been reassured. He saw French rule in that province not just as the likely outcome of a new invasion but as a possible springboard to the domination of America. "Canada would

be a solid acquisition to France . . . because of the numerous
inhabitants, subjects to her by inclination, who would aid
in preserving it under her power against the attempt of any
other." And once "possessed of New Orleans, on our Right,
Canada on our left and seconded by the numerous tribes of
Indians on our Rear," France "would have it in her power to
give law to these states."[58]

At the time of this letter, in fact, Washington had more
immediate reasons to look upon the French Alliance as a
mixed blessing. A series of unfortunate incidents had dogged
d'Estaing's fleet during the first months after its arrival off
Sandy Hook in July 1778 from Toulon. In the bitter aftermath
of the joint attempt on Newport, General John Sullivan's men
felt they had been betrayed by their new allies. His officers
drew up a formal protest in which they observed darkly that
"the honor of the French nation must be injured by their fleet
abandoning their Allies" for the safety of Boston "in the midst
of an expedition agreed to by the Count himself." It was one
thing to keep Boston in mind as a last resort, but such a plan
could not "be supposed to extend to the removal of his whole
fleet . . . on account of an injury . . . to two or three of his
ships." This behavior did not meet American expectations of
the alliance or bode well for its future. Rather, it "must make
such an unfavorable impression on the minds of Americans at
large, and create such jealousies between them and their hitherto esteemed Allies, as will in great measure frustrate the
good intentions of his most Christian Majesty and the American Congress, who have mutually endeavored to promote the
greatest harmony and confidence between the French people
and the Americans." The alliance's debut, in other words, had
been a grave failure of public relations as well as of military
tactics.[59]

The combination of old prejudices, new ill will, and physi-
cal proximity soon led to more serious expressions of mutual
displeasure. In Charleston, South Carolina, a fight broke out
between American and French sailors on the night of September 6, 1778, "when the former made use of indecent, illiberal,

and national reflections against the latter, which provoked resentment." The matter escalated to "open hostilities" in which the French were chased onto their ships, "whence they fired with cannon and small arms, which was returned by the Americans from the adjoining wharfs and shore." The militia was called out and "obliged to be under arms a great part of the night," but only after "several lives" had already been lost. In the aftermath, the government of South Carolina took "proper measures . . . to prevent a repetition of the like disorders," and the president and assembly "expressed their deep concern, that the slightest animosities should prevail between any citizen of America, and the subjects of their illustrious and good ally." [60]

A similar melee took place two days later in Boston. At a time when food was in short supply, prices were high, and resentment at the "successless expedition against Rhode Island" was still strong, a mob attacked a bakery belonging to d'Estaing's fleet.[61] The bakers defended themselves, and when two French officers tried to intervene to stop the fighting, one of them was struck on the head and mortally wounded. He was the chevalier de Saint-Sauveur, a young nobleman and first chamberlain to the comte d'Artois, the king's brother.[62] In this most awkward situation, efforts to control the political damage consisted mainly of an agreement on the part of d'Estaing and the Boston authorities to blame the attack on English sailors. Conveniently, there was a batch of them, prisoners of war, serving aboard a Continental privateer then anchored in Boston Harbor. A local newspaper also nominated as culprits the remnants of Burgoyne's army being held in the city. The General Court referred carefully to "certain riotous persons unknown" and voted to erect a memorial to the chevalier.[63] The comte d'Estaing, when thanking the court for this gesture, in turn cast suspicion on local Tories or British secret agents acting as provocateurs.[64]

There were further outbreaks in Boston involving local residents and French sailors in late September and early October.[65] It became increasingly clear that an active propaganda campaign would be required in order to prevent a serious deterioration of allied goodwill. James Warren expressed the party line this way in a letter to John Adams. "The French officers and Seamen" had behaved themselves "Extreemly well" and were "indeed the most peaceable, quiet and orderly set of men in their profession I ever saw." There had, nevertheless, "been several disagreeable riots and Quarrels between them and the English Sailors here. I believe set on by the Tories, who wish to blow up a Breeze between us and our New Allies." Keeping tabs on the situation from his headquarters in Fredericksburg, New York, George Washington was even more to the point. He wrote to Heath, his commander at Boston, to express his pleasure at hearing that the Saint-Sauveur affair had been "terminated in such a manner as to convince the French gentlemen that no public harm or insult was intended by the people of the town of Boston." He urged the adoption of "all possible means" to "cultivate harmony between the people and the seamen," an effort in which, according to Gordon, "the cooler and more judicious part of the community employed their services." [66]

Those would-be shapers of public opinion had their work cut out for them as violence involving their French guests continued to erupt. In September 1779 an English prisoner of war serving on a Contintental ship—the *Queen of France*, as it happened—picked a fight with a group of Frenchmen in the Boston market and was shot dead. It was a disturbing event but easy to explain away as the work of a lout who had gotten what he deserved. On the other hand, when six French sailors and a Bostonian set upon one James Bass in December 1780 and stabbed him to death, there was no such convenient excuse. One of the Frenchmen escaped, but the other five and their local accomplice, Philip Eliot, were arrested. Louis Dessuages was indicted for murder and the rest for "aiding helping abetting comforting assisting and maintaining the said Lewis Dessuages the felony of Murder aforesaid to do and commit." A jury of reliable Whigs, of which Paul Revere was the foreman, acquitted the defendants on all counts. Whether or not it was an honest judgment, it was certainly an expedient one.[67]

While Washington, Heath, and Revere did their best to protect and defend the popularity of the alliance, others took positive steps to promote it. Chief among these in New England was Samuel Cooper of Boston. A Congregationalist minister, Cooper early befriended the comte d'Estaing and the chevalier de La Luzerne, who succeeded Conrad Gérard as French minister to the United States in 1779. Cooper was an ardent champion of Franco-American cooperation in many fields, the arts and sciences as well as American independence and the emancipation of Canada. His correspondence with La Luzerne highlights what the two men saw as the main obstacles to greater acceptance of the alliance.[68]

La Luzerne wrote to Cooper in the fall of 1779 in anticipation of news of d'Estaing's exploits in the West Indies and the Carolinas. He offered detailed instructions as to how best to turn any French success there to the general advantage of the alliance. Any public announcement, the diplomat suggested, should stress "the union and good sense which will have reigned among the allied troops" and give equal credit to both countries. Cooper and his colleagues should make it clear that in turning from the islands to the defense of Georgia and the Carolinas, the admiral had followed the express orders of the king. Finally, La Luzerne reminded his friend that "the English will apply themselves incessantly to spread germs of jealousy between the United States and France," and that it would be necessary to work actively against them.[69]

The following summer, after Rochambeau had disembarked his army at Newport, La Luzerne wrote to Cooper to transmit an example of just such Tory propaganda and to offer a remedy. He quoted from the *New York Gazette* of July 15, 1780: "The prospect of a french army landing in the Northern provinces, alarms the Republican fraternity in connecticut and Massachusetts: should these Roman catholic allies ever nestle themselves in one of the revolted states, it is apprehended their independence must give way to the establishment of a french government, laws, customs, &c. &c. ever abhorrent of the sour and turbulent Puritans." La Luzerne gamely dismissed this as a "quite gay" idea that "does honor to the imagination of its inventor." Rhode Island, the Tories would have it, was "sold like Joseph by his brothers to the merchants," while "the French, these papists, these Monsters who eat their protestants raw," schemed to take possession of it as security for American debts. Such scurrilous tripe reminded La Luzerne of "an old governess who sees her little charge again after 25 years and wants to scare him with the bogeyman again." It was too late, he declared; "the time of illusions and lies" was past.[70]

Just what were those illusions, though? Itemizing them even as he dismissed them, La Luzerne revealed both the specific lines of Tory attack and how much they weighed on his mind. His little catalog of supposedly obsolete considerations was unintentionally eloquent. Speaking for the Americans, he wrote, "We no longer believe that an English vessel can overwhelm a French one of the same strength; that a French officer spends the whole morning performing his toilette, wears rouge but refuses to carry a rifle; that an English Grenadier can put a company of French soldiers to flight by breathing at them; that the tallest of them doesn't come up to the shoulder of a Briton." Warming to his subject, La Luzerne mentioned other accusations further removed from martial honor. The Tories had dared to suggest "that the kingdom of France makes only faulty manufactures; that its wines are weak and unhealthy, the nation enslaved, the prince a despot." But none of this would stand. "It is too late, Messieurs: we have seen France and there we have seen liberty, without license; a powerful monarch who yet does not abuse his power; a constitution flourishing in the shade of the laws; and authority and submission tempering one another through the love of the ruled for the prince and the paternal tenderness of the king for his people."[71]

This flattering picture, La Luzerne asserted, had taken the place of former notions. The reformed American, elevated above old prejudices, was acquainted with the French and their many virtues. La Luzerne's imaginary friend of the alliance was so fond of French goods, for instance, that he would not trade his Louvier sheets for British linen. Above all, he was pragmatic. "As for wine, that's another affair: I would not wish to give up Madeira, but Burgundy and claret are excellent liquors nonetheless. Very well, let there be no exclusions. Let us drink what pleases us best: toast our generals with Madeira, our friends with Burgundy, and our mistresses with champagne."[72] Given the French reputation for libertinism, Cooper may have found the choice of image a little unfortunate. Still, it was the thought that counted: Americans ought to put aside impractical preconceptions and make use of whatever was best suited to the task at hand.

It was in fact a rather bold claim. It was easier for La Luzerne than for most New Englanders to compare taste in allies to taste in wines. The Tories had passed from the enlightened religious tolerance of the Quebec Act to the familiar anti-Catholic vocabulary of their attacks on the French Alliance. The Americans were being called upon to shift in the more difficult direction, against the grain of habit. Those who sought to convince them to do so needed either to deny the importance of old beliefs or, better yet, to explain how those could be reconciled with recent events. La Luzerne described the scope of the problem and in the same breath declared it solved, but he knew more than he wrote. The resort to French patronage seemed likely to carry the young United States into uncharted and perhaps troubled waters. If La Luzerne complacently believed in his own role as the agent of American enlightenment, his clients were not always so sanguine.

On the New England side, it was easier to acknowledge the growth of French influence than to stake one's reputation on its unalloyed wholesomeness. The sense that something might be lost, something old and precious traded away for something new and of uncertain worth, placed a chill on the effort to rally support for the alliance. It was not enough to announce that one welcomed the generosity of the French; or rather, that was already saying too much. It was judicious to begin more modestly, explaining why one thought it safe and wise to accept the French offer. In making this case supporters of the alliance found it useful to reexamine and refine popular notions about the French national character. It would not do to sit idly by while Americans continued to think of the French the way that William Greene did. A "new Frenchman" was needed to replace the overenlightened, or arch-Catholic, and at all events antirepublican creature of Greene's imagination. Undergirding as it would the popularity of the alliance itself, a new way of imagining the French could greatly benefit the American cause. But its usefulness would depend on its plausibility, and circumstances did not permit a carefully orchestrated campaign to nudge public opinion in the right direction. Improvisation was more the order of the day.

# 5

## The Greatest Prince on Earth

On May 2, 1778, Silas Deane's brother Simeon arrived at York with copies of the treaties of alliance and commerce with France. The joy and relief these occasioned were heightened by the fact that the Americans had had no official word from their representatives in Europe for over a year. Wasting no time, Congress ratified both treaties on the fourth. George Washington organized a celebration by the army two days later. The soldiers assembled by brigade in the morning and heard the news from their chaplains, who followed it with sermons of thanksgiving. The men then formed two lines for a thirteen gun salute, and "at the firing of the last, a running fire of infantry began on the right, and continued through the whole front line; it was then taken up on the left of the second line, and continued to the right. A signal was given, and the whole army huzzaed, 'Long live the King of France.'" [1]

On the eighth, Congress announced the alliance in an address "To the Inhabitants of the United States of America." After describing the treaties and the benefits they would bring, the address warned the Americans not to think all their problems solved. They had "still to expect one severe conflict." Even if French aid eventually secured their independence, it could not "secure your country from desolation, your habitations from plunder, your wives from insult or violence, nor your children from butchery."[2] Having thus lowered expectations of the alliance and guarded against complacency, Congress went on to say that it would behoove the recipients of this largesse to show proper gratitude and respect to their benefactors. They should treat the French "as their brethren and allies" and "with the friendship and attention due to the subjects of a Great PRINCE, who, with the highest magnanimity and wisdom, hath treated with these United States on terms of perfect equality and mutual advantage, thereby rendering himself THE PROTECTOR OF THE RIGHTS OF MANKIND."[3] The campaign to promote the French Alliance had begun in earnest, and the depiction of Louis XVI as the champion of the Rights of Man would not prove its strangest result. Many old ideas about the French and about Catholics in general would be revised or discarded, often in ways that proved easy for Tories to ridicule. As one satirist described these efforts of rebel propaganda:

> With doctrines strange in matter and in dress,
> Here sounds the pulpit, and there groans the press.[4]

It was under the weight of more than a century of their own anti-French and anti-Catholic invective that the pulpit and press of the Revolution labored. New England almanacs and magazines had long been filled with tales of corrupt priests and effete Bourbon nobles. John Tulley's Boston almanac for 1695 made room for only two items beyond the obligatory twelve calendar pages: a table of eclipses and "An Account of the Cruelty of the Papists Acted upon the Bodies of Some of the Godly Martyrs."[5] The Seven Years' War focused particular attention on the French. An item on the "Character of the French Nation" which appeared in 1759 said they were a people lacking in depth and substance. They were "full of levity" and "civility," but "with little sincerity," too "fond of outside show and grandeur." The women in France were "very free in their behavior," the common people "the poorest, and at the same time the merriest," in Europe. They were "devout in their churches," except when distracted during festivals by the "musick and trappings" of papist rituals. In politics they groveled before their king, in the service of whose glory they would do anything, since, "being slaves themselves," they "would gladly reduce all mankind to their own miserable condition."[6]

This last charge, that French inconstancy extended into politics and led them to violate gladly any oaths they might make to others, was not the quirk of one writer. It was an application of the frequently repeated accusation that Catholic doctrine did not require believers to keep faith with heretics.[7] The French were typical of the papist breed, said another writer, likely to "speak one thing and mean another; they make great promises, but never perform any; their mouths flatter, whilst their hearts betray; and they have no friendship without design." In diplomacy France was "the Proteus of the age," the last nation one would want as an ally. "She enters like a lamb, transforms into a fox, and thence becomes a devouring wolf."[8]

These caricatures dated from wartime and thus were not necessarily relevant to the period, a generation later, of cooperation between the Patriots and the French. Yet there had been no gentle tapering off of unfriendly sentiments during the years of peace in North America after 1763. William Greene's diary of his travels in France in 1778 shows him to hold the same prejudices—of the French as frivolous, priest-ridden slaves—that were current in 1759. Up to and following the outbreak of the Revolution, the French continued to be seen this way, both in the press and in private expressions of opinion. The image of superficiality, for instance, was reinforced in 1773 by an almanac anecdote about a French marquis who stopped for dinner at an English public house and began to boast "of the happy Genius of his Nation, in projecting all the fine Modes and Fashions, particularly the *Ruffle*, which he said, *Was de fine Ornament to de Hand and had been followed by all de other Nations.*" The publican "allowed what he said, but observed at the same Time, *That the English, according to Custom, had made great Improvement on their Invention, by adding the Shirt.*" Another swipe at French morals came in a gardener's playful claim that besides being "master of the *mint*" and knowing how to raise "his *celery* every year," he made "more *beds* than the French king" and kept "more *painted ladies*" in them. Americans were, if anything, freer with their contempt for French character when expressing themselves in private. Abigail Adams, despite being impressed by the good behavior of the French officers at Boston, could not shake the conviction that the French as a nation were dissolute. Writing from Paris, she told Mercy Warren that there "the Business of Life" was "Pleasure." The Catholic religion, she thought, bore much of the blame. In a Protestant family she had seen a rare "Decorum and Decency of Manners. . . . But whilst absolutions are held in estimation and pleasure can be bought and sold, what restraint have mankind upon their Appetites and Passions?"[9]

French religion, then, was one of the contributing factors to the low state of the national character. Yet it was a problem that from the Patriot point of view cut both ways. If many Americans were in the habit of ascribing the moral and political defects of the French to the influence of the Catholic Church, many others traced the same effects to the opposite cause, that is, the decline of religious faith at the hands of decadent philosophes. The public relations campaign waged on behalf of the alliance thus was obliged to protect two flanks at once, simultaneously presenting the French as skeptical and devout. Few American writers faced this problem squarely, since it was more convenient to make one point at a time than to articulate a position complex enough to resolve the contradiction.

One place where this scattershot method left its mark was in the pages of New England almanacs. These annual pamphlets contained recipes, interest rate tables, schedules of eclipses, lists of inns along the post roads, humorous and instructive anecdotes, and a considerable amount of terrible poetry. The centerpiece of any almanac, however, was its calendar. Each month received a page with much other information wedged in and around the dates: tides, phases of the moon, weather predictions, court sessions, assorted words to the wise, and notations of important anniversaries. In the early 1770s most New England almanacs made room on June 4 for King George's birthday, although they compensated somewhat for this by recalling Charles I's execution on January 30. Another date regularly noted was November 5, the Gunpowder Plot.

The *Freebetter's Connecticut Almanac* for 1774 is a good example of the pre-Revolutionary style. It noted the beheading of Charles I, the repeal of the Stamp Act, Queen Charlotte's birthday, the restoration of Charles II (on his birthday, conveniently for almanac editors), King George's birthday, the taking of Cape Breton by New England forces in 1744, King George's coronation, and the Gunpowder Plot.[10] Once the Revolution began, space on June 4 became available for weather forecasts instead. Mention of the Gunpowder Plot dropped off as well, although not as quickly or completely.[11] Other names, previously unthinkable, began to appear in the calendar pages. Readers of a 1780 Rhode Island almanac came across a "List of the Princes of Europe" at whose head was

> France. Louis XVI (whom God preserve) born August 23, 1754; succeeded his grandfather May 10, 1774; married Maria Antonietta, of Austria, May 16, 1770.

Next came

> Spain. Charles III (whom Heaven prosper), born January 20, 1716. Issue 5 sons and 2 daughters.

There followed entries for Portugal, Denmark, Rome, and only then one for

> Island of Britain. George III, the sanguinary tyrant, born (to dismember the British empire, and render America independent) June 4, 1738.[12]

In the editions of 1781, prepared in 1780, Louis's birthday and the signing of the treaty of alliance (February 6) became staples of the almanac calendars. By 1786 *Bickerstaff's Boston Almanack* found space for these two dates, Louis's accession to the throne, and the birthdays of Marie Antoinette and the dauphin.[13]

Almanac anecdotes were even more explicit about seeking to enhance the reputation of the French, both commoners and aristocrats. The ordinary people were now "comely and well-shaped, very active and lively, with a great share of wit, and a natural disposition and aptitude for all bodily exercises." That is, their peculiar physicality had become a virtue. Nor was their "affection and obedience to their Kings" any longer a defect. Their "sociality," formerly a sign of frivolousness, was "directed by good sense, excluding all restraints and affected gravity from conversation." As for their natural charm, it now produced such "commendable qualities" as "complaisance and a readiness to oblige, which they practise not only towards relations and acquaintance, but likewise to strangers, who they treat with great civility, contracting friendship with them as readily as with their countrymen, and shewing themselves not only disinterested, but even generous and noble in their friendship."[14]

Similar character assessments of the French nobility helped shore up the reputation of the officer corps. Marshal Montluc, the veteran and chronicler of the Hundred Years' War, began to surface in almanacs as a model of piety and valor. According to the excerpts of his memoirs that appeared in several editions, this noble figure had never let a day pass without beseeching God's help and forgiveness or entered battle without gladly offering up his life to him. An even more improbable item managed to transform a French admiral's raids along the Scottish coast during the Seven Years' War into an honorable enterprise. The said Admiral Thurot "at first spread terror," but this "soon gave place to admiration inspired by his humanity." True, he pillaged, but he "paid a full price for everything he wanted" and "behaved with so much affability" that a local resident actually dared to complain when one of the admiral's officers robbed him of fifty guineas. "Thurot ordered the officer to give his bill for the money, which he said should be stopped out of his pay, if they were so fortunate as to return to France." Here was a Frenchman worthy of emulation. "Such incidents," the editor suggested, "ought to be held up to the public as examples of true heroism." [15]

The praise American printers lavished on their allies reached its highest pitch in a thoroughly revised attitude toward the House of Bourbon. Thus one almanac called attention to an instance of "TRUE GREATNESS . . . in Henry IV. of France." Another, printed shortly after the signing of the alliance, extolled the virtues of the French and singled out the "lively genius" of Louis. It also described Marie Antoinette, unusually, as "of a most chearful temper, extremely affable and obliging, easy of access to all ranks of people, and most generously condescending to converse with the meanest of her subjects." [16] Everywhere one turned after 1778, New Englanders had good things to say about the French royal family. August 23, Louis's birthday, became an occasion for extravagant celebrations in Philadelphia which New England newspapers in turn reported with approval. The *Massachusetts Spy*, *Continental Journal*, and *New Hampshire Gazette* all reprinted descriptions of the "due decorum, festivity and popular joy" that marked the day in 1779. Flags bedecked a liberty pole on the Market Street wharf and ships in the harbor, and a delegation from Congress delivered formal congratulations to Conrad Gérard, the outgoing French minister. All afternoon the bells of Christ Church rang out and ships' cannon and city artillery fired salutes, "whilst the healths of the illustrious monarch and his Royal Consort were liberally toasted at the many festivities held" around the city. At nightfall there was "a grand exhibition of fireworks, &c." [17]

That same month, the new French envoy, the chevalier de La Luzerne, arrived in Boston on his way to take up his post in Philadelphia. John Adams, just recalled by Congress from his own foreign assignment, crossed the Atlantic in the same ship. Landing late one afternoon at John Hancock's wharf, the chevalier and his party were met by a committee of the Massachusetts Council and a thirteen-gun salute from Fort Hill. Having received these and "every other mark of respect . . . which circumstances would permit," they proceeded in carriages "to the house late the residence of the Continental General." The council soon invited the minister to address it, which he did in French before an audience of "a number of principal Magistrates of the State, the Clergy, and other Gentlemen of distinction."[18]

A few days later Adams escorted his guest to Harvard College, the citadel of Congregationalism and the setting of the anti-Catholic Dudleian Lectures. The students turned out "in their academical habits, their heads uncovered," to form two lines across the Yard on either side of the official party's path. The visitors were greeted at Harvard Hall by "the President, Corporation, Professors and Tutors, and conducted to the library." The president, Samuel Langdon, solved the language problem by delivering his speech in Latin, "making the most respectful mention of our illustrious ally, His Most Christian Majesty." He expressed his "warmest wishes for the perpetuation of the alliance, and the completion of its important and happy design, and for the prosperity of religion and learning throughout the world." La Luzerne responded "in the most polite manner, and in the same language." He pronounced himself pleased to see "a country once indeed the region of ignorance and barbarity" become a beacon of learning. Langdon and his faculty, for their part, took the opportunity to show their visitor "the rich variety of books reposited in the Library" and "the Philosophical apparatus fabricated by some of the best artists in Europe."[19]

A few days later, preparing to set off for Philadelphia with an escort of light dragoons and a train of more than twenty wagons, the chevalier published a letter to the Massachusetts

Council that reflected his hopes in the area of public relations. He acknowledged his kind reception in Boston as a testimony of goodwill toward France and said he could "venture to affirm that this affection is reciprocal." The more frequently the two nations had opportunities "to become acquainted with each other," he said, "the greater will be their mutual esteem." He was "very certain" that the leading men of the state would "employ every exertion to cherish sentiments so natural" and promised to do his own best "to nourish the affection of the French for Confederated America." For his own part the envoy had done his best to display the most progressive aspect of French culture. His visit to Harvard was an encouraging nod to American science in the teeth, so to speak, of American religion.[20]

The city fathers did not miss their cue. They feted La Luzerne as they had d'Estaing and his officers the previous fall. The *Massachusetts Spy* devoted the entire first page and much of the second of its issue of October 7, 1779, to a glowing tribute to King Louis. The article invited its readers to recall their bleak condition before "the noble soul of Louis XVI burst forth" and "espoused our cause." George and Louis were "living in the same age," but posterity would find them utterly "unlike in temper, . . . dissimilar in fate," and "unequal in . . . fame"—as different, in short, as "Cain and Abel." Straining for a sufficiently lavish form of praise, the writer compared Louis to "the sun who kindles up the sleeping sparks of fire diffused throughout the system." He had "re-animated, in the early years of his reign, all the love of honour, courage, gallantry and heroism that has long adorned the annals of the nation."[21] This rightful heir of the Sun King, this prince whose "magnanimity and goodness" were "sufficient to irradiate the system of an hundred kingdoms," not only had introduced several new virtues to the catalog of the French national character but had managed to expunge the vices as well. He had shed his image as a cruel tyrant and squanderer of the nation's wealth. William Gordon recorded the applause in

Boston when Louis, on his birthday in 1780, abolished the use of torture in the French courts. Another decree of the same date ordered "a prodigious reform in his houshold," abolishing "no less than 406 offices in that department . . . in order to lessen the burdens of his people." [22]

American Patriots drank toasts to the alliance and to Louis on any suitable occasion. A Tory wag mocked this practice by proposing "The King of France!" at a gathering where most of the company were Whigs. Challenged as to the sincerity of his toast, he alluded to the old Plantagenet claim, saying, "You may drink *your King of France*, and I will *mine.*" Most New Englanders were busy drinking the health of Louis. The third anniversary of the battle of Bennington, for instance, called for "festivity and public rejoicings" in that town, at which "the militia officers and other principal gentlemen of the State of Vermont" drank to the king and queen of France, the king and queen of Spain, and Admiral de Ternay and General Rochambeau. A week later the French monarch's birthday brought forth the same toasts. In perhaps the ultimate encomium to the House of Bourbon, Robert Treat Paine—the attorney general of Massachusetts, member of the Continental Congress, a chaplain at Crown Point in his youth, the son of a minister and great-grandson of the Reverend Samuel Willard—baptized a daughter Maria Antonietta Paine.[23]

As La Luzerne's exhortation had suggested, and as New England traditions would lead one to expect, there was something forced in all these protestations of love for France. This came near to the surface, if it did not quite emerge, on the occasion of the birth of the dauphin in October 1781. George Washington, for his part, oversaw a very elaborate celebration at Fishkill. His camp on the Hudson was the scene of feasts, toasts, songs of praise, fireworks in the shape of fleurs-de-lis, and the construction for the occasion of a 220-by-80-foot colonnade. "Sixty-four columns of the form of palm trees, sixteen feet high," supported the structure, which had "forty-two oval windows (of five feet by four)." It enclosed tables for five hundred, with room for an orchestra and "ample vacuity at the centre" for dancing. Although its newspapers reported these details, Boston observed the event with more restraint. Governor Hancock first informed the house and senate that he had received an official announcement of the dauphin's birth. As for how they might wish to respond to the news on behalf of their constituents, Hancock could "only say, that I shall most readily and cheerfully concur with you, gentlemen, in every measure which your lively feelings shall dictate, and your judgment determine to be proper for expressing in some publick manner our common joy." The next day a joint committee of the two chambers replied that while its members certainly shared "the lively joy which this happy event has given the most Christian King," they respectfully declined to make any suggestions as to a celebration. Instead they passed responsibility for the decision back to Hancock, asking him "with advice of Council, to take such measures as in your wisdom shall be thought proper to express in a publick manner the common joy upon this auspicious occasion." [24]

One way or another, June 12 became "the day appointed by the government" for the festivities, which included the ringing of church bells and firing of cannon in the morning, a large public dinner in the senate chamber at noon, and fireworks and more gun salutes at night.[25] Recording all this, a Boston newspaper observed that

> Every order of men, in its own way, shouted benediction to the Dauphin, which is a compliment not only upon the patriotism, but the good sense of the people, who did well to consider of what importance (in an hereditary kingdom) is the birth of a Dauphin; who not only from his infancy may be educated for the throne, but (life preserved) may save immense bloodshed, which so often happens where the right of a crown is disputed. This alone is a reason why even Republicans (as far as they are friends of mankind) may rejoice when the heir to a great Empire is born.[26]

This passage brims with ironies: the dauphin died before he was ten, and the idea of disputing his family's right to the crown soon took on a whole new dimension. Even at the time, however, the suggestion that "even Republicans" could take part in the celebrations struck a distinctly apologetic note. Despite strenuous efforts to present them as compatible, the Revolution and the alliance remained an odd fit in 1782.

From the outset there had been signs that the alliance was not receiving a warm welcome everywhere in America. In July 1779 New England newspapers printed a message from Congress aimed directly at this problem. It was a long defense of the alliance that acknowledged its awkwardness and sought gamely to present that awkwardness as an advantage. If the Tories and the British were dumbfounded that American Protestants would accept French protection, then surely this must recommend the policy. "The Resentment and Confusion of your Enemies," Congress told the people, was a good sign, one that "will point out to you the Ideas you should entertain of the Magnanimity and consummate Wisdom of his Most Christian Majesty on this Occasion." King Louis, it said, had "cemented the Harmony between himself and these States, not only by establishing a Reciprocity of Benefits, but by eradicating every Cause of Jealousy and Suspicion." The New Hampshire House of Representatives must have found this plausible, since it voted to have the address "printed, and dispersed throughout this State." It also recommended that upon receiving it, ministers "read the same to their respective Congregations . . . immediately after the Divine Service," and that selectmen have it read at town meetings."[27]

There was more than a little "Jealousy and Suspicion" lurking in New England, however, and to label it unnecessary was not to dispel it. Realizing this, Congress made use of such other devices as the unbridled revisionism displayed in a collection of old and new papers issued in 1779 as *Observations on the American Revolution*.[28] The introduction to this pamphlet managed in a few pages to make several ambitious historical claims, all of them intended to defuse anti-French feeling. The authors denied, for instance, that America had originally been settled under British protection. Rather, the colonies in the early days "were in fact so many independent states, whose only political connection with each other and with the several parts of the British empire, was by means of a common sovereign." The sole reason this fragile arrangement had not "crumbled to pieces at a much earlier period" was that it had "been cemented by the sameness of manners and language, a striking similarity of civil institutions, a continued intercourse for the purposes of commerce and other circumstances of the like kind."[29]

The Protestant religion was conspicuously absent from this list. The omission had the virtue of making it less jarring to present the role of France during this period in a benevolent light. French possession of Canada, it was now claimed, had not posed any threat to New England all those years. True, it was "a neighbour" who "cramped our growth and repressed our efforts," but only for a time. More importantly, the proximity of an alternative patron for the settlers had served as a check on British power. If their colonial masters ever pushed the Americans too far, the French could step in with "effectual aid in case of rupture." The Peace of 1763, in other words, did not free New England from a horrible popish threat, as Jonathan Mayhew would have said; it only emboldened the British by removing the last barrier to their imperial ambitions. The alliance of 1778 was thus nothing new or strange but a natural outgrowth of the balance of power in North America. France had always waited in the wings to answer America's call and free it from its chains.[30]

However impressive a performance, the *Observations* give an idea of the demands the French Alliance placed on the ingenuity of American propagandists. Still, the explicitly religious aspects of the problem could not be ignored. A way would have to be found to confront the Catholic Question head-on. There eventually emerged two streams of propaganda designed to reconcile the alliance and the Protestant values in whose defense the war was supposedly being fought. One was a distinction between "Frenchness" and Catholicism—that is, a claim that the French were no longer actually Catholic. If this was true, then the problem at once disappeared, since support of the alliance no longer implied an endorsement of Catholicism.

The article that appeared in the *Pennsylvania Ledger* shortly after the announcement in America of the signing of the treaties with France was not unusual in mocking the way the Congress had changed its tune on the subject of religious toleration. What distinguished this attack was a second argument, one that anticipated the strategy of the other side. The rebels, the writer charged, would say "that the French are no longer such a bigoted people as they were . . . , and that we need not fear imbibing any improper sentiments from her maxims of religion and government." It was a prescient remark, as this is exactly what the rebels did say: that the French (and the Spanish) had lost their Catholic faith and with it their desire to enforce the will of the pope.[31]

The Patriots did not have to concoct this thesis out of thin air. Part of the anti-French prejudice formerly common to Americans and Britons was the belief that French libertinism pointed to a weak religious faith whose decline was most advanced in the upper reaches of the aristocracy. William Greene subscribed to this view, and while in France in 1778 recorded what he considered several instances of the progress of the decay. He certainly found French morals loose and Benjamin Franklin already well acclimated to them.[32] Visiting Franklin, Adams, and Lee in Paris, he marveled "to think how different we now spend our Sundays to what we formerly did at Boston, then going to church all day, and not to walk till after the sun set." They now spent their Sundays "either going to the play, into large company or some amusement to kill time." He found it "astonishing what different customs" obtained "in different climes. I hope I shall keep fast my integrity in the midst of every temptation I shall meet with."[33]

Greene was not to prove a very successful ascetic. A few weeks later he found the Italian opera a feast of beautiful scenery, elegant dress, and bewitching music. "I was enchanted beyond measure," he confessed, and "never was so pleased with any thing of the kind in my life." Still, he did think that when laxity "gets so far it is to the discredit of a nation." The fact that Sunday was "the greatest day for all kinds of frolicking in the week" was a glaring indication that "this nation from the height of superstition are dropping fast to no religion at all." This decline was due to "the effects of the Romish Priest." Idle, cynical churchmen were at the root of the problem, causing the rapid erosion of Catholic faith in France. An abbot in Nantes confided to Greene that he saw his colleagues as a class of "useless beings, so little do the priests themselves believe in the numerous rites and ceremonies of the Church of Rome." All they did, Greene added, was "to endeavour to deceive, and to keep in error their fellow creatures and to be examples of the greatest debauchery and most licentious lives." An Irish abbot confirmed this, telling Greene that the priests "believe not a word of the service they perform" and "are the most dissolute sett of people in the Kingdom, and of the most debauched morals."[34]

Greene took heart, though, from the belief that this state of things would not endure. The cracks in French Catholicism were so deep that the whole edifice might soon collapse. "The eyes of the French begin to open with regard to religion." The king himself had recently taken the step of abolishing six feast days. "They proceed as fast as prudence will permit to throw off the many superstitions they use. Six or eight months past the priests fear'd an entire alteration in religion" and "were obliged to take great pains to prevent it."[35] If Louis himself was on the verge of reformation, then how dangerous a force could French Catholicism be? One of Greene's hosts in Paris, John Adams, lost no time in applying the same logic to his own defense of the alliance. Writing to James Warren, he betrayed his anxiety on the question by demanding rhetorically whether there was "a sensible Hypocrite in America who can start a Jealousy that Religion may be in danger" there. And if so, "from whence can this arise? not from France." Times had changed, and old fears lost their foundation. "The Spirit for crusaiding Religion is not in France. The Rage of making Proselytes which has existed in former Centuries is no more. . . . Nothing can be clearer than that in this enlighten'd tollerant Age, at this vast Distance, without Claim or Colour of Authority, . . . this, I had almost said tollerant Nation can never endanger our Religion." [36]

Adams no doubt protested too much, but the escape route he indicated was one that many apologists were quick to follow. Congregationalist ministers who supported the alliance were especially eager to demonstrate that doing so was consistent with Protestant values. How convenient, therefore, that the French were no longer in the papist camp. Louis's apologists could point to the fact that he had restored the toleration of French Protestants first proclaimed by Henri IV in the Edict of Nantes but abrogated in 1685 by Louis XIV. This welcome news demonstrated that to be French and to be militantly Catholic—or to be Catholic at all—were not necessarily the same thing.[37] The *New-Hampshire Gazette* helpfully produced what it claimed was a clause of the treaty of alliance stipulating that "if a society of 15 or 20 persons shall settle in any town within the kingdom of France, they are to be tolerated in the exercise of their religious worship, according to the custom of their country." [38] Joseph II, the Holy Roman Emperor, received similar credit from Americans for championing the toleration of Protestants and having "suppressed most of the religious orders of both sexes, as useless to society." [39]

This last point was key, since it touched on how independent Catholic European monarchs were from that supposed embodiment of pre-Enlightenment, the pope. Hannah Adams reminded American readers that the "Galacian clergy" were "more exempt than others who profess the Romish religion from the Papal authority." They recognized that authority in no area but "things relating to salvation." Louis was an important beneficiary of this arrangement, she said, since the pope lacked the power to excommunicate him or to absolve his subjects of their duty of allegiance. Such assurances departed sharply from the customary Protestant insistence that the pope's sway over Catholic rulers and their subjects made him the de facto tyrant of a huge international empire. According to the old view, as enunciated by Samuel Cooper in the 1773 Dudleian Lecture, every Catholic monarch groveled before the pope. "The Emperor Frederic the first held the styrup of his horse, and was chided for holding it on the wrong side. Another Emperor, Henry IVth, waited three days at the gates of Pope Gregory VIIth to obtain an audience. Frederic fell prostrate in St. Mark's church at Venice before Alexander the III, in presence of the people." And these were only symbolic representations of a far more dangerous power. "The Prelate of Rome has deposed Kings and Emperors; absolved their subjects from all allegiance to them; and authoritatively required their taking arms against them." [40]

It therefore mattered greatly that Louis and Joseph were standing up to the pope, defying and frustrating his will. If true, it meant that the French were less dangerous than a cautious New Englander might have thought. Either they no longer believed in the Church of Rome, as Greene and Adams said, or they were at last bestirring themselves to reform it. Once again, Patriot writers pointed to the lesson. Ezra Stiles delivered an election sermon in Hartford calling Louis and Joseph "two young Princes . . . raised up in providence to make their people and mankind happy." Louis, he said, had allowed the French Protestants, "formerly oppressed with heavy persecution," to "enjoy a good degree of religious liberty, though by a silent indulgence only." [41] As for Joseph, his rescript disclaiming "all subordination to the pope in secular affairs" had greatly alarmed Pius VI. The pontiff had conferred with his cardinals and decided, "notwithstanding his great age," to travel to Vienna and discuss the matter in person. Joseph had casually replied that the pope could make the trip if he wanted. Pius had then done so in the spring of 1782, but only to spend a month in Vienna and leave again without changing the emperor's mind. This act of defiance received prominent treatment in several American newspapers.[42]

There were encouraging signs in other Catholic countries as well. David Tappan hailed "the downfall of the hellish Inquisition in Spain, and the liberal institutions which begin to take place in that country, so remarkable, hitherto, for a blind, narrow, furious, persecuting bigotry." According to William Gordon, Americans ranked the duke of Modena's banishment of the Inquisition from northern Italy "among the remarkable circumstances, that have distinguished the year 1780." In Reggio, in the south, the local prince had seized the occasion of the death of the Grand Inquisitor to order "that tribunal to be for ever abolished," its buildings destroyed and its funds "applied to laudable purposes."[43] A Boston almanac contributed an anecdote in which Don Pedro of Portugal simultaneously dispensed justice and humiliated the Catholic Church by allowing a commoner to assassinate a corrupt and abusive bishop.[44]

Another blow to papal power had been the suppression of the Jesuits in 1773, what Timothy Dwight called "the most fatal wound popery hath received, since the Reformation." As the pope's influence grew more and more restricted, Americans perceived a fresh breeze of toleration blowing across Europe. Hannah Adams gave credit for newfound liberality to the rulers of Bohemia, Hungary, and Slavonia. Jews, she reported, could worship openly in Rome itself, "and the professors of a religion which once stigmatised all others as unworthy the sacred rights of humanity, now openly avow the liberal sentiments of mildness, forbearance, and moderation." In an incremental way all these instances helped Americans feel that they could support the alliance, even drink the health of the king of France, without giving aid and comfort to the Church of Rome.[45]

Catholicism was not only divisible from Frenchness, it was even something separate from the bigotry and tyranny of those who had ruled the faithful for so long. Ordinary Catholics, Americans said, were retreating from hateful practices of the past. This was another novelty, since traditional anti-Catholicism had held that Catholics could never change for the better.[46] With the coming of the French Alliance, Americans became more optimistic. Perhaps the alliance itself would have a salutary effect, allowing the French serving in America to absorb enlightened ways of thinking and carry them home. One could even say that America, far from taking lessons from France, was giving them instead. James Dana of Connecticut held out this hope in an election sermon in 1779. Since popery and arbitrary government depended on one another (as the Quebec Act had once again proved), an effective way of undermining the Catholic Church in France would be to welcome the French allies and expose them as much as possible to the political ideals of the Revolution. Once they had "their eyes opened on the blessings of such a government," Dana predicted, they would "at once renounce that superstition" of their religion.[47]

For Dana, the political and religious struggles were closely intertwined, almost one and the same. American independence would free France of its Romish notions, while "should we lose our freedom, this will prepare the way to the introduction of Popery." Dana was an unreconstructed anti-Catholic who managed to see the French Alliance not as a compromise with Rome but as a chance to strike a secret blow against it. Ezra Stiles took a more generous view of the alliance as a good influence on the French. In an election sermon of his own, he pointed to the "friendly cohabitation of all sects in america" as a "precedent" which the French, Dutch, and Germans had "intently studied and contemplated for fifteen years past." It might have "already had an effect in introducing moderation, levity, and justice, among european states." The Bible, Stiles recalled, told of such redemption by example. "And who can tell how extensive a blessing this american Joseph may become to the whole human race, although once disciplined by his brethren, exiled and sold into egypt?"[48]

While this was hardly the lesson James Dana hoped the French would learn during their stay, both ministers believed that time in America would improve the visitors. Later commentators continued to cherish this notion. Echoing Dana, Jeremy Belknap interpreted the upheavals of 1789 as a sign that "the French by their intercourse with America have caught the spirit of civil liberty." His "fervent wish" was "that they would also review their religious system, and . . . no longer pay an implicit deference to fathers and Councils and Popes and what they call the Church." Mercy Otis Warren also thought the experience of the alliance had helped the French to break the "shackles of superstition" already weakened by the subversive "atheistical opinions" of Voltaire, d'Alembert, Diderot, and others. The French had not, she claimed, made "any remarkable struggles . . . in favor of civil liberty, until the flame was caught by their officers and soldiers, and resistance to tyranny taught them, while in union with the sober and pious Americans." They had learned of civil and religious liberty together, and bishops and kings had both felt the effects. It was a final vindication, after the fact, of the alliance. American Protestantism had been absorbed by its French patrons after all, and in a way of which Republicans could be proud.[49]

The French, having turned out on closer inspection not to be very Catholic in the first place, were only hurried along the path of enlightenment by participation in the alliance. This was one version of events by which Americans could mitigate the awkwardness of their role in the arrangement, but it was not the only one. Beside it ran another argument that, rather than deprive anti-Catholicism of its target, sought to deflect that sentiment away from the French and toward the British. This required something more than hopeful reports on the decline of religious faith and obedience to the pope in Europe. It involved the more abstract proposition that the proper object of Protestant hatred was not the Catholic faith itself so much as the modes of thought and action it engendered in its followers.

On this view, practicing Catholics could be decent people by Protestant standards as long as they transcended their parochial environment and learned to think for themselves. What was evil in Catholicism, in other words, was not so much the religion per se as the cultural style. Not all Catholics partook of it, and not everyone who partook of it was Catholic. It was the bootlicking Tory, for example, that toady of Anglican bishops and willing slave of the king, whom true Protestants ought to guard against and despise. The same writer in the *Pennsylvania Ledger* who had predicted that the Patriots would say the French were no longer Catholic also anticipated this second argument and indeed adopted it for his own partisan use. If French Catholicism was in truth "little more than an outside show to cover a general infidelity," he wrote, then that was all "the more cause to fear and distrust her views, as the less real religion she has at heart, the more will she be disposed to encourage the political tenets of the Church of Rome, on account of the advantage they afford to her ambition, in the pious work of enslaving mankind." Catholic faith was unimportant; the danger was Catholic style.[50]

Samuel Johnson, who prided himself on being above sectarian hatreds, made the same point when he accused "the exquisite Protestants of the Congress" of having "adopted what they abominate as papistical tenets" in their devious policy toward Quebec. The accusation was soon flying both ways: having agreed that the French were not actually very Catholic, English and American Protestants vied to depict each other as the heirs to popish political tactics. In 1776 Johnson could ridicule Congress for saying that Corsican separatism proved Catholics were "as strenuous in support of freedom as Protestants," because most Americans still claimed to shun all Catholics everywhere.[51] By 1778 they no longer did so, though they made some nice distinctions. American writers performed some clever research in support of their efforts to redirect anti-Catholic feeling toward the British. They exhumed, for instance, the origin of the word *Tory* as an epithet for Irish Catholics. After the rupture with Britain, a Connecticut almanac informed its readers that "this name was first given by the Protestants in Ireland, to those Irish robbers and murderers who stood outlawed for robbery and murder." Since that time it had been "applied as a nickname for such as call themselves high church-men, or the partisans of the Chevalier de St. George." Here was a useful etymology for the Patriots, one that linked St. George and the Church of England to popery as well as to the "robbery and murder" of the current war.[52]

In a similar vein those describing Catholic cruelty to the Protestant martyrs began to avoid examples from the Continent (like the Spanish Inquisition) in favor of the crimes of British Catholics.[53] Thus another almanac recalled Bloody Mary's attempt to exterminate the Irish Protestants in 1558, a plot foiled only by the quick hands of Elizabeth Edmonds. (Mrs. Edmonds, "being well affected to the Protestant religion," substituted a deck of cards for the commission from Mary in the carrying case of the royal emissary when he stopped at her house in Chester. By the time he reached Dublin Castle and discovered the switch, Mary had died. Queen Elizabeth rewarded Edmonds with a pension.)[54] A third New England edition combined fulsome praise for the French national character in one item with another describing the "fearful death of a popish bishop." This was the story of John Cameron, bishop of Glasgow and "a Man given to violence and oppression." He suffered "a fearful and an unhappy end" on Christmas Eve, 1446, struck dead with terror by "a voice summoning him to appear before the Tribunal of Christ, and give an account of his doings." It was, the author observed, "a notable example of God's judgment against the crying sin of oppression."[55]

The tendency of the hierarchical Catholic Church to deal harshly with dissenters from its orthodoxy led naturally to comparisons with the court of King George. Perceived royal favoritism toward the Canadian Catholics in granting the Quebec Act had caused New Englanders to suspect the king of papist tendencies as early as 1774. Once the war began, ministers likened the British and the Catholic threats. Judah Champion interpreted the clause in the Quebec Act concerning the king's supremacy as setting him "at the head of the Romish church in Canada." Americans, he said, must "be zealous in a good cause, defending the truths of the gospel . . . without the least shuddering at the impotent thunders of papal mandates." What connected papal and British tyranny in Champion's mind was the "usurped authority" which "in church and state" had "shed rivers of blood."[56]

Champion gave his sermon in 1776, when it was possible to curse Catholics and Tories with equal venom. One could still afford to ignore the Quebec Expedition, or even disapprove of it, as Champion did. Charles Lee was equally within bounds in 1774 when he derided a group of New York Tories as "high-flying Church of England Romanised Priests." Imagining them in a religious procession, he singled out the Reverend Thomas Chandler as "their Reverend Pontifex himself, whom I conceive marching in the front, an inquisitorial frown upon his brow, his bands and canonicals floating to the air, bearing a cross in his hands, with the tremendous motto, *In hoc signo vinces*, flaming upon it in capital letters of blood, leading them on."[57] The alliance with France, however, required a more discreet vocabulary, one that associated the British with Catholic traits but stopped short of explicitly identifying those traits as Catholic. "The Last Will and Testament of Old England," printed in a Connecticut newspaper in 1779, managed to link British decline to creeping Catholicism there while at the same time giving credit to the secular national power of France and Spain. Old England blamed his "very weak and languishing state" on "voluptuousness and loss of blood" and proceeded to divide his estate. He left his "power by sea and land to the French King" and his "integrity to the King of Spain." The witnesses to the document were "Pagan," "Mahomet," and "His Holiness Pope."[58]

The assertion of a general affinity between Tory and Catholic habits—one that made use of easily recognized terms of abuse but rarely named the religion—became a mainstay of Patriot propaganda. The Tories often facilitated this tactic, as when Miles Cooper provoked old resentments by toasting Archbishop Laud in New York.[59] For their own part the American Whigs observed the survival of Catholic ritual in the Church of England and concluded that its adherents still believed in "the doctrines of the divine right of kings, and the duties of subjects of unlimited submission, passive obedience and non-resistance."[60] One instantly recognizable slur on Catholics was that they considered it no sin to break faith with heretics and thus felt free to lie and cheat in their dealings with Protestants. Under the pressures of Revolutionary politics this became a Tory trait instead. Commenting skeptically on the likelihood of British adherence to the Saratoga Convention, Congress referred to its enemies as those "with whom it was a favorite maxim that no faith was to be kept with rebels." Congress returned to the theme a few months later when announcing the alliance. Its message on that occasion scorned the idea "that the least shadow of liberty can be preserved in a dependent connexion with Britain." America's only guarantee of any new arrangement would be the word "of a parliament who have sold the rights of their own constituents." This "slender security" was "still farther weakened" by the fact that it would be pledged to those whom the British regarded as rebels and "with whom they think they are not bound to keep faith by any law whatsoever."[61]

Patriot writers were not always content to rely on such

understated innuendo. In the case of Guy Fawkes, a Connecticut almanac editor followed the new thinking to a logical if somewhat startling conclusion by transforming the notorious Catholic terrorist into a dedicated Tory. In this dialogue Peter, a Loyalist "Newsmonger and Politician," assures Dick, a "Country Man," that the rebels will soon go down to defeat.

> P. And we're going to conquer 'em too.
> D. Well how do they do that Peter?
> P. . . . They're to blow up the parliament men at Villa-delphia.
> D. Aye! how Peter?
> P. Why, they're to bring Guy Faux to life again and he's to dig a way under the zea, till he gets right under them and then up they go.[62]

With this the game had turned upside-down: the Gunpowder Plot, that resonant symbol of Catholic treachery against the crown, had become a metaphor for the royalist opposition to American independence. If Guy Fawkes was a Tory, then all bets were off. Anti-Catholicism no longer bound English and American Protestants to one another, and Catholicism no longer implied a particular political stance. A Catholic Tory was an enemy, a Catholic Frenchman a friend.

The sympathetic portrayal in Patriot discourse of the situation of the Catholics themselves offered corroboration for the idea that Catholicism per se no longer counted for anything in politics. It also neatly complemented the discovery of the old dreaded papist traits among the British. If a close examination of supposedly Protestant Anglicans showed them to be voluptuous, treacherous bootlickers, then a clear-eyed look at individual Catholics revealed little to warrant the customary hate and fear. It became accepted among Congregationalist supporters of the alliance that sophisticated Frenchmen and Spaniards were quite immune to the obscurantism of their faith. Discussing the doctrine of transubstantiation in the 1781 Dudleian Lecture, William Gordon said that "persons of the first character for wisdom and learning among the Papists have acknowledged the insufficiency of scripture to prove it." The problem was not that such persons did not reason for themselves; Cardinal Cajetas had made a judicious argument against the literal interpretation of the host as the body of Christ. The problem was the pope, who found the cardinal's ideas "so express and therefore obnoxious" as to merit censorship. As for other fairy tales spread by Jesuits about "Beasts, Birds, and Insects" that had been seen to worship at Catholic altars, Gordon thought they would "receive little more credit with sensible persons, whether *Papists or Protestants*, than the histories of Rawhead and Bloody-bones, of Tom Thumb and Jack the giant-killer." Such denominational evenhandedness also characterized David Tappan's sermon of thanksgiving on the occasion of the peace in 1783. He saw hope for the future in "the secret contempt, in which almost all the learned and more knowing, in Popish countries, are said to hold the absurdities and fooleries of that religion." John Lathrop was equally confident that "the well-informed Catholics of the present day despise the superstition and folly of the dark ages." Like their rulers, Catholics were emancipating themselves from the power of Rome.[63]

The notion of this dissociation—the separation of Catholic faults from people who happened to be Catholic—made it possible to tie those faults to the enemies of America. The element of anti-Catholic ritual in the reaction to Benedict Arnold's treason takes on added significance in this context. Even though Arnold cited staunch anti-Catholicism as his motive for going over to the crown, his effigy was carted around Philadelphia in exactly the manner previously reserved for the pope. The discovery "in the private correspondence of his family and himself" of "illiberal abuse" in the form of "the most sarcastic and contemptuous expressions of the French nation" did not give good Patriots pause. Rather, it showed that an honest French Catholic counted for more than an Anglophile Protestant of such "baseness and prostitution of affairs and character, as it is hoped this new world cannot parallel." Arnold's hatred of the French reflected only on himself. One Patriot wit made the point by rewriting Arnold's address and putting these words in his mouth: "Even a Frenchman, whom I had treated with so much friendship as to borrow of him twelve thousand pounds to pay for a country seat and plantation . . . had assurance to hint he would be glad to take a pair of my horses for eight thousand pounds of the money lent. But this I refused, and therefore could hope for no farther favour of the like kind from him, and consequently have a right to abuse and hate him and all his countrymen." The religion of traitors and allies no longer mattered; it was their character and honor to which Americans ought to look. Arnold deserved the pope's treatment not because he was a Catholic but because he was a bad man.[64]

This transformation in perspective, however well suited to the immediate needs of Revolutionary politics and diplomacy, could not take place without some uneasiness in New England consciences. With Congress at mass, Guy Fawkes a Tory, and Benedict Arnold a self-described Puritan, some Congregationalists felt they had lost their bearings. A tongue-in-cheek item inserted in the *Massachusetts Spy* a few months after Arnold's treason spoke to that sense of confusion. The previous winter, it announced, there had "escaped in a private manner from the Jury Box in Rattlehampton (a few days before the Court) the names of six Protestants" slated to hear the case of a person "to be tried for an expression against P—p—y." [65] The entire item, starting with the existence of "Rattlehampton" itself, appears to have been of whole cloth. That even in a joke a New Englander should be arrested for defamation of the pope revealed its author's slightly cynical awareness of how strange life had become.[66] By rendering the old vocabulary of anti-Catholicism obsolete, the French Alliance exposed the need for one that could square old truths with new considerations. Given the flat contradiction of the former by the latter, there was no entirely satisfactory way to do this.

The more importance a person assigned to Calvinism, the less enthusiastic he or she could be about the alliance, and vice versa. However embarrassing it might be to discuss the dilemma openly, its general (if tacit) acknowledgment opened the way for frank avowals of pragmatism. Without having to say so in as many words, those who had chafed at Puritan pieties could present themselves as forward-thinking men and women who were willing to look past theological pettifogging to such pressing issues of the day as politics and trade.

The idea that making the best of one's opportunities was a positive virtue began to acquire a sheen of respectability. An almanac item in 1781, for instance, took what once would have seemed a highly irreverent view of the English Civil War. It told of "a memorable small coal-man in Kent-street, (London) who lost most of his customers by endeavoring to be civil to all." Hitting upon a way out of his predicament, he pretended to go insane. His ruse prompted both sides to offer him support: "the Puritans, because this loss of his wits was a visible judgment from heaven," and the Royalists, because his madness only reflected "too quick a sense of the times." The moral of the story was that "a fellow who was ready to starve by his industry" in the end "lived in plenty by his cunning." [67]

The alliance presented a similar choice between scrupulous adherence to principle, which might lead to ruin, and a more worldly willingness to adapt. From the start its promoters stressed the benefits it would bring to the most worldly pursuit of all, American trade. John Adams might fret in 1776 that "the Spirit of Commerce . . . is incompatible with that purity of Heart and Greatness of soul which is necessary for an happy Republic." [68] Congress nevertheless cited the commercial benefits first when making the public case for the alliance in May 1778. The increase in the flow of goods that trade with France would bring meant that prices would fall and "those who have engrossed commodities may suffer (as they deservedly will) the loss of their ill-gotten gains." Besides dealing this overdue retribution to hoarders, "the sweets of a free commerce with every part of the earth" would at the same time enrich honest Americans. "The full tide of wealth will flow in upon your shores, free from the arbitrary impositions of those whose interest and whose declared policy it was to check your growth." The alliance marked the culmination of a movement for unrestricted American trade that had begun with the Sugar Act protests of hallowed memory—or so Congress maintained. The coda of the May 1778 address returned to this theme of the uplifting power of business. In America's shining future "the enterprise of extending commerce" would "wave her friendly flag over the billows of the remotest regions." Industry would "collect and bear to her shores all the various productions of the earth . . . by which human life and human manners are polished and adorned." The benefits of these connections would not be material only but would help make America more cosmopolitan in outlook. "In becoming acquainted with the religions, the customs and the laws, the wisdom, virtues and follies and prejudices of different countries, we shall be taught to cherish the principles of general benevolence. We shall learn to consider all men as our brethren, being equally children of the Universal Parent."[69]

While few apologists for the alliance were quite so open about trying to link free trade with religious toleration, the first part of Congress's message certainly fell on receptive ears. John Adams proved able to bring himself to promote the alliance's beneficial effects on the very commerce he had so recently denounced. While representing the United States in Holland in 1780, he wrote a series of public letters arguing the case for American independence. In them he stressed the gains to American commerce that had resulted from the association with France. In the worst, first years of the war, he said, only "one vessel in three went and came safe" in the trade with Europe. "At present there is not one in four taken." Americans benefited from supplying the French fleet and army in their midst, and for that matter the British troops as well.[70] James Warren, always readier than his friend to welcome the alliance, echoed Adams's new enthusiasm for its material rewards. As the French cleared the coast of British warships and privateers, "great advantages" had consequently "derived to our Trade." Warren mused that "perhaps in a War which seems to be a Tryal whose Purse shall hold out the longest the advantage may be general." [71]

New England merchants certainly agreed that the alliance was good for business. John Hancock had made a show of his wariness of the French by failing to attend the council's "Elegant Entertainment" for the first French naval officers to arrive in Boston in May 1778. [72] Within a few years he had come around. In the fall of 1781 he was enjoying the role of intermediary between the gentlemen merchants of Boston and the commodore of the French squadron in the harbor. The comte de Barras, then at Newport, had expressed his "warmest Gratitude" in July for "the Resolution passed by the Body of Merchants of the State of Massachusetts, to take Measures for restoring to me the Deserters from my Squadron who may offer themselves to be employed in their Vessels." The comte looked on this no-poaching agreement as a "new Proof of Attachment to the common Cause," one that gave the commerce of Massachusetts a special "right to my most particular Attention." In October, Hancock wrote to a committee of the gentlemen merchants to explain that although he had expressed their wishes to the French commodore during a conference at his house, the comte would not be able to put to sea in the near future. Nevertheless, Hancock assured his colleagues, "as soon as the Commodore Receives his orders, he will communicate them to me, and will be Ready at all Times to Render every Service in his power to the Trading Interest consistent with his Instructions." [73]

When the marquis de Vaudreuil arrived in Boston with a fleet and army in August 1782, en route from Yorktown, his nation was still popular with Boston's traders. Their spokesman, William Phillips, said in a welcoming address that they had "experienced in every opportunity of intercourse with the

Subjects of that wise and excellent Monarch a fresh occasion for the unbounded confidence and esteem their Virtues first founded." In his equally courteous reply, the marquis assured his hosts of his willingness to "do everything in my power to fulfill the intentions of my Sovereign in protecting the Commerce of a City and a Country with Which he is united by such ties of amity and in which I have already received so many obliging Civilities." [74]

Vaudreuil did not feel surrounded by men who would let religious differences stand in the way of business. The New England merchants' enthusiastic pursuit of French trade and the constant complaints of their ministers about the evils of extortion and covetousness made for a sharp contrast with the highmindedness of 1774 and 1775.[75] Then, Protestant zeal and mercantile self-restraint had combined in the moral and commercial strictures of the Continental Association. Now worldly interest seemed everywhere to have won out over simple virtue. The response of a Boston editor to news of a French fleet off Cape Ann in 1787 shows how unself-conscious the spirit of commerce had become.

> The vicinity of this town, from the plenteousness of the season with which heaven has been pleased to bless us, being capable of a supply of animals and vegetables, fully adequate to the consumption of this fleet, we with pleasure welcome our generous allies to our shores, to partake with us the blessings we enjoy; assuring them of a continuation, in all ranks of our people, of that friendship which was formed in the hour of our adversity, and cemented by the blood of both nations.[76]

Cemented by blood, an old Puritan might have said, and lucre.

Once it was asserted that politics and trade ought to take their own course without answering to kings and priests, it followed that Americans should not content themselves with establishing a regime of enlightened pragmatism at home. They should promote its spread abroad or, if they lacked that power, at least offer their encouragement and applause. Nowhere was it more satisfying to discern such progress than in France. Any movement toward a more liberal political economy in that country would have twofold benefits for its American friends. It would increase their opportunities for trade, the loss of which with Britain still smarted; and it would vindicate those who had argued in favor of the alliance.

All through the Revolution, Patriot writers had sought to revise the traditional and very unfavorable American stereotypes of the French. That the task was still under way in later years is clear in the revision of Jedidiah Morse's *American Geography* as it went to press in 1789. This compendium of facts about America and the world included abridgments of two other works, Zimmermann's *Political Survey and Present State of Europe* and Guthrie's *Grammar*. Morse's aim, as he explained it, was to provide "the minds of American Youth" with not only "an idea of the superior importance of their own country" but also "a simplified account of other countries, calculated for their juvenile capacities."[77] The entry on France was quite unflattering and played to standard Anglo-American prejudices. Under the subheading of "Government," one read that France was "one of the absolute monarchies in Europe," in which the king was not only "exclusively possessed of the supreme power of the state" but actually "considered as the viceregent of God, from whom alone he derives his authority." Under "Religion" one learned that Roman Catholicism was the established faith, and that, the repeal of the Edict of Nantes being still in effect, "no other christian sect is legally tolerated." Only in "Alsatia" did French Protestants "enjoy the free exercise of their religion." For good measure the editor included the information that France possessed "18 archbishops, 111 bishops, 166,000 clergymen," and "5400 convents, containing 200,000 persons devoted to monastic life."[78]

Oddly enough, Morse was not in agreement with the picture of the French he had cribbed from Zimmermann and Guthrie. In the section on America, which he wrote himself, he spoke of "the absolute need we have of a government, invested with powers adequate to . . . a system of commercial regulations." Fortunately, the "newly established Federal Government" would enable Americans "to meet the opposers of our trade," that is, the British, "upon their own ground" and thereby to act as good trading partners with more benevolent nations. "Our good and faithful allies and friends, the French," for instance, deserved better treatment than they had been receiving from the disorganized American commercial regime.[79] To make it clear on which side of this editorial contradiction he finally came down, Morse inserted a special section at the very end of his volume entitled "Corrections respecting France." It was a distillation of the campaign, by then a decade old, to remodel American opinion in this area. Morse claimed that the revision was a response to recently arrived news. "Since the Abridgement of Zimmermann's *Political Survey* was made and printed," the addendum began, "a better acquaintance with facts has given room for the following observations concerning the Religion and Government of France." Rather than relying on a tacit toleration, for instance, Louis XVI, "who has been styled by the United States, 'the Protector of the Rights of Mankind,'" had chosen to promulgate "a solemn law" granting French Protestants "all the civil advantages and privileges of their Roman Catholic brethren." In another striking development, Morse decided that "His Most Christian Majesty is far from being, or styling himself, an Absolute Monarch." The untrammeled despot of page 496 became a devotee of constitutional government on page 537: "In the ceremony of his coronation, he takes the oath of never infringing the rights and privileges of the nation, or altering the constitutional laws without their consent. Like his Britannic majesty, he styles himself *King by the Grace of God*; but it is not more understood in France than in England that the king is the viceregent of God, and holds his power by divine right."

In his refurbished state Louis had become a federalist as well. He had reestablished the Estates "in all the provinces" and "upon the most perfect system of representation yet known." Just recently he had called a meeting of the Estates General for May 1789 with the "intention of establishing with them, the constitution of the nation upon the enlightened principles of the eighteenth century." This was good news to Americans, Morse reported. It pleased them greatly "that the same sovereign, who has generously supported their independence, is no less liberal in restoring to his subjects their unalienable, but long neglected rights." The fact that "the parliaments, the clergy, and part of the nobility" were as fiercely opposed to him in this endeavor as "the arms of Great Britain" had been during the late struggle only proved what a gallant warrior he was in good causes.[80]

Ten years after it had begun, the attempt to recast the image of France in New England imaginations was still under way. To the charge that the French were too priest-ridden to be fit associates of free men came the reply that their faith was less powerful and less obnoxious than formerly. The same was said of their politics. The haughty French kings of old had given way to a good and mild man. The persistence of such claims strongly suggests the persistence of skepticism about them. However relieved some New Englanders may have been to be able to endorse the French Alliance without having to feel guilty, there were others who refused to ignore its less attractive features.

Furthermore, and like the earlier embrace of the French Canadians, it was not just the suitability but the larger meaning of the alliance that proved contentious. Its supporters went from arguing its merits to pointing to its eventual success as evidence for the underlying principle that there was nothing wrong with Catholic allies. In reply, those who still harbored doubts could not deny the contributions of Rochambeau and de Grasse to the American victory. What they could do, however, was caution against the drawing of inappropriate lessons. If it had been necessary to accept French help, that did not prove that Louis's motives had been pure or even benign. Nothing was ever entirely as it seemed. From their own point of view, the Congregationalist clergy were the best suited to shed light on the essential truth of the affair. They were also in a sense professionally obliged to do so. As defenders of the Protestant faith, they would be the first ones called upon to explain the sudden marginalization of anti-Catholicism. It was an explanation many looked forward to with interest.

# 6

# *Romanists in Disguise*

Unlike the new image of the French, the new image
of Catholicism put forward by the American Revolutionaries was a bald denial of received Congregationalist doctrine. Put simply, any attempt to redefine Catholicism as less odious than previously thought was at the
same time an admission that Calvinist anti-Catholicism was no
longer a signal virtue. In this light a Congregationalist minister who endorsed the French Alliance had answered only one
question and begged several others. Was the relaxing of old
Puritan strictures a temporary expedient or a recognition that
God preferred New Englanders to love Catholics rather than
hate them? Whoever took the latter view had to explain the
provenance of this sudden revelation in favor of ecumenical good feeling. For it was not just a matter of reexamining
the difference between Protestants and Catholics; there were
other implications as well.

Within English Protestantism, the Congregationalists were
heirs to a dissenting tradition whose fundamental objection
to Anglicanism was that it retained too many vestiges of Catholic belief. From the time of the Puritans to the very eve of the
Revolution, New Englanders had taken comfort in the align-
ment of their political and theological views of the world. At
one extreme was France, that dungeon of slavery and priestcraft. At the other was free and pious New England. Britain
lay in between, its constitution and its Protestantism given

little more than lip service. The events of the Revolution thoroughly disrupted this picture and undermined the Congregationalists' formerly keen sense of exceptionalism. With France and America allied against Britain, it grew difficult to argue that degrees of liberty and degrees of Protestant faith necessarily coincided. To make matters worse, the members of the Standing Order differed among themselves on how to respond to the evolution of Patriot diplomacy. Caught somewhat off guard, they used a variety of means in trying to regain their balance. Their differing responses were the occasion of considerable awkwardness, since lay people were naturally curious to know on what grounds their ministers disagreed. The alliance was only the most obvious issue to pit ministers against each other in this way. The questions and doubts it raised led inexorably to further disputes over the relative merits of Calvinism on the one hand and unfamiliar ideas of toleration and enlightenment on the other.

The appropriately named John Devotion, pastor of the Third Church in Saybrook, stood by traditional wisdom when addressing the delicate topic of alliances in his Connecticut election sermon of 1777. Although the agreement with France had not yet been concluded, Devotion knew that the politicians in his audience were contemplating some dubious attachments. He reminded them of God's command to Isaiah to dissuade the people of Judah from any defensive alliance against the league of Syria and Samaria. The Lord had told his prophet, "Say not, A confederacy, to all them to whom this people shall say, A confederacy." These instructions, Devotion said pointedly, had made Isaiah "strong against the principles of the people who at that day, seemed to think of no other way of deliverance." Such doubters in the Lord's protection had "neglected repentance and reformation, and were about to guard themselves against distressing fear, by a confederacy." [1]

John Devotion may have had in mind a close alliance between Connecticut and the other colonies rather than the proposed ties to France; it is impossible to tell from the text of his sermon. In any case, he added footnotes to the published version in which he insisted that he had only meant "to handle the subject theologically, not politically . . . lest any might suspect an innuendo from his use of the word confederacy." Such a disclaimer seems naive in an election sermon, suggesting that a number of listeners objected when Devotion first aired his contrarian views. The minister replied that it was his responsibility as "a divine, not . . . a politician," to warn of the sinfulness of any arrangement that put faith in worldly allies before faith in God. "Making a league, and trusting in that and in man for salvation out of the hands of enemies," he said, "are opposite to satisfying the Lord of Hosts himself."[2]

While some of Devotion's colleagues likely shared his distaste for political developments, few came even as close to expressing opposition as he did by his ambiguous reference to "confederacies." Ministers who could not stomach the French Alliance but who declined to attract attention to themselves by criticizing it in public could resort to damning it by faint praise or no praise at all. In the Massachusetts election sermon for 1780, Simeon Howard chose this recourse. Amid gloomy complaints about the "low and declining state of religion among us" and "that spirit of infidelity, selfishness, luxury, and dissipation, which so deeply marks our present manners," he found no room for even a passing acknowledgment of French assistance.[3] Most election sermons gave at least grudging credit to France. James Dana, for instance, while listing the steps by which the young country had "collected strength and firmness," did not elaborate on his mention of "stores . . . brought to us from abroad" and "the interference of foreign powers."[4] Henry Cumings observed that victory at Saratoga "gave us respectability abroad, and induced one of the first European powers, heartily to espouse our cause," but he neither named the ally nor described the help received. A similar fastidiousness marked Jeremy Belknap's 1785 election sermon in New Hampshire. Describing the ineptness of British efforts during the Revolution, he recalled that "with proper exertions on our part, and by the help of our allies, they fell into our hands by whole armies at a time."[5]

An occasion on which it would have been especially embarrassing to mention the alliance was the quadrennial Dudleian Lecture on the Catholic Church. On the one hand, the fact that the third in the cycle of four endowed lectures proceeded on schedule in 1777, 1781, and 1785 suggests that unlike Pope Day celebrations, some manifestations of anti-Catholicism lay beyond George Washington's power to suppress. On the other hand, the thinly veiled references to France in the election sermons and the noticeably diminished virulence of these lectures show that even the unreconstructed felt some need to tone down their zeal. When Edward Wigglesworth delivered his lecture on November 5, 1777, for instance, he made no reference to the date—an omission that would have been unthinkable for any of his predecessors. Rather than look to the past at all, Wigglesworth stressed the danger of becoming hidebound by tradition. He took as his text Jesus' reproof of the Pharisees, "Thus have ye made the commandment of God of none effect by your tradition."[6] Although his obligatory point of departure was the imminence of this danger within the Church of Rome, his sermon was open to other interpretations as well. A Patriot minister preaching on so delicate a topic might reasonably hope his listeners would apply the same line of reasoning to traditional prejudices of their own. Wigglesworth criticized Catholicism for its overreliance on doctrines and habits of thought for which there was no scriptural authority. The Bible, of course, was also silent on the proper treatment of Catholics, an area in which New England had long-standing traditions of its own. Wigglesworth may have sought to prepare his listeners for a new way of thinking when he reminded them that the first and last authority for a Protestant was Scripture.

Thus one option was to adhere, however formally, to anti-Catholic doctrine and accordingly to ignore or even oppose the French Alliance. This risked the sort of political unpopularity that seems to have prompted John Devotion's disclaimers. Most ministers chose instead to endorse the alliance and then reason backward, as Wigglesworth had begun to do, to show that it was justified. In 1781 the task of giving the Dudleian Lecture fell to the Reverend William Gordon of Roxbury.[7] The alliance was by then three years old, and Rochambeau's army was poised to march south with Washington's toward Yorktown. On the day of the lecture, John Eliot, a fellow Congregationalist minister, took a certain pleasure in contemplating the predicament in which Gordon's assigned topic placed him. He suggested to Jeremy Belknap that it might be interesting to "meet at Cambridge, for the Dudleian Lecture sermon is to be preached there by Dr. Gordon, and upon a subject I wish to hear at this time, Popery being a delicate point to handle, where people boast of their alliance with Roman Catholic powers."[8]

If he looked forward to some rhetorical leaps and twists on Gordon's part, Eliot was not disappointed. Straining credulity, the speaker explained that vigilant criticism of "the erroneous tenets of Popery" not only was consistent with a political alliance with "Popish powers" but actually contributed to the stability of such an arrangement. Any relaxation of the Protestant creed embodied in the Dudleian Lectures would, "instead of recommending us to our allies, . . . sink us in the opinion of the most sensible among them." If they saw the Americans "become indifferent to Protestant truths" and depart from "their solemn compacts with their God," the French could only conclude that their allies were just as liable to break "their own engagements with men, when future interest may dictate" it. To devote an afternoon in September 1781 to an anti-Catholic diatribe was not, therefore, as inappropriate as it might seem: it served to prove America's good faith as a partner in the alliance. Even so, Gordon went on to offer a picture of the shortcomings of Catholic doctrine that fell far short of the passionate attacks of those who had preceded him. His labored reasoning in defense of the alliance and stress on the past extremes of popish corruption, rather than present behavior, pointed to diminished room for maneuver.[9]

Not all ministers who favored the alliance bothered with such contortions. Ezra Stiles gave an election sermon in Hartford in which, far from shrinking from the topic, he relished the idea that future Americans would "celebrate the names of a Washington and a Rochambeau, a Greene and a La Fayette, a Lincoln and a Cha[s]tellux, a Gates and a Viomenil, a Putnam and a duc de Lauzun." God had "raised up for us a great and powerful ally, an ally which sent us a chosen army, and a naval force." This was an occasion for rejoicing, but also for humility before the inscrutable wisdom of the Lord. "We live in an age of wonders," Stiles admitted. "We have lived an age in a few years: we have seen more wonders accomplished in eight years than are usually unfolded in a century." The Lord worked in his own ways, and his ends justified even the most peculiar of his means. If God made use of His Most Christian Majesty to rescue true religion in New England, so be it. Like Stiles, James Dana urged a suspension of judgment on the part of mere mortals. Some might ask, "Why doth not God govern the world without the instrumentality of subordinate agents?" They might as well wonder, Dana said, "Why did he not determine to save the world without the intervention of a mediator?" that is, Jesus. "With respect to both it should satisfy us, that *so it seemeth good in his sight.*"[10]

Such attempts to stave off skepticism about the divine will are notoriously ineffective, however. The flat assertion that everything happens for a perfectly good reason cannot satisfy those who seek to distinguish between good and evil in the world. Consequently, some partisans of the alliance ventured further in their attempts to address the paradox. Like good Protestants, they sifted through the Scriptures for precedents. Deriving divine approval for congressional diplomacy might require some neat exegetic tricks, but more than one Patriot writer rose to the occasion. At the most general level, one could assign to George and Louis the roles of Cain and Abel and let the reader draw his or her own conclusions.[11] Turning from Genesis to the end of the Bible, one could mine the Book of Revelation—traditionally used to identify the Church of Rome as the Antichrist—for allusions better suited to new purposes. The dragon in chapter 12, for instance, could be read as "the arbitrary, unjust, haughty, and cruel court of Britain" that had "sent a flood, that is, a powerful fleet and army, to overturn our American free states," which in turn were represented by the pregnant woman flying into the wilderness. In verse 16 the earth rescues the woman by opening up to swallow the flood. If the earth was construed as "some civil powers," then "this seems remarkably to point out the seasonable relief our independent states received from the generous interposition, the noble and almost disinterested friendship of France."[12]

The end of the Second Book of Chronicles and the first verses of the Book of Ezra told a story more obviously relevant to the matter at hand. This was the tale of Cyrus the Great of Persia, who had protected the Israelites in Babylon and sponsored the rebuilding of the temple in Jerusalem.[13] As a powerful Gentile monarch who had freed the Chosen People from slavery and preserved their religion, Cyrus fairly leaped out at Congregationalists seeking a model for Louis XVI. Philips Payson gave the election sermon in Massachusetts just weeks after the alliance became public knowledge. Throwing back the charge that consorting with Catholics was a sign of impure faith, Payson impugned the faith of the doubters. "We must be infidels," he admonished, "the worst of infidels, to disown, or disregard the hand that has raised up such benevolent and powerful assistants, in time of great distress." After all, the Lord had used similar methods before. "How wonderful," Payson exclaimed, "that God, who in antient times, 'girded Cyrus with his might,' should dispose his most Christian Majesty, the King of France, to enter into the most open, and generous alliance, with these independent states."[14]

This comparison of the cases of Louis and Cyrus became

a popular device, and Patriot ministers repeated it from their pulpits on several occasions. Jonas Clark, preaching three years after Payson from the same platform, elaborated on the comparison. God, he said, had once called Cyrus "his shepherd, to raise up his afflicted people, oppressed under the Babylonish yoke," and directed him "to restore them to their country, their religion, and their possessions." Now he "inspired the King of France . . . to favour the cause of these injured infant states." Like John Devotion in Connecticut, Jonas Clark resorted to footnotes in the published version of his sermon to recognize some awkward political implications of his remarks. In Clark's case the implied objection was that just as the Jews had remained vassals of Cyrus rather than completely free, so the Americans might find they had only exchanged British rule for French. In a lengthy note Clark "readily granted" that "the children of Israel were not restored to a state of perfect freedom and independence" and "were still dependent on the Persian kings." But this was only a matter of timing. Since they were "just emerging from a long and distressing captivity," the Jews needed a powerful friend; and God, as the prophets had foretold, provided one in the form of Cyrus. To quibble over their exact status while under "the wing of his patronage and protection" was to confuse the issue. "I will only add," Clark explained, "that, in my reference to Cyrus . . . the judicious reader will easily see, that the main point in view, was not to illustrate the compleatness, or degree, of that freedom and liberty, to which God's people were raised; but the hand of God and the wisdom of his all superintending providence, in directing the measures, influencing the policy and overruling the conduct of men, princes and kings." [15]

In a 1783 sermon marking the signing of the peace, David Tappan showed that the analogy had not lost its usefulness. He referred to the Jews' "instant deliverance" from slavery "by a most unlikely instrument indeed, a Pagan, idolatrous Monarch, a stranger and an enemy both by nation and religion,

the King of that very empire, which held them in servitude."
Clearly there remained some misgivings along these lines. Tappan tried to dispel them by calling Louis XVI "the Cyrus of
our Israel, whose paternal, liberal, effectual aid, afforded to
us in our low estate, so remarkably resembles the conduct of
that ancient, noble Prince, whom Heaven inspired, though
an alien from their religion, to proclaim and effect the great
deliverance celebrated by God's Israel" in Psalm 126.[16] The
emphasis on Cyrus's strange religion and great power, not to
mention his willingness to separate the two in his dealings with
the Israelites, suggests that the unease to which Jonas Clark alluded in his footnotes had not entirely dissipated with victory,
peace, and the French evacuation. It was not helpful that others seized on the comparison for their own purposes, as when
the Anglican Charles Inglis suggested that a more apt precur-
sor of Louis was the Roman general Titus, conqueror of Jerusalem and destroyer of the temple.[17] The war for independence might have been won, but there remained the question
of who would assert what degree of authority in recording and
interpreting its history. The defeat and (for the most part) departure of the Tories did not put an end to this hermeneutic
struggle; it merely opened a new phase in which erstwhile Patriot allies were pitted against one another. Different groups
had different ways of accounting for the peculiar twists and
turns of recent developments in the religious sphere.[18] The
hurried reconciliation with the old papist enemy had left
more than one Congregationalist eager for assurances of divine sanction for the change. Furthermore, the limits of that
change were themselves another source of doubt. If anti-
Catholicism could be dispensed with when it became inconvenient, what other tenets might qualify for the same fate?

In June 1783, the Reverend Jeremy Belknap answered a letter
from the townspeople of Wakefield, New Hampshire. They
had asked him to explain what constituted orthodoxy and
heresy among Congregationalists. In his reply Belknap admitted that the two terms had "changed their meaning oftener

perhaps than any other words in the whole compass of language." The party in power always called its own opinion orthodoxy "and the contrary opinion Heresy." The best one could do, he advised, was to fall back on "the two main pillars of the Reformation," namely, "That the Scriptures are the only standard of faith and practice, and That every man has a right and is obliged to judge of himself of the sense of Scripture." This pair of rules not only defined Protestantism, they were its best defense. "So long as we act upon these two principles, we can maintain our seperation from the Chh. of Rome by unanswerable reasons; but every deviation from them is retreating a step towards the bosom of that mother of harlots and abominations." If Belknap's invocation of the dreaded Catholic Church was to be expected in any discussion of heresy, it was not obviously relevant to what troubled the people of Wakefield in the summer of 1783. Their concern was the new doctrine of Universalism and the controversy that raged about it.[19]

There are several ways to characterize Universalism, one of which is to frame two fairly blunt questions: Does hell exist? and if so, Who is going there? Calvinists did not flinch to answer "Yes" to the first of these and "Just about everyone" to the second. The damned were all those not among the elect; the elect were the few predestined for salvation according to God's inscrutable plan. The inscrutability of the divine plan, it should be noted, was an important Calvinist tenet. No mere mortal could tell that he or she or anyone else was among the saved. To claim such knowledge was an act of great impertinence and proof that one was prideful and therefore not, in fact, saved. In short, if you said you were definitely not going to hell, it only meant that you were. During the Great Awakening of the 1740s, neither the revivalists nor their conservative critics departed from this dogma. New Lights and Old Lights alike upheld it while eagerly applying it to each other. Each said, in effect, "Hell certainly exists, and you who are so proud to think yourselves spared will soon be meeting there."

Universalism broke entirely with this construction of God's

relationship to men and women. Salvation and the knowledge that one was saved, said the Universalists, were available to all; Christ redeemed every one of us. Hell, if it exists at all, is populated only by those hardened sinners who rejected the offer of eternal life. These ideas were not new. Throughout Christian history the tension between perfect justice and perfect mercy has lent itself to any number of solutions, some more nuanced than others. One of these is the assertion that mercy always outweighs justice in the end. The mainstream of the English Reformation, for instance, neither endorsed this view nor condemned it as heresy. But Calvin thought otherwise, and that fact made Universalist ideas highly controversial when they began to circulate in New England during the period of the American Revolution.

What made Universalism so contentious in New England was not just the challenge it posed as a set of ideas but the disturbing presence of the Universalists themselves, men and women dedicated to explaining and propagating these strange beliefs. One of the most prominent of them was John Murray. Born in Hampshire, England, in 1741, Murray passed from his parents' Anglicanism through George Whitefield's Calvinist Methodism before eventually becoming a follower of James Relly. Relly was a radical Universalist who held the redemption of all men and women to be not just a possibility but an accomplished fact. Murray sailed to New Jersey in 1770, became an itinerant preacher, and made enemies quickly when he moved to New England in 1772. The Congregationalist clergy were hostile to him, and an angry Boston crowd threw rocks at him in the fall of 1774; but he attracted a sizable lay following and Winthrop Sargent's sponsorship for the pulpit of the First Church in Gloucester. In February 1775 the *Salem Gazette* printed a somber "warning against the dangerous doctrine" of the newcomer, and Murray's appointment in May as a chaplain to Rhode Island troops at the siege of Boston brought indignant protests from the other chaplains. George Washington eventually felt obliged to intercede, announcing that "the Reverend Mr. John Murray is appointed Chaplain to the Rhode Island Regiments, and is to be respected as such." Murray continued to excite hostility, however, and a few years later the town authorities of Gloucester tried to expel him. Instead he gathered his followers, several of whom had been suspended from the First Church along with him, and in January 1779 formed the Independent Church of Christ. He managed to remain in Gloucester for several years, marrying Sargent's widowed daughter in 1788. He became pastor of a Universalist society in Boston in 1793 and died in that city in 1815.[20]

A less extreme but, in conservative eyes, even more egregious influence of this sort was exercised by the Reverend Charles Chauncy of Boston. Unlike Murray, Chauncy was a full-fledged member of the Congregationalist establishment. A Bostonian born in 1705, he attended Harvard and was ordained a minister. He was an arch-opponent of George Whitefield and of what he perceived as the emotional excesses of the Great Awakening and a defender of traditional forms of church government. In the words of one of his biographers, however, the later stages of Chauncy's life saw "his affirmation of certain theological convictions which were distinctly unorthodox."[21] Living until the age of eighty-two, Chauncy enjoyed a long second career as a theological liberal. In 1762, when he was fifty-seven, he offered the first hints of his growing belief in universal salvation as opposed to the damnation of the nonelect.[22] He waited twenty years before publishing a pamphlet on *Salvation for All Men* and then a much longer work setting out his beliefs in full.[23] He was at pains to disavow any connection with Murray, referring to him as "the stranger" and agreeing with those who thought public morality would suffer if all sinners felt assured of salvation.[24] Chauncy tried to stake out a middle ground between Murray and the Calvinists. Whereas Murray simply denied the possibility of damnation, Chauncy wanted to retain at least some concept of punishment for those who rejected salvation even when they knew it was available. This was not Rellyism; in his preference for rationalism over emotionalism and orderly church government over itinerancy, Chauncy distanced himself from Murray and laid the groundwork for what would soon take the name of Unitarianism. But it was a far cry from Calvinism as well, a fact that conservatives had no difficulty recognizing.

Chauncy's apostasy, as it seemed, caused a confusion among Congregationalists that members of the sect could not deny and others could not overlook. In September 1782 John Eliot wrote to Jeremy Belknap, his friend and fellow minister, to report on the sensation Chauncy's avowal of Universalism had occasioned. "We are all in a flame," he wrote from Boston, "about the controversy concerning the duration of future punishment." [25] Like Belknap, Eliot had been introduced to Chauncy's ideas while his student, but both younger men were cautious about the advisability of publishing them at a time when "Salvation Murray" (as he was called) was attracting so much attention.[26] In the current climate of opinion it was most unlikely that Chauncy would succeed in getting a fair hearing for his own more subtle doctrines. By joining in the argument when he did, Eliot wrote, Chauncy had only "let the cat out of the bag." Respectable citizens thought "this time was the improper to start a controversy" and "that it will admit of very bad consequences," what with Calvinists attacking from the right and "Murrayites" and Baptists poking fun at the spectacle of feuding Congregationalists. Wearily surveying the scene of havoc that all the disputing parties had wrought, Eliot confessed: "In short, I am mad about their whole conduct, and think that they have gotten us into a direful hobble. And if I could run away from Boston, I would be content not to see the place for 7 years, and heartily repent my setting down here in the ministry." [27]

So dim an assessment of the situation was not confined to those within the Congregationalist fold. On the contrary, as Eliot had gloomily noted, the level of dissension had become something of a spectacle to those without. In the same year of 1782 there appeared in Boston an irreverent satire called "A Treatise on Orthodoxy." This purported to relate the honest struggle of a seeker after truth to make sense of the conflicting doctrines then current among those claiming to share a Calvinist faith. The narrator attended two sermons in the same Congregationalist church, one based on traditional notions of predestination and the second on universal salvation. Finding himself troubled by the contradiction, the narrator then had a dream in which he went "into one of the temples dedicated to Calvin" in the hope of understanding better. What he saw made him conclude that "their god was asleep, and the lethargy contagous," since the congregation were emitting "a kind of music resembling a concert of swine." [28]

It was an undignified picture to draw of the heirs of the Puritans. How had it come to this? Universalism was fundamentally repugnant to those who believed in the salvation of the elect only. But it was just one of the many obnoxious beliefs and errors to which mankind was prey; why should it particularly exercise New Englanders in the 1780s? Certainly the resistance to it was deep-seated and vociferous. Surveying "the moral countenance of the land" in the wake of the victory at Yorktown, Timothy Dwight regretted that the prospect did not give him "a fairer opportunity of commendation." The times, he said, were "a period of eminent delusion." The war itself, "a judgment which ought to awaken repentance and humiliation," had only "produced a dissipation of thought, a prostitution of reason, a contempt of religion, a disdain of virtue, and an universal levity and corruption of soul, before unseen and unimagined." The list of transgressions is interesting not least for its order, which in Dwight's opinion described a causal chain. For centuries, he said, a relaxation of intellectual rigor had allowed "the moral system" to be "branched into innumerable schemes of error." With the abandonment of careful thought and correct reasoning, "ridicule and sophistry" had undermined respect for religion, with the result that "multitudes" had been "swept away into the regions of eternal ruin." [29]

Universalism, Dwight said, was the latest and most flagrant manifestation of this unhappy sequence of events. Proceeding from weak and self-serving logic, it led only to skepticism and moral dissipation—the classic European vices from which America might yet be saved. The idea that anyone at all could be saved struck Dwight as a cowardly evasion of hard moral and theological problems. It was the work of "limited minds, who cannot discern the relations and consequences of important truths, and who hate the pain, the labour, and the attention necessary to think in a methodical and comprehensive manner." Human pride bridled at the thought of divine justice and had sought "in every age" to "remove this pain, and bury every reflection on so disagreeable a subject." The Universalists offered to do so at a single stroke, retaining the scriptural promise of eternal life while deleting such inconvenient elements as depravity and punishment.[30]

To preach this doctrine, conservative Calvinists believed, was to make every individual his or her own moral judge, an absurd and highly dangerous affront to God. It was on just this point that Joseph Buckminster took the Universalist Isaac Foster to task. Foster, in a sermon at his son's ordination, had interpreted the depiction of Christ in Romans 10:4 as "the end of the law for righteousness" to imply that no sinner was beyond the reach of redemption.[31] The criteria of salvation, Foster explained, were not the same for all people. The "remedial law, or law of grace," operated to lower the minimum level of good behavior to just that level, however low, of which a given person was capable.[32] To Buckminster, this was nonsense. It read into the New Testament a complete break with the Old, from a command that one "do" to a far weaker requirement that one merely "endeavour." What then could remain of the idea of sin? "Who is there than cannot do as well as he can?" he fumed. "If the law says do, but the gospel endeavour, and this is the difference between them, let us never hear more; strait is the gate, and narrow is the way, and few there be that find it; but let us rather say, wide is the gate and broad is the way, that leadeth unto life, and he must be very slothful and negligent who misseth it."[33]

To identify Universalism as a symptom of declension, of the falling away from an ancestral faith, was one way for conservatives to attack the recent innovations of Murray and Chauncy. A related approach, another way to characterize the new doctrine as the antithesis of New England's "true religion," was to compare it to Roman Catholicism. This was the gravest charge one Calvinist could level at another, and as such it increased the bitterness of the Universalist controversy. At the same time, however, the accusation turned out to be a problematic one; for quite aside from raising the level of partisan invective, the assertion that Universalism was crypto-Catholic would have some unintended consequences.

From the point of view of its opponents, Universalism bore an alarming resemblance to Catholic doctrine in two different respects: the criteria for church membership and the punishment that awaited sinners. In the first place, by rejecting predestination and the concept of the chosen few, the Universalists had abandoned the Puritan attempt to restrict church membership to the outwardly righteous. If anyone who felt like joining a Universalist congregation could do so, then this was no better than the Catholic practice of inviting those who sinned six days a week to worship and confess on Sunday. The Church of England had retained this inclusive attitude after the Reformation. It was because the Puritans found it repugnant—or more precisely, because they believed it to be repugnant to God—that they had separated from the Church of England. It was, they said, a prime example of the Anglicans' failure to make a real break with Rome. In literal terms, of course, the Puritans were right. Universalism was and is another word for Catholicism.

This was not the only doctrinal point at issue, however. When a moderate Congregationalist like Ezra Stiles dismissed

John Murray as "a Romanist in disguise," it was not only because they disagreed about church membership.[34] Even more
telling was the related question of eternal punishment. Not all
Universalists went so far as to agree with Murray that Jesus'
death had rescued absolutely everyone from the danger of
being damned.[35] But less radical formulations of universal salvation still begged the question. If a sincere deathbed conversion opened heaven's gate to any sinner, then what reward was
there for good behavior here and now? Sensing the need to retain some acknowledgment of divine justice as well as mercy,
Charles Chauncy settled on a compromise position. Since it
would not please heaven to extend the same welcome to the
righteous and the sinner alike, the latter would first have to
suffer a painful but temporary punishment.[36]

Far from mollifying the traditionalists, Chauncy's subterfuge only made it easier for them to pin the Catholic label onto
Universalism. Chauncy's idea of temporary rather than eternal
punishment had a very familiar ring. "However dressed up
in soft terms and smooth expressions," the Reverend Samuel
Chandler charged, it was "the very popish purgatory."[37] The
title of Stephen Johnson's 1786 pamphlet, *The Everlasting
Punishment of the Ungodly*, gives a fair idea of his stance on
the question. Writing in reply to the book-length defense of
Universalism that Chauncy had published in 1784, Johnson
denounced "his doctrine of purgatory" as equaling and sur-
passing "the popes, clergy, and church of Rome itself." The
audacity of the Universalists in denying that anyone suffered
in hell forever was almost more than Johnson could bear.
"Catholicks and protestants, lutherans, calvenists, arminians,
and in general christians of all denominations," he exclaimed,
"have unanimously believed, the future state shall be one
of retribution." Who could have the audacity to pretend
otherwise?[38]

Distressing as it was to see such heresies in print, conservatives could not help wondering further what effect they
might have on those who heard them from the pulpit. Joseph

Buckminster of Rutland, for one, was confident that church members would prove immune to such crackpot ideas. Addressing an audience of like-minded colleagues in 1779, Buckminster predicted that "the people of New England will not long endure such doctrine. They have been too well instructed. And when the warmth is a little abated, they will recover their senses, and then such preachers will be despised as much as they were carest and admired."[39] In hindsight he was certainly overconfident. Universalism and Unitarianism did not turn out to be passing fads but quickly took root in Massachusetts. The conservatives' strategy of damning liberalism by associating it with Catholicism did not evoke the ingrained anti-Catholic reaction they had counted on. It turned out that the question of who had the right to accuse another of Catholic tendencies was one that religious liberals were quite willing to contest. Rather than accept the Catholic label, they would fling it back at the traditionalists.

The situation was almost absurd. In New England in 1780 it took a good eye to spot an actual Roman Catholic anywhere outside the French expeditionary force, yet here were the two wings of the Congregationalist establishment calling each other Catholics. The expedient abandonment of ordinary anti-Catholicism (the kind directed at Catholics) does not of itself explain the rise of Universalist and other irenic beliefs in New England during this period. But the attendant confusion as to what constituted respectable religious opinion did allow new ideas a wider hearing than they would otherwise have enjoyed. The question Who is Catholic? was one that Revolutionary propaganda had deliberately set out to confuse. In the context of the Universalist controversy that swelled to such a pitch at the end of the war, this helps explain the otherwise puzzling fact that liberal and conservative Congregationalists were so eager to abuse one another in these terms. After so much effort had gone into detaching the term from its denominational meaning, there existed a kind of semantic vacuum available to whoever appropriated it first.

There were more far-reaching repercussions as well. By placing in question the whole notion of Catholicism, the Revolutionaries simultaneously did the same to that of anti-Catholicism in a way that struck to the heart of Congregationalist identity. Those who raised this point were not for the most part Catholics, of whom there were still so few in New England. More numerous, and better placed to draw attention to the self-inflicted damage recently sustained by the Standing Order, were members of other Protestant denominations. Anglicans, for instance, now wondered aloud what justification could remain for Congregationalist dissent. An eloquent exponent of this point of view was Margaret Mascarene Hutchinson, a Boston Huguenot and Tory who fled to Halifax during the Revolution. In a series of letters to her sister-in-law who remained in Boston, Hutchinson commented drily on the Universalist controversy and other recent shocks to the New England Way. As she summed up the situation, the more liberal Congregationalists were simply owning up to what they had long believed without caring to admit. They were Universalists; they were not anti-Catholic; and given these two facts, little remained to separate them from the Mother Church. The exchange of letters on these matters began in the spring of 1785 when Margaret Hutchinson, still in Halifax, learned that New England's first Anglican bishop would soon take up residence in Connecticut. Taking the opportunity to tweak the religious sensibilities of her more pious Congregationalist relative, she wrote Margaret Holyoke Mascarene in Boston to ask what she thought of the news. She suggested the occasion was a good one for the so-called dissenters, and especially the Chaunceans, to shed their pretense of harboring any serious disagreement with Anglican doctrine. "I suppose for the novelty of the thing, your parsons will all take orders," she joked, "for the new Doctrine they preach may as well be delivered by the one Clergy as the other, and then Fare well all sanctified faces and Hypocritical grimace which has lurked under their black coats for many years." [40]

Although her letters in reply have not survived, it is clear that Margaret Mascarene took exception to the tone of Hutchinson's remarks, for the latter was quick to apologize. When she wrote again in August, Hutchinson said she was "sorry to find you were a little miffed at what I wrote about the Bishop and Clergy." But whereas Mascarene had claimed not to understand what new religious ideas she had been referring to that might render old distinctions meaningless, Hutchinson persisted. Surely her dear correspondent "could not be at a loss to know" that she had been referring to "the Doctrines . . . which Docr. Chauncy has lately published which treat of universal Redemption." As to "how far it agrees with the bible," Hutchinson conceded that "those that read his book are the best judges." She had not read *The Mystery Hid from Ages* and had no wish to read it, "as I think it would only have a tendency to unhinge those principles which having imbibed in youth I have no cause to alter in old age."[41]

All the same, she pressed Mascarene to face the implications of the fact that so many Congregationalist ministers shared Chauncy's opinions. "And pray my dear Sister," she gently insisted, "let me ask you whether those are not the very Doctrines the Dissenting Clergy differ'd with the church of England clergy about, that they favour'd too much the Roman Catholicks and th[eir] notions and in short were only a little reformed from that Church." It was a pertinent question, if not a kind one. If latitudinarians like Chauncy thought that church membership could be universal, then what reason was there for them to remain separate from the Anglicans? And if they believed in universal salvation, had they not abandoned the last vestiges of Calvinism? Furthermore, they could hardly have come to this realization overnight upon reading Chauncy's book but must have harbored secret doubts about their own doctrine for some time. Implacable in her logic, Hutchinson drew the obvious conclusion. "I think you will agree with me there, and pray if this is true have not some of your clergy play'd the Hypocrite in keeping those principles so long concealed and then publishing them even in favor of purgatory?"[42]

As Margaret Hutchinson saw it, the middle ground of liberal Congregationalism had become untenable. One ought either to admit that one was a Universalist (and therefore no longer a true dissenter) or stick to a Calvinism that, however harsh and anti-Catholic, at least had the virtue of being consistent. Her opportunity to say so in as many words came four years later, when Mascarene wrote to tell her that Boston's old Huguenot church on School Street had been converted for use by the first Catholic parish in Massachusetts.[43] In reply, Hutchinson once more aired her progressive and slightly jaded opinions.

> You ask what I think of the french Church being turned into a Mass house. I have done thinking any thing strange, there is no wonder or it is all a wonder. I don't know what Mrs. Royal and some of the old puritans would say, how it would grieve their righteous souls to see popery introduced and the notions of a purgatory established. . . . For my own part I am no bigot, tho' I would not wish to Change my religion yet I don't know why I should think, that every person, that worships his maker in a different manner from my self must necessarily be in the wrong. No my dear far be it from me to have such narrow old notions.[44]

Though far removed in every sense from the arguments taking place among Chauncy, Murray, Buckminster, and Johnson, Hutchinson nevertheless put an unerring finger on what it was that made their disagreement so bitter and the stakes so high. If the Calvinists were to succeed in turning back the tide of laxity and innovation they detected, then the liberals might find themselves cut off from their ancestral church and forced to seek refuge among the Anglicans. On the other hand, should these same liberals prevail, and the recent opening to Catholics become a frank endorsement of religious toleration, then the "old puritans" risked being reduced in the eyes of their community to a sorry collection of self-righteous bigots.

In such an atmosphere it was clear that anti-Catholicism, like Catholicism itself, had been divorced from its familiar meaning. Having long endured as an axiom no New Englander would expect to be called upon to defend, anti-Catholicism had become instead a partisan platform from which one group of Congregationalists attacked another. By identifying Universalism with popery, Dwight and Buckminster reasserted the vitality of Calvinist rigor and declared their desire to turn back the clock on the liberal excesses of the recent past. The response of their opponents was to make a virtue of their supposed apostasy. Rather than defend their reputations as orthodox Calvinists, they abandoned the field to rejoin the struggle on a different plane, whether as warm Univeralist radicals or prophets of cool Unitarian rationalism. Arguing for a more liberal Protestantism, they implied the folly of attempts to return to the rules and definitions of a bygone era.

Ezra Stiles, for instance, disdained Murray's radicalism but counted himself a liberal colleague of Eliot and Belknap.[45] Like them, he eschewed Chauncy's flamboyance in favor of a more measured reformist style. In a 1783 sermon he suggested that changes taking place within the Catholic world justified a lessening of the pitch of Protestant opposition. Popery, he said, was a "species of idolatry" indistinguishable from "that of the Druids or Zoroaster, of the Bramins or . . . that of the great Lama of Potola."[46] This was standard abuse, as far as it went. What is remarkable about Stiles's critique of Catholicism in this instance is its overall restraint. By May 1783 the French army and fleet had left America, so Stiles was not simply being cautious. On the contrary, he spoke as if with a new confidence that—whatever might be true of deists and atheists—Catholics no longer posed a threat to his religion. Toleration would reign in the United States, and Stiles was prepared to welcome its extension to "all the religious sects or denominations in christendom," including "the romanists." All would be able to "enjoy their whole respective systems of worship and church government, complete."[47]

In defense of his declaration that even idolaters deserved freedom of worship, Stiles pointed to three considerations, each of which had wide currency among his Congregationalist colleagues. First, the Catholic Church was losing its temporal powers and having to mend its imperious ways as a result. Second, an age of enlightenment was spreading over the world, awakening a spirit of inquiry that was inherently resistant to the superstition and obscurantism of Catholic dogma. Third, this new combination of a weakened Catholic Church and a robust freedom of the human mind meant that Protestants had nothing to fear and much to gain from open competition among Christian denominations. Whatever their concerns about internal dissent, it was with a magnanimity born of unaccustomed self-confidence that Congregationalists beheld their old Catholic rivals in the 1780s.

Those New Englanders who were not convinced theological conservatives found it comforting to believe that it was the Roman Catholic religion, and not their own, that was changing. This belief drew equally from two sources: simple assertions that it was the case and observations about the gradual diminution of the pope's temporal powers. Thus, Stiles praised the suppression of the Jesuits and the recent demonstrations of independence from Rome by Louis XVI, Joseph II, and the king of Spain.[48] Others eagerly agreed that the decreased influence of the pope over the thrones of Europe would allow wiser counsels to prevail and was itself a sign that "the hierarchy of Rome, which is now waxed old, and hath been long decaying, is ready to fall."[49] Joseph Willard considered these developments "happy presages of the total cessation of the tyranny of this church."[50] Wishful thinkers pointed first to Louis's rise to prominence and eventually to his overthrow in 1789 as evidence that Catholic political power was steadily draining away.[51]

The result of this deterioration, some said, was a willingness on the part of the Catholic Church to "refine" its doctrine "so as to depart from the old staunch popery of former times." By the time of his Dudleian Lecture in 1793, John Lathrop felt able to couch his anti-Catholic critique in historical rather than contemporary terms. The Roman Church was now so "humble and dejected," Lathrop said, so soon to become merely "a huge pile of magnificent ruins," that it was not worth the effort to make "the charge of tyranny and usurpation" based only on "her present claims, and the exercise of the powers which she *now* possesses." Instead he would have to refer to its haughty past. His theme was not the present danger of popery so much as the gratitude New Englanders ought to feel for the passing of that threat. Quite independently of the "check" the church had "received . . . from opposing princes" in Europe, the force of numbers would protect Protestants from its influence in America. Describing himself as "under no apprehension, that the Catholic church will greatly prevail in this country," Lathrop felt emboldened to waive the usual objections to "a doctrine, which obliges all who embrace it, to acknowledge subjection to a foreign power." American Catholicism was sufficiently small and weak, and Protestantism well enough rooted, that the new country was safe for religious toleration.[52]

In this view America had nothing to lose and perhaps even something to gain from the presence of Catholics. In the Massachusetts election sermon of 1782, Zabdiel Adams predicted that such competition between Christian denominations would have a salutary effect on all who took part. He not only agreed to the toleration of Catholics, he welcomed it. Diversity of religious opinion, he said, was a good in itself. "Coertion" might "bring mankind to a uniformity of sentiments," but "no advantage would result therefrom." On the contrary, Adams thought it "best to have different sects and denominations live in the same societies. They are a mutual *check* and *spy* upon each other, and become more attentive to their principles and practice. Hence it has been observed that where Papists and Protestants live intermingled together, it serves to meliorate them both." This new notion, that reli-

gious competition had an invigorating effect, like the economic kind, eventually received the ultimate sanction of inclusion in the Dudleian Lecture on popery. In 1793 John
Lathrop agreed with Adams that Protestant churches could
benefit from having their errors pointed out to them "and
would thank the members of any church whatsoever, for assistance in so good a work." [53]

Ezra Stiles and Jeremy Belknap were even more confident
that it was safe to tolerate Catholics. Rather than taking the
view that coexistence would be mutually stimulating, they
thought Catholicism would be unable to stand up to equal
scrutiny and reasoned comparison and consequently would
wither away. In Stiles's words, "a friendly cohabitation of all
sects in america" would afford religion "its last, most liberal,
and impartial examination." Stiles looked forward to "the
annihilation of the pontificate," a process that "a liberal and
candid disquisition of christianity" would cause to begin in
America and then spread to Europe. The extermination of
Catholic beliefs, in other words, required not their suppression but their exposure. Jeremy Belknap reacted in a similar
way. It was "no unpleasing Circumstance," he told a French
priest, "to see your Churches set up in this Country." He
could conceive of no "more striking emblem" for Catholicism in America "than the burning of tapers in the beams of
the sun." He believed "that Popery, destitute of wealth and
power and surrounded by the light of science and free en-
quiry," would, like the candles, "unavoidably be absorbed
and lost." [54]

There was also, the liberals said, a more principled reason
to look favorably on the decline of anti-Catholic feeling. Religious toleration was not just something Americans could afford to practice, it was a Christian duty. Joseph Willard, the
president of Harvard, made this proposition the theme of his
Dudleian Lecture in 1785. "Nothing can appear more irra-
tional and absurd," he said, "than persecution on the account
of religion." The gospel's injunctions against persecution were

"consonant to the dictates of sound reason and the voice of an enlightened understanding." That lengthy invocation, an echo of Chauncy's proto-Unitarian rationalism, appears at several points in the manuscript of Willard's sermon, inserted in a different ink and smaller hand.[55] Willard considered "enlightened understanding" both a happy development in New England and a recent one. To illustrate the change he began his sermon by contrasting the mildness of the New Testament with the "thunderings and lightenings" of the Old Testament, "which struck terror and amazement into every heart." The "Mosaic oeconomy" had been "in many respects severe" and made use of "sanctions . . . of a temporal kind." The new dispensation established by Christ, on the other hand, "was to be mild and gentle, and its arms were to be no other than reason and persuasion." Should it prove that "these would not gain men," then "they were to have no temporal punishments inflicted upon them, but were to be left in the hands of God."[56]

The formulation was revealing. Although Willard scattered perfunctory remarks throughout his sermon on the persecuting spirit of the Catholic Church, his real target was New England Puritanism in its old unenlightened form. Catholic bigotry and persecution were terrible, he granted. He mentioned them, however, not as evidence of what was wrong with Catholics but as evil in themselves. They were to be watched for and shunned when they cropped up "by slow degrees" in places much closer to home. The danger he evoked was the willingness of some Protestants to adopt the worst tactics of their religious enemies. It was one thing to "abhor the persecuting principles of this corrupt church," he said, but another to "imitate her even by wishing the destruction of her members who hold them." Willard closed his lecture with a direct appeal to the young undergraduates in his audience, exhorting them once more not to act, so to speak, more Catholic than the pope. They should not "endeavor to control—never even dispute the right of private judgment" but should try to "live

179

peaceably with all denominations of Christians." He addressed these recommendations "in a particular manner" to those of his listeners who planned "to devote yourselves to the work of the Gospel Ministry." By being "gentle to all men," they would "recommend, by your own lives, the excellent Religion" they preached, and "shine as lights in the world."[57]

As championed by its supporters, the toleration of Catholics in New England was safe, salutary, and pleasing to God. By implication, any return to the habits of an earlier time was both unwarranted and dangerous. The cruelty of those who would persecute others for their beliefs proved to President Willard that "pride in being opposed in their own religious notions, and hatred to their opposers, and not regard to God and Christ, nor benevolence to men, have strongly characterized their conduct." In those cases where men and women had been "urged on to persecution by religious zeal, it has been a zeal without knowledge, unwarranted by the Gospel of the blessed Jesus." It was for keeping temporal power out of the hands of such men that Willard praised the "excellent Frame of Government in this State" and its protection of religious minorities.[58] The separation of church and state was also conducive to the separation, for their mutual benefit, of pragmatic politics and diplomacy on the one hand and true religion on the other. If Willard's warning against "zeal without knowledge" signaled his desire to see religious opinion guided by men of understanding, it resonated outside the ministry as well.

Many lay people showed themselves receptive to the twin notions of toleration and a diminished role for religion in government. The idea that a sophisticated person was also tolerant had applications, after all, beyond the sectarian realm. Isaac Collins, when setting forth the mission of his newspaper in 1777, announced that while he would "ever think it his peculiar Duty to support the Interests of Religion and Liberty," he was bound "at the same Time, to treat with disregard the intemperate Effusions of factious zealots, whether religious or political." [59] Similarly, an article in the *Massachusetts Spy* urged readers not to choose men of blind enthusiasm in the elections of 1780. Writing under the name "Cosmopolitan," the author made it clear that it was enthusiasm of the religious sort he had in mind. The "business of our rulers," he wrote, was "to guide the reins of government," and not least "to pass with advantageous steps through the intricate and untrodden paths of foreign treaties." Religious probity, no matter how unimpeachable, was not a sufficient qualification. "It is not every honest man that is competent to these purposes. Those natural good parts, which would carry a man with reputation through an office in the church . . . will fail at the board. Honesty is but one security against error. Uninformed zeal is a blind principle, the source of much trouble." [60]

The notion that traditional religion exerted a drag on politics—that honest but obstinate zealots might obstruct wise policy—had also emerged in the extremely discreet response of New Englanders to the anti-Catholic Gordon Riots that raged in England for several days in June 1780. Newspaper reports dwelled on the ugliness and destructiveness of the mob rather than the Protestant Association's fear and anger at the rapid progress through Parliament of a bill for Catholic emancipation. They described the rioters as simple thugs and thieves and in general lent their editorial support to the forces of order. The *Massachusetts Spy*, for instance, printed an account denouncing the "popular fury" as "a demon of the most outrageous kind" and reported in detail the damage to Sir George Saville's furniture, Sir John Fielding's office, and Lord Mansfield's library. The *Gazette Françoise*, produced for Rochambeau's forces at Newport, devoted its entire first page to the similar horrors perpetrated at Bath. There a band of rioters "led by the servant of a gentleman" had terrorized the city until confronted by Captain Dupere and twenty volunteers. They threw sticks, stones, and insults at the soldiers until "one of the mutineers was killed by a pistol shot, believed to have been fired by an officer." This in turn so enraged the crowd that they beat back the small armed squad and proceeded to burn down a chapel, its rectory, and four other buildings before a larger detachment from the army finally restored order.[61]

Samuel Cooper was understandably eager to overlook the sectarian aspect of things when passing on news of the riots to the chevalier de La Luzerne. He characterized the participants as "a great Mob" that "seemed to have no digested Plan, nor to be supported by any Persons of Consideration." Cooper did mention Lord George Gordon, leader of the Protestant Association, but quickly added that he was "supposed by many to be Insane."[62] John Adams, commenting on the events in a letter to Mercy Otis Warren, gave equally short shrift to the rioters. "What they will come to, in the End, I don't know," he mused. "It seems hitherto a fanatical Business. Their civil Liberties, and most essential Interests are forgotten, while they are running mad for their own contracted notions."[63] This was not the time, Adams thought, to put narrow religious ideas ahead of broad political goals like the establishment and protection of civil rights. Indeed, New Englanders seemed to bend over backwards to avoid noticing that anti-Catholic grievances had fueled the riots. A newspaper writer searching for precedents found them not in the religious wars of the sixteenth and seventeenth centuries but in the peasant revolts of Wat Tyler, Jack Straw, and Jack Cade. The *Massachusetts Spy* went so far as to reprint without comment an announcement by the Protestant Association disavowing "any connection with those lawless rioters, who have . . . under pretence of opposing Popery . . . committed the most flagrant and dreadful depredations in and about the metropolis."[64]

While this was certainly disingenuous, it was in keeping with the general tenor of the Patriot response to the Catholic Question as posed by the French Alliance. In 1778, when that bond was still new and unaccustomed, John Adams stoutly insisted to James Warren that he himself was free of anti-Catholic taint. Such bigotry was a remnant of English influence and so deserved to be cast off by every American. "Narrow and illiberal prejudices peculiar to John Bull, with which I might perhaps have been infected when I was John Bull, have now no Influence with me. I never was however much of John Bull. I was John Yankee and such I shall live and die." [65]

Adams was confident that independence itself would usher in a new American age, one in which religion was not a divisive force but a unifying one that at the same time knew its place. Others were more skeptical about the ability of progressive ideas to take root in New England. The most ardent proponents of a new religious and political culture took seriously their conservative opponents' boast that New England's Calvinist heritage would withstand any such innovations. When charged with unorthodoxy, the Universalists and other liberals were not as complacently assured as John Adams. They instead replied that orthodoxy itself was unworthy of the reverence in which New Englanders held it. They proposed the future as more important than the past. In a word, they championed the idea of enlightenment, by which they meant (among other things) the assertion that religious toleration was intrinsically good. This allowed the proponents of a new religious culture to draw a line separating enlightenment and religious toleration on one side from superstition and bigotry on the other. Since New England tradition had always placed Catholicism squarely in the second category, it suited liberal purposes to try to locate the Puritan ancestors and their hardline followers there as well. If Puritans shared the vices they imputed to Catholics, then what was there to choose between them? One might as well make a clean break and start anew. The historians Mercy Otis Warren and Hannah Adams were among those who frankly identified liberal Protestantism with enlightenment and Puritanism with its opposite.

A Republican and an admirer of Jefferson, Mercy Warren

was extremely wary of those who invoked religious tradition in support of any course of action. "Mistaken ideas of religion," she wrote, had been the source of untold human misery. "The ignorant, the artful, or the illiberal children of men, have often brought forward the sacred name of religion, to sanction the grossest absurdities, to justify the most cruel persecutions, and to violate every principle of reason and virtue in the human mind." [66] Reason and virtue were always at risk from religious fanaticism, Warren believed, and religious liberty was their best defense. She viewed the "variety of opinions among mankind" on religious questions as a progressive cultural force, one that served "to improve the faculty of thinking, to draw out the powers of the mind," and "to exercise the principles of candor." [67] Far from considering religious diversity a social problem or sign of error, Warren took it as given that "the variety in the formation of the human soul" made it "impossible for mankind to think exactly in the same channel." The worst possible response to this diversity was to insist on the uniformity of belief, an ancient but primitive longing whose unattainability was perhaps becoming apparent at last. "The modern improvements of society, and the cultivation of reason, which has spread its benign influence over both the European and the American world, have nearly eradicated this persecuting spirit; and we look back, in both countries, mortified and ashamed of the illiberality of our ancestors." [68]

Hannah Adams cast an equally skeptical eye on the Puritan founders. She recalled with regret their "determined resolution to enforce uniformity in religion" and their "mistaken idea, that it was their duty to use coercive measures to suppress erroneous opinions." Like Warren, Adams saw in the history of Christianity the slow but deliberate advance of liberal thinking. To those living "in an enlightened age," she wrote, "the conduct of the early settlers of New-England must appear truly astonishing; and we may be led to asperse them with censure." Still, she said, one ought to "consider the influence which the prevailing prejudices of the age, in which they lived, must have had upon their minds." It was only recently that "any party of Christians" had risen above the atavistic urge to impose its beliefs on all others. "The bloody persecutions in the annals of Popery, fill the mind with horror; and we find traits of the same intolerant spirit in the conduct of the reformers." The Church of England, for instance, "by enforcing uniformity in religion, had driven the Puritans to seek an asylum in the new world." Once arrived there, these refugees from persecution "considered it a duty to suppress those religious beliefs, which they supposed diametrically opposed to Christianity." With her critical lay vision, Adams saw the Reformation and Puritanism not as historic victories that had turned back the high tide of popery but rather as successive phases in the development of the liberal idea. They were not even very distinct stages at that. To her, Puritanism did not mark any great qualitative advance over the Inquisition, and whoever clung to Puritanism also resisted enlightenment. Like the disillusioned creatures in *Animal Farm*, Adams looked from the Calvinists to the Catholics, and from Catholics to Calvinists, and found it hard to tell one from the other.[69]

So, perhaps, for Mercy Otis Warren and Hannah Adams. But their assertions that a liberal and tolerant Protestantism was equivalent to enlightenment did not convince men like Joseph Buckminster to go quietly. Nor did one have to be a conservative Calvinist to think it unfair of the liberals to present themselves as the sole repositories of virtue. Reflecting in 1789 on the recent changes, the minister and geographer Jedidiah Morse observed that "since the war, a catholic tolerant spirit, encouraged by a more enlarged intercourse with mankind, has greatly increased, and is becoming universal."[70] A cause for rejoicing by some, for gnashing of teeth by others, this relaxation of old rules and definitions struck Morse as a mixed blessing. He called attention to the danger that New Englanders might "break the proper bound, and liberalize away all true religion."[71] Seen in this light, the Puritans were not so unattractive. The "supposed severity" with which they had "composed and executed" their laws, "together with some other traits in their religious character," Morse granted, had "acquired, for the New Englanders, the name of a superstitious, bigoted people. But superstition and bigotry are so indefinite in their significations, and so variously applied by persons of different principles and educations, that it is not easy to determine whether they ever deserved that character."[72]

Indeed, it was not easy; but it was necessary if one was to arrive at a coherent understanding of the way political events during the Revolutionary period had forced people to choose between traditional and progressive religious orientations. Morse was quite right to point out that portraying the Puritan ancestors as noble but unenlightened was a convenient way to excuse oneself for having abruptly discarded their principles. It was also a way to rescue the moral reputation of the Revolution from unkind suggestions that it had been as self-serving as most human enterprises. As such, the liberal interpretation of events was perhaps less than reliable.

Morse's observations about the Puritans, like Belknap's on orthodoxy and heresy, openly acknowledged the interested character of religious historiography. The Universalist controversy of the late eighteenth century was not simply a theological dispute that happened to arise at this time but a symptom of the jarring effects of the Revolution on the religious culture of New England. Having first held aloft the flickering candle of Puritanism as long as it served their purposes to do so, the Patriots had subsequently hidden it under a bushel. In religion even more than in politics, the burden of justification lies on those who change their minds in such haste. The abandonment of Puritan anti-Catholicism cried out for explanation, and the explanation the Revolutionaries offered was one that only some people found convincing. Seeking to excuse their recourse to Catholic aid, the Patriots reexamined Catholicism itself and announced that it was not what they had formerly believed it to be. It followed, they said, that fear and hatred of Catholics had outlived their usefulness as guardians of true religion and actually had become obstacles to the full flowering of American Christianity. It is not difficult to imagine the appeal such reasoning held for New Englanders of the Revolutionary generation. What is also clear, however, is the repugnance it aroused in those who rejected its blandishments. It was one thing to revise religious doctrine in order to give moral sanction to one's political preferences. It was something quite different to adhere to traditional religious mores and in doing so find oneself condescended to as a primitive and a poor Christian to boot. Small wonder, then, that the rival attempts to reconstitute Congregationalism in the wake of the Revolution were the occasion of such bitter recrimination and such free use of that most cutting of epithets, "papist."

# 7

## *Coming to Terms*

In 1788, reacting angrily to Anti-Federalist complaints that the United States Constitution was a betrayal of Revolutionary ideals, an item in a Boston newspaper used the language of Revelation to compare such views to the anarchic devices of the Antichrist. "Anti-christ," the writer declared, "is a despiser of governments. . . . This many-headed foul mouthed monster barks incessantly at men in office, snatches at the leg of a governour, tears the gown of a chief justice, wets her long serpent's tail, and splatters the stinking urine on Congress, Councils, and Assemblies." Catholics might call Mohammed the Antichrist, and Protestants "compliment the Pope with the title, as a reward of his cunning." But it was the Anti-Federalist faction that practiced the most "Satannick delusion," for had not "Anarchy made all America believe that paper was gold?" To defend against such wiles, the author called on "all good Christian people" to stand together "heartily to hate this cursed Antichrist, who for so many years fooled you, cheated you, and threatens utterly to devour you." Denominational differences counted for nothing before this common political peril. "Catholicks, Presbyterians, Lutherans, Baptists, Episcopalians, Quakers, and whatever other names! Come, bear a hand to destroy this monster of anarchy, by strangling, hanging, burning, drowning, or any other means;

then ye shall secure liberty, peace, plenty, and all manner of happiness ever."[1]

For this writer, who signed himself "A Friend to Sound Politicks and Rational Religion," anti-Catholicism was no longer a necessary component of either. Even so, his biblical phrasings revealed a belief that religious forms still had resonance in American politics. The difference from the style of the previous generation lay in the fact that the crucial distinction was no longer between Protestants and Catholics but between true Christians and misguided deists and atheists. These were the terms in which the Federalist cast his dispute with the political opposition: instead of calling them papists, as his parents might have done, he called them faithless.

Jeremy Belknap tended to agree. As early as the winter of 1780 he had confided to a friend that Catholicism, having become "ridiculous even to children," was no longer a threat to New England's religious or moral well-being.[2] Many of his colleagues took a little longer to feel as sure. Presenting the Dudleian Lecture on popery thirteen years later, John Lathrop cited the danger of prosletyzing among children as justification for continuing the practice of the quadrennial sermon.[3] Still, the fact that Lathrop felt the need to offer an explanation underlines the secure position from which Congregationalists took the measure of the Church of Rome in 1790. This is not to say that anti-Catholicism itself had vanished. No change of heart, after all, dissuaded New England editors from printing and reprinting a list of "Reasons for Being a Papist" that consisted of old chestnuts about breaking faith with heretics and trafficking in dispensations.[4] Sentiments of the kind had nonetheless suffered a perceptible decline in prestige in Boston. There was now a French newspaper in that city dedicated, according to its publisher's manifesto, to printing whatever might diminish "the force, the folly of national and religious prejudices."[5] There was a Catholic parish in Boston, established in the fall of 1788. According to a Frenchman residing in Boston at the time, the unprecedented event was treated not as an outrage but as a spectacle. As he wrote to a friend in the West Indies, "The liberal part of the inhabitants (and to their honour there are but a few who are not liberal) are highly pleased with it; and many of the Boston people attend" the Catholic services, "some from motives of curiosity, and others to evince that liberality which shines so conspicuous in the character of the Americans." [6] The celebration of holy mass in Boston thus provided both an opportunity for interesting diversion and a chance to display one's own tolerant principles.

Another occasion for such display arose two years later, when the death of a visiting French official made it necessary to arrange a public Catholic funeral in Boston. The priest of the School Street church was out of the city, and the family of the deceased did not want John Thayer, the somewhat eccentric convert, to officiate. This left the Anglican rector of Trinity Church, Samuel Parker, as the most plausible substitute. What would once have been deeply shocking and viewed as final proof that the Anglicans were no more than secret Catholics was still controversial when Parker performed the funeral. [7] Belknap nonetheless contented himself with the observation, in a letter to Ebenezer Hazard, that such displays of Catholic ritual, far from upsetting him, helped to expose the "absurdities" of that religion. [8] The following summer, Parker and the visiting John Carroll, the first American Catholic bishop, acted as joint chaplains at a public reception. This time it was John Eliot who wrote in his diary on the occasion, "How would our fathers have Stared! Tempora mutantur, &c. And much to the credit of modern times." [9]

*Tempora mutantur:* The times are changing. Even those who disapproved of recent trends felt constrained to be discreet in their complaints. Anti-Catholicism was no longer quite fashionable in Boston. As the French visitor wryly put it, the inhabitants "have prejudices it is true, but they do not unguardedly show them to strangers. . . . They have the politeness to wait until they are gone, to abhor the Frenchmen comfortably among themselves."[10] The persistence of such behavior in private, if it was the rule, still represented a change. The impersonation of liberality is after all a step toward its establishment. Furthermore, even the most hypocritical profession of religious tolerance acknowledged its new status as a virtue to which vice was willing to pay tribute. In its most public manifestation—the sermons and other writings of its ministers—Congregationalism had moved a great distance in the generation since the Seven Years' War. Those who sought classic expressions of no-popery in the style of Jonathan Mayhew would have to look elsewhere than the sacred desk from which he had delivered his election sermon of 1759. Still, fashionable Boston in 1788 is not the most reliable gauge of the lasting impact of the French Alliance on New England mores. Whatever pragmatic adjustments wartime needs had dictated in elite ideology, they did not include or result in the permanent demise of anti-Catholicism. At the same time, the outbreak of revolution in France in 1789 put back in play whatever understandings had been arrived at during the 1780s about the proper balance of civil and religious powers in the new nation. As a result, what emerged in the formative years of the American republic was a complex and in some respects ironic relationship between Catholicism and anti-Catholicism, Francophilia and Francophobia. It is no simple story of the decline of religious and ethnic prejudice, but it is no less interesting for that.

For ordinary New Englanders in the 1780s, as much as for John Locke a century before, Catholicism marked the firm boundary of the Protestant imagination. As Locke had defined it, the idea of religious toleration applied only to relations among Protestant denominations, not between Protestants and Catholics. Without mentioning Catholicism by name, Locke's *Letter concerning Toleration* used its easily recognizable signifiers to place it outside the bounds of civil protection. Enumerating a list of "opinions contrary to human society, or to those moral rules which are necessary to the preservation of civil society," Locke mentioned the supposed Catholic tenets that "dominion is founded in grace," that "kings excommunicated forfeit their crowns and kingdoms," and that "faith is not to be kept with heretics." He asserted flatly that those "who upon pretence of religion do challenge any manner of authority over such as are not associated with them in their ecclesiastical communion . . . have no right to be tolerated." [11] As many have pointed out, this formulation of the relation of civil to religious power reversed the Puritan assumption that religious needs dictated the proper scope of government authority. For Locke, "the preservation of civil society" required that the "right to be tolerated" be reserved to those religious groups alone whose beliefs were consistent with and supportive of the principles of liberal individualism.

This construction of the idea of toleration may have been at odds with the beliefs of the Puritan fathers, but it took root and flourished in New England nonetheless. So it was that the Massachusetts Constitution of 1780, written and ratified even as the citizens eagerly awaited the arrival of French forces, exposed the persistence of ideas that conflicted with the spirit of ecumenical evenhandedness so conspicuously displayed in Quebec. When the convention adopted language requiring that governors and other civil officers declare their belief in "the Christian religion," the objection this elicited from voters was not that it was unfair to Jews and atheists but that it was overly indulgent of Catholics.

The members of the town meeting in Paxton, Massachusetts, were unusual in their willingness to make some nice distinctions on this point. After reminding the convention that "our forefathers did not only go under that extensive word Christians but Protestants" and that "we mean not to have any other but Protestants to rule over us," they made a nod to practicality by allowing an exception to this rule "as occasion may require in the army." The willingness to make such allowances was itself exceptional, however. Those towns that felt moved to comment on the use of the word *Christian* instead of *Protestant* in the requirements for office holding lobbied for the more restrictive formula. Drawing directly on Locke, the western Massachusetts town of Sandisfield declared that "since it is a community of Protestants who are covenanting and emerging from a state of nature, . . . it is necessary to say that not only the Governor but all executive, legislative, judicial, and military officers shall be of the Protestant Christian religion." In an earlier communication the voters of Sandisfield had spelled out that whereas they hoped the new constitution would secure "the free exercise of religious principles" to "Protestant Dissenters of all denominations within this State," they reserved "the right of instructions to our Representatives" should the legislature ever to take it into its head to extend "toleration to other denominations of Christians." [12]

In so stipulating, Sandisfield at least left open the possibility of granting such an extension of rights to non-Protestants. Wareham, in Plymouth County, took a similar view. Its citizens preferred an explicit rule "that Roman Catholicks may not enjoy equal priviledges with Protestant Christians" and offered the justification that "the Papists are generally known to be . . . of a restless disposition" and "a persecuting nature . . . whenever the power is in their hands." Still, Wareham was willing to grant that Catholics might "enjoy a toleration in particular places as the legislature shall direct." The boundary between Protestants and papists need not, in other words, be identical with the boundary of Massachusetts but might be redrawn within it. Other towns preferred a more traditional separation. Wilmington, in eastern Middlesex County, wanted "free liberty of conscience allowed to Calvinists and Arm[i]nians" only. In the district of Maine, the people of Wells cited "that authority and jurisdiction which the Bishop of Rome claims over the whole Christian world" as incompatible with "the safety, peace, and welfare of a Protestant Commonwealth." More specifically, they pointed to the fourth article of the proposed Declaration of Rights—stipulating the "sole and exclusive right" of the people of Massachusetts to govern themselves—as proving the unsuitability for office of "whose who are of the Church of Rome." [13]

The least compromising of all in its assertion of Protestant supremacy was the petition from Lexington. It staked its claim on a literal-historical understanding of "the word Protestant, . . . a Word which took rise from the pious, noble, and truly heroic stand which Luther and the first reformers . . . made . . . against the Errors, Superstitions, and Hierarchy of the Pope and Church of Rome." The draft constitution, Lexington complained, proposed to dispense with "a term which our venerable ancestors brought with them . . . and held, in a manner, sacred, as an expression of their character . . . ; in opposition to the blasphemous absurdities of the Church of Rome." Nevertheless, and despite further animadversions on the difference between "popery" and "the true religion of the Gospel," even here the ultimate recourse was to John Locke, not John Cotton. It was the civil rather than the spiritual danger of popery that most worried the voters in Lexington. What made it so important to bar Catholics from "offices of trust and places of power in the government of this State" was that their "Religion itself leads them to hold principles inimical to Liberty, subversive of Government and dangerous to the State." [14]

Anecdotal evidence of this sort suggests the ambiguous status of anti-Catholicism by 1780. The right to hold office, after all, is not of the very same order as the right to vote, or indeed to live and worship within the commonwealth. None of these more fundamental civil rights was at issue, partly because there were so few Catholics to be found in Massachusetts but also because what excited Protestant concerns was not so much Catholic citizenship as Catholic power. The relative importance of these two factors, the scarcity of Catholics versus their perceived dangerousness, is itself a matter of debate among historians of the period. [15] In any event, the language of the oath required of officeholders in the 1780 constitution amounted to a de facto anti-Catholic religious test and was not repealed until the Convention of 1820—whereupon voters promptly rejected the repeal.[16] Furthermore, up until the formal disestablishment of Congregationalism in 1833, Massachusetts Catholics were obliged to contribute tax monies for the support of Protestant ministers. The restriction of such support to "Protestant teachers" was no more controversial on account of its impact on Catholics than on atheists or Jews. Father Matignon, the curate of the first Catholic parish, tested the limits of toleration in 1799 and found them robust. When he tried to sue for control of his parishioners' tax contributions, the Massachusetts Supreme Court rebuked him with a stern reminder that "papists are only tolerated, and as long as their ministers behave well we shall not disturb them. But let them expect no more than that."[17]

The upheavals of the Revolution apparently had done two things. The opening to Catholics at the level of pragmatic diplomacy had split elite opinion, diminishing the influence of the Congregationalist establishments and their revivalist challengers alike in favor of a more avowedly liberal climate of opinion regarding the diversity of religious belief. At the same time, in the realm of constitutional politics, the ground had shifted from the blanket exclusion of Catholics to a carefully delineated toleration of the private if not public manifestations of their faith. The constitutional settlement proved quite stable until such time as the sheer pressure of Catholic numbers, together with the Unitarian-Trinitarian split within Congregationalism, unleashed the most pragmatic of all forces in a democracy: organized political pressure for disestablishment.[18]

"The language of toleration," as Stephen Carter remarks, "is the language of power," and the declining ability of New England Protestants to impose legal and political disabilities on Catholics reflects the fracturing of a once coherent majority into a competing array of denominational interest groups.[19] But the political is not the only sort of power. In the realm of

ideas and opinion, the absorption and digestion of the changes
brought about in religious affairs during the Revolution was a
far less even process than the slow but fairly steady progress of
Catholic emancipation. Neither the decision to grant toleration nor the realization that it would get harder and harder to
delimit that right obliged Protestants to modify their private
views. The Universalist controversy had shown that not all
the recognized molders of opinion were devotees of the new
broad-mindedness. As if to underscore this fact, the eruption
of the French Revolution breathed new life into the counter-
argument. As it wore on, the strife in France inspired many a
New England divine to reconsider the part of Catholicism in
the work of Providence. The effect of this reconsideration was
to divert the religious-intellectual discourse on Catholicism
from the meliorist path of the legal-constitutional one. If the
latter concerned the fashioning of useful institutional arrangements for the future, the former addressed a separate though
related task: to reexamine the Catholic alliances and make of
them a usable past.

Pressed by a correspondent in 1807 to explain the origins
of the French Alliance, John Adams demurred. "Others en-
tangled us with France, not I," he remarked testily, "the whole
history of which I could detail; but it is not necessary here." [20]
Adams's reticence is easy to understand in light of his difficult
relations with the French court and much worse problems
with the revolutionary government during his presidency. Yet
many of his compatriots, friend and foe alike, reacted in just
the opposite way. They saw in the events of the 1790s more
reason than ever to reflect on the prophetic role, for better
or worse, of the French Alliance. Ezra Stiles approached the
question from an oblique angle, couching his apology for the
French Alliance within a book-length defense of Oliver Cromwell. His *History of Three of the Judges of Charles I*, published
a year before he died in 1795, sought to clear the air of growing doubts about Cromwell's place in the American pantheon.

To this end Stiles set out to establish the affinity between "the republican martyrs and heroes of the twenty years period from 1640 to 1660" and the revolutionaries of his own day both at home and abroad. The godly Puritans were "now in resurrection in France, Poland, and America," where they were already "beheld with spreading estimation" and would "in future be contemplated with justice and veneration by all nations." As his use of the word *justice* suggests, Stiles did not think public opinion had yet arrived at a sufficiently appreciative attitude toward the first modern republicans. The very willingness of an old man to devote several hundred pages to defending "the enlightened upright and intrepid Judges of Charles I" indicates that he did not consider their reputation well enough established to be left as it was. Stiles set out to remind his readers that God had been squarely on the side of the Roundheads.[21]

The criticism of Cromwell unleashed by the anti-Universalists and others in the aftermath of the Revolution had made great advances by the 1790s, and it disturbed Stiles that Americans should try to distance themselves from the legacy of the English Commonwealth. His choice of topic underscored this point for New Englanders in particular. His study concerned Whalley, Goffe, and Dixwell—three English Puritans who, having sat in judgment of Charles I, had to flee for their lives at the time of the Restoration. They went first to Boston, expecting to find refuge among the like-minded Puritans who had enjoyed nearly complete autonomy during the long disruption of central government. To their chagrin, however, they soon discovered that the colonists knew which way the wind was blowing and were most reluctant to provoke Charles II. Stiles gently reproached the Bostonians for shunning the erstwhile heroes of their cause: "Indeed all New-England were their friends, although they did not wish to be too knowing about them."[22] He went on to recount the embarrassed way in which those who were privately sympathetic arranged to smuggle Whalley and Goffe to Hartford and New Haven, and finally, when the scrutiny of royal spies made it impossible to hide them there, to Hadley, "then an exposed frontier" in the Connecticut River valley. The Reverend Mr. Russell took them in during the fall of 1664, and Dixwell joined them later that winter. Dixwell stayed "for some time," but the other two never left their hiding place. Either in Russell's house or Peter Tilton's, Whalley and Goffe lived out their days "in dreary solitude and seclusion from the society of the world," Whalley dying around 1678 and Goffe around 1680. Only several years later, after the Glorious Revolution had overthrown the potentially vengeful Stuarts, did it become safe to tell the tale in Hadley and the rest of New England.[23]

In retrospect this struck Stiles as shabby treatment. It irked him all the more that, a century later, there were those in America who refused to give Oliver Cromwell and the English Puritans their due. Even the American Revolution, so reminiscent of the English one, had not been enough to lay to rest the reservations of Cromwell's critics. If anything, they now felt freer to speak ill of him, since they no longer felt a common duty to rebut the Tory slurs against him. It had once again become respectable, Stiles complained, to call the Lord Protector a liar, a praying hypocrite, and a usurping tyrant whose power had rested on a huge standing army.[24] Begging to differ, Stiles hailed Cromwell as "a Phoenix of ages" and set out to correct the record.[25]

In the first place, Cromwell had not been a liar. "With respect to dissimulation," Stiles wrote, "I never found a man freer from it." True, he "sometimes concealed, but when he spake, he ever spake his mind." It had to be said that "*no man ever misunderstood Oliver*; they dreaded him, but they knew what he meant." Nor was he an illegitimate ruler. His "elevation" to power had been "regular, and legal, and no usurpation." (Perhaps aware of the difficulty of proving this statement, Stiles contented himself with repeating it. His next sentence reads, "He was no usurper, but legally and constitutionally invested with the supremacy in dominion.") For Stiles, the problem was not the establishment of Cromwell's government but the way "these happy beginnings were never firmly finished, and the whole fabric was overturned at the Restoration." While it lasted, "the whole great enterprize of the Long Parliament and Protectorate" had marked "by far the most distinguished and glorious" period in English history "from Alfred to the present time." It was just absurd, Stiles thought, to call Cromwell a tyrant. His government had been "impartial, peaceable, mild and moderate, but energetic and efficacious, and firm as the mountains." In a word, "it was excellent"; and like Washington, Cromwell had refused a crown.[26]

Political theory, however, was not Stiles's only concern when defending Cromwell's right to a place of honor in American memory. What bothered Stiles most of all was the unending "stupidity of charging Oliver with hypocrisy." In truth, "hypocrisy was unnatural to him, it was abhorrent to his very nature. He needed it not." Yet the accusation was so common that "the purity of his principles are called into question, or rather now with one consent reprobated by all."[27] Here Stiles drew the line, willing to stand alone, one Puritan defending another against that most dreadful of insults. Why did people say this of Cromwell, he demanded to know. Was it because he had "established liberty of conscience"?[28] Or because he had led a strong army and a strong government and therefore could not possibly have remained entirely virtuous? When would such ridiculous narrow-mindedness cease? "At least is not one hundred and fifty years long enough to cast reproach and derision upon a man for asking counsel of his God upon every important emergency? Great God! shall it be a disgrace for mortals to supplicate thy throne?" Cromwell had been "a sincere Puritan." What was needed was not more carping at him but more emulation of his character and his "open, . . . unabashed, . . . undissembled and undisguised religion."[29]

What lay behind this cri de coeur from the president of Yale? Stiles acknowledged that reasonable people could disagree with him, that "many of the best and wisest patriots, and the firmest friends of liberty" were uncomfortable, for instance, with the New Model Army as a precedent for a standing force in the United States. But one ought to judge things by their results, and any sweeping judgments were bound to be inaccurate. For his own part Stiles considered "Oliver's army powerful and victorious, but not dangerous to liberty in England," while on the other hand he agreed that "they were so in Scotland and Ireland, in the unjustifiable war he carried on in those two kingdoms." The same cause could produce different effects in different circumstances; one had to know which factors counted for most. Consider, Stiles proposed, the conditions that produced either tyranny or civil liberty. "Even Oliver's army would not be dangerous to a country whose inhabitants were possessed of a diffusive property," since an army of yeomen would be too independent to be bought and sold like mercenaries. Pursuing this line of thought, Stiles pointed out that it was their systems of land tenure that made England and America safer than Scotland and Ireland against invasion and military dictatorship. "Let the experiment be tried all over the world, and the effect will be the same. Freehold property had too much footing in England . . . to permit ultimate danger from armies." Ten thousand yeomen "are worth three times the number raised in the usual manner of conscribing venal armies. This, much more than religion, was the secret of the invincibility of Oliver's and the American army. They had a motive to fight for liberty a[n]d property." [30]

Property, then, not faith, had won the day for the Commonwealth and for American independence. The same had just happened in France, where there were now enough of these yeomen to defend the Republic. "And they will do it effectively," Stiles predicted. Observations of this sort were consistent with his exhortation that Americans become less strident and dogmatic in their own politics. In calling for an end to the pillorying of Cromwell as a hypocrite, he appealed for recognition of the fact that principled behavior and rigid adherence to established positions were not the same thing. Stiles admitted that he had long made the same mistake; he had formerly "entertained such ideas" about Cromwell as made him out to be "a tyrant and an usurper, full of religious enthusiasm, and of unexampled dissimulation in religion and politics."[31] But after "more thoroughly entering into the genius and spirit of his character," he had seen his error and "altered my sentiments." Understandably enough, one of the great virtues Stiles had subsequently discovered in his subject was that "like all discerning and wise men, in different circumstances, upon new views and upon new evidences he altered his mind."[32]

The idea that to change one's opinion when the circumstances changed did not make one a hypocrite was perhaps of more than casual or historical interest to a Congregationalist minister who had completed the intellectual migration from orthodox anti-Catholicism to ardent support for the alliance with France. Stiles was correspondingly generous in his treatment of the late, unfortunate Louis XVI. "Louis Capet," as the French radicals renamed him, "was a sovereign justly esteemed and loved by America." Charles the First of England "was a tyrant at heart," Stiles thought, but "Louis XVI was not." Stiles suspected his readers of harboring a less favorable opinion of "the mild and clement" Louis.[33] "The truth," he insisted, was that "Louis was of lenient principles in government, and was disposed to yield to his subjects a rational and less despotic government than that of his predecessors."[34] "There was a time," Stiles assured his readers, "when Louis XVI . . . really had these beneficent ideas." Furthermore, in his comments on the French Revolution Stiles made it clear that he was not one of those who took malicious pleasure in the misfortunes of the French church. He had come to believe that there were more dangerous things in the world than a Catholic. Louis XVI had been a Catholic, but no worse a king for that. Rather than pretend that the French had little religious faith and so did not really qualify as Catholics, Stiles insisted on the authentic faith of the great majority of the population. He tried to dispel the image of the French as a collection of jaded deists. On a close examination, he said, "the collective aggregate of this learned, this philosophic and licentious description would prove a small and inglorious, though brilliant minority: and . . . of twenty-five millions in France, above twenty-four millions, and perhaps nine tenths of the other million, would now be found christians." [35]

For himself, whether in the foreign or domestic contexts, Stiles was "in decided opposition to the deistical ideas, which have usurped too much influence in the reformation of politics at this day." It was well and good for toleration "to be cultivated among all sects of christians," but that did not mean "that a christian republic ought either to renounce christianity, on the one hand, or on the other hand, to extend charity" to the point of "the equality, indifference, and nullification of all religions." Some sects might be more deserving of public encouragement than others, but Ezra Stiles preferred a devout Catholic to an indifferent deist. He recounted a conversation he had had in 1779 with M. Marbois, secretary of the French minister to the United States, the chevalier de La Luzerne. Stiles had been relieved to learn that "most of the bishops, and the body of the ecclesiastics, with the main body of the people, were not only not deistical or disbelievers of revelation, but were even," according to Marbois, "superstitiously devoted to religion." [36]

By now Stiles had wandered quite far from his brief, which after all had been to vindicate the three judges of Charles the First. He had digressed into a vigorous defense of Cromwell and then more widely to encompass recent events. By covering so much ground he was able not only to illustrate the difference between hypocrisy and pragmatism in the conduct of others but also to display some flexibility of his own. His protest against the rising tide of indifference to religion ("which seems to be agreed to be shut out of modern politics") located Roman Catholicism as the ally rather than the enemy of Protestantism on the newly redrawn map of human values. Like the devout Congregationalist and venerator of his ancestors that he was, Stiles recoiled from the notion that his support for the French Alliance or the toleration of Catholics made him a hypocrite. If Cromwell had been a good Puritan and had shown the ability to adapt to new facts, then a New Englander could do the same in the late eighteenth century without needing to apologize. Like Cromwell, he would be sure to have his detractors: traditionalists would call his religion impure, while cynics would call it a charade. Like Cromwell, and like the current revolutionaries in France, such a person would have to answer for certain actions whose only excuse was the greater good they had helped to achieve. For "though many tumults and cruel events may arise in the cause of a just revolution, which would be unjustifiable, and which no friend to order, no judicious and upright civilian would justify, but reprobate, in an ordinary and righteous course of government; yet the cause itself, and *every thing essentially subservient to it*, is justifiable on the highest principles of public right."[37] This was true of the execution of the tyrannical Charles I, and even of the well-meaning Louis XVI. "I am a Jacobin," Stiles declared on hearing news of the French invasion of Holland in 1793. "I glory in the name."[38] Later, at the height of the Reign of Terror, he called for "more use of the Guillotine yet" to remove "hurtful poisonous Weeds" from "the Field of Liberty."[39] How much more then was it true of the French Alliance. Ezra Stiles's conscience, as he had demonstrated, was clear. Yet in the very elaborateness of his vindication of the English and American Revolutions one discerns a recognition that the passion of his argument outstripped its logic. Try as he might to square the circle of Puritan tradition and Revolutionary politics, Stiles was too honest to believe he had entirely succeeded. As an indelible instance of moral ordinariness, the French Alliance still represented America's dirty hands.[40]

Ezra Stiles, the moderate Old Calvinist and venerable college president, was writing when it was still possible to see in Jacobinism the defeat of tyranny rather than the triumph of infidelity. It was a wholly different exegesis of the Catholic alliances that caught the imagination of Stiles's successor at Yale,

Timothy Dwight. He and Stiles had never gotten along well, and not only because they inherited the doctrinal feud between Isaac Stiles, father of Ezra, and Dwight's grandfather Jonathan Edwards. More personally, Ezra Stiles suspected Dwight, who had been a rival candidate for the presidency when Stiles was chosen, of harboring designs on his job and of plotting to poach students away from Yale to Dwight's own academy in Northampton.[41] It was all the easier, then, for Dwight to distance himself from his late colleague by swinging sharply against the French Revolution over the course of the 1790s. Dwight's own literary testament elaborated a wholly different way of absorbing and representing the religious history of the Revolutionary generation.

Timothy Dwight's *Travels in New England and New York* was a compilation of materials he amassed during trips he took each fall from 1796 until just before his death in 1817. Like Stiles, though, Dwight intended far more in his book than the title suggested. In the guise of a travel writer, he expounded and defended his own version of New England's history with particular attention to its religion. Again like Stiles, he included a defense of Cromwell and an account of the unlucky Whalley and Goffe; but these were of only passing concern to Dwight. What mainly interested him were the recent injuries to New England's Calvinist heritage, not least the authority of ministers of the gospel, and the possible means of restoring the same.[42] So whereas Stiles had written in the fading twilight of Protestant harmony, when Puritan piety could still be reconciled with amity toward France, Dwight was having none of it. Speaking for the arch-Federalist faction of the New England clergy, he described the French Revolution and the French Alliance alike as baleful foreign influences of which New England might yet be cured.

Before proceeding to Dwight's thorough inversion of Stiles's argument and its implications for public as well as private configurations of Catholicism, it is worth noting that Dwight faced more determined supporters of the French Revolution than

Stiles even among his fellow ministers.[43] The Baptist John Leland was well placed to act as Dwight's foil in this debate. Leland was Dwight's age, both having been born in the early 1750s, and a fellow Massachusetts native. Raised by a Presbyterian father and a "high-flying, separate new-light" mother, Leland grew up puzzled by denominational controversies and arrived at a Baptist faith grounded in abiding doubts as to the ability of men and women to discern and act upon God's will in political affairs. Like many before him, Leland deduced from this skeptical epistemology the conclusion that humility required governments to practice religious toleration.[44] This in turn made him a convinced opponent of religious establishments and a relentless critic of the quasi-establishment enjoyed by Congregationalists, Presbyterians, and Baptists alike under the Massachusetts Constitution of 1780. A supporter of the Federal Constitution and its ban on religious tests, Leland called the Massachusetts Constitution only "as good a performance as could be expected in a state where religious bigotry and enthusiasm have been so predominant."[45] Leland was unusual in his eagerness to expose not only the operation but the origins of church-state arrangements in Massachusetts. Not at all content with the sop to Baptists in the constitutional provisions for the support of "Protestant teachers," Leland asked why the legislature had felt justified in taxing "Pagans, Turks, and Jews" for the purpose.[46] More to the point, he objected to the treatment of Catholics. Despite its pretensions to evenhandedness among Christian denominations, he argued, the state government in fact put Catholics at a great disadvantage, forcing them "to pay men for preaching down the supremacy of the Pope."[47] Of this arrangement, Leland said, "one of two things must be granted; either that Papists are no Christians, or that there is a partiality established" in the Massachusetts Constitution. He was as sure of the truth of the latter possibility as he was that most New Englanders, in their hearts, believed the former.[48]

By the turn of the century, Leland felt he had arrived at an even better understanding of the behavior of the Standing Order. Fourteen years in Virginia had made a convinced Democratic-Republican of Leland. He saw the predominantly Federalist clergy's attacks on the French Revolution as nothing but a smoke screen for their self-interest. It suited them perfectly to exaggerate "the growth of infidelity in France" and "French influence in America" in order to justify their own status as government-supported guardians of public morality. "Reverend gentlemen," he chided them, "if you wish to stop the spread of Deism, seek to remove the cause. Come forth . . . and renounce the scheme that Mr. Cotton first introduced in Massachusetts, to support preachers by law." [49] Protestants who actually believed in their principles, Leland insisted, would not hide behind "the Papal maxim, that government is founded in grace." [50] This equation of establishments with popish tyranny was an old dissenters' theme, much used by New Lights in their struggles against antirevivalists enemies during and after the Great Awakening. John Leland managed to combine it with a spirited defense of Catholic rights and the French Alliance. As late as 1802 he cast his lot with France, whose "alliance and communication with Americans enkindled the spark of liberty among them," as against those pseudo-Protestant Anglophiles who clung to the skirts of power and pleaded for legal privileges they scarcely deserved. [51]

It was this living outrage, then, and not just the ghost of Stiles, that confronted Timothy Dwight. He did not shrink from either challenge. Where Leland attacked the postwar Massachusetts and Connecticut establishments, Dwight would defend them. Where Stiles had excused the compromises with Catholicism that the Revolution had necessitated, Dwight would utterly disavow them. By enunciating his own version of recent history, Dwight would repair the damage the Catholic alliances had caused and restore the foundation of American, and especially New England's, distinctiveness. A true polemicist, he chose his ground with care. Rather than venture into the thicket of the Quebec Act and the overtures to the habitants, for example, he simply ignored them. This tactical decision freed him to give full rein to his unabashed anti-Catholicism and accompanying contempt for the French Canadians. Throughout the *Travels*, when reflecting on the history of the locales he visited, Dwight recalled in gruesome detail the miseries of the long conflict with New France. His hostility was not tempered by the slightest acknowledgment of the bond that had united Yankees and Quebecois in 1775–76. The "Canadian French" were "a miserable, unanimated race, without ambition or energy, without intelligence or taste." Their sole contribution to the history of New England, according to Dwight, had been the infliction of great suffering. For 130 years, from the restoration of Quebec to Champlain until Montcalm's defeat, "Canada was the baleful spring whence issued these waters of bitterness." As a result, even four decades after the Plains of Abraham, horrific memories of French and Indian brutality were "the thoughts which instinctively crowded" into his mind on a visit to Crown Point.[52]

Not content to record his selective reminiscences, Dwight offered to explain them, and specifically to explain them as the product of French national character. If not for the French, he claimed, New England would have enjoyed peaceful relations with the Indian tribes. Indian "cruelties" were "only the customary consequences of a Canadian irruption"; it was the French who "stimulated the savages to every inhuman act." Dwight quoted with approval the bland assertion by Governor Shute in 1718 that Massachusetts might have "always lived in perfect ease with our neighboring Indians had it not been for the instigation, protection, supply, and even personal assistance of the French." The refusal of the French to own up to such practices, much less desist from them, was the clearest evidence of their moral turpitude. When they disclaimed any ability to control the depredations of their Indian allies, they were only smiling behind their hands. Their conspicuous success in penetrating the "peculiar secrecy" of the Indians might have gratified them, but to Dwight it revealed their own true nature. It was "the sinuous ingenuity of that singular nation" that gave it such an advantage in situations calling for shameless flattery and manipulation. Well-honed skill in "rendering themselves agreeable to those from whom they hope for any advantage" had "for ages been a primary characteristic of the French."[53]

Two fundamental facts, Dwight thought, accounted for French behavior. One was their lack of principle, their ruthlessly selfish pragmatism. "No nation was ever so eagerly attentive to its political interests as France, and no government ever pursued its interests with equal fraud, cruelty, or destitution of principle." The second factor, the primordial flaw underlying even political crimes, was a literally bad faith: French Catholicism. When assigning blame for the Indian raids, Dwight pointed a finger straight at the Canadian clergy. "No men were ever more zealously engaged in making proselytes, . . . or less encumbered with moral restraints." While "the government demanded scalps" from the Indians, "the clergy called for captives whom they might convert to the Romish religion." The resulting "diffusion of fire and slaughter" was that much worse for being "sanctioned by the ministers of religion," men who "caressed and cherished" the Indian "bloodhounds" while all the time "professing themselves to be followers of the Saviour."[54]

Dwight did not confine his attacks on Catholicism to its baleful influence on Indian relations. Recalling the early days of his native Northampton, he was happy to note that the settlers had quickly abandoned the "very improper custom" of burying their dead "in the center of towns and parishes," a rude practice that "plainly had its origin in the superstition of the Romish church" and its idolatrous notion of holy ground. Commenting at another juncture on the comparative merits of different immigrant groups in New York, he singled out "the dissocial nature of Popery" as the fatal defect of the Irish. Their "extreme ignorance . . . concerning moral obligation" was traceable to "the doctrines taught in the Romish church concerning absolutism, indulgences, and other licentious tenets." The French Huguenots in New Rochelle, on the other hand, were living proof that what most afflicted Frenchmen was their religion. These French Protestants, unlike the Irish "Papists," had proved easy to assimilate. They were well on their way to becoming "mere Americans, in no way distinguishable, except by their surnames, from the descendants of the English colonists." [55]

In choosing Protestantism as his standard of rectitude, Dwight underscored his desire to contrast the ancestral heritage of New England with the Catholic influences that had always lurked at the edge of the wilderness. Quebec's geographical proximity and unremitting hostility (as recalled by Dwight) made it the perfect antitype of New England. To drive the point home, Dwight speculated on how different a prospect the nineteenth century might offer "had the American states been colonized from France."

> The lands would have been parceled out, as were those of Canada, between a numerous noblesse and a body of ecclesiastics probably not less numerous. The great body of the New England people, instead of being . . . an enlightened independent yeomanry, would have been the vassals of these two classes of men, mere Canadian peasantry, sunk below the limits of civilization, unable to read or to think; beasts of burden . . . , satisfied with subsisting on maize and tallow with an occasional draught of whiskey; Roman Catholics of the lowest class, their consciences in the keeping of ecclesiastics prostrating themselves before a relic and worshipping a crucifix or a cake.[56]

Dwight was sure his countrymen shared his horror at the mere idea of such a contamination, or at least he hoped so. "How mightily would the inhabitants of Boston or Salem, Hartford or New Haven find their circumstances changed," he declared, "were the ground on which they live to become, like the island of Montreal, the property of a convent!" [57]

The question would shortly take on a more than rhetorical significance when a Protestant mob burned down the Charlestown convent in 1834. Timothy Dwight was dead by then, but his image of New England's embattled purity long survived him. It was a theme he developed at length in the last volume of the *Travels*, in the course of an account of the history and current state of "the religion of New England."[58] It was an account that stressed the effects of the American Revolution, albeit with some distinct editorial biases. Dwight read the Quebec Expedition out of the record entirely. The French Alliance, by contrast, he was able to put to good use.

Unlike his illustrious grandfather, but like his friend Jedidiah Morse, Dwight was a mediocre theologian and an energetic shaper of public opinion. Consequently his religious history passed over fine philosophical and denominational differences in favor of sweeping judgments that would support such immediate concerns as the endorsement of the quasi-establishments and attacks on Revolutionary France. To these ends Dwight constructed a past in which the Puritans and their descendants fought tirelessly for the right to be left alone. It was to quarantine themselves against infection by a depraved world, he said, that the Puritans had crossed the ocean, only to be set upon almost immediately by marauding Catholics. Even peaceful interlopers, the interfering Quakers and Baptists, had received the treatment they deserved. "They cordially hated the people of New England. Why did they not stay among those whom they liked better? The only answer is, they came to make proselytes: the most uncomfortable of all intruders."[59] Proceeding from this somewhat dour position, Dwight sketched the course of religious developments since the 1750s—that is, during his own lifetime—as a series of encroachments by a variety of "intruders." Far from inviting denominational competition in the confident spirit of Stiles, Belknap, and Zabdiel Adams, Dwight's taste for the New Divinity led him to stress the risks over the rewards of the vogue for religious toleration. Concerned above all with the preservation of New England's "true religion," Dwight kept a watchful eye on the ever-changing enemy at the gates.

Dwight's religious history, like his treatment of Quebec, is as interesting for what it leaves out as for what it includes. In keeping with his concern for the integrity of New England Calvinism, he paid scant attention to the controversies over revivalism and itinerancy during the 1740s. He gave no hint of a connection, so self-evident to many later historians, between the Great Awakening and the Revolution. He began instead in 1755 with the outbreak of the Seven Years' War, which he characteristically preferred to call the French War. On the face of it, this imperial conflict between Britain and France was what had made North America safe for Protestantism once and for all; but that is not the way Dwight described it. More significantly, in his view, the war was the time when "foreigners for the first time mingled extensively with the inhabitants of New England." The results had been unfortunate. The unworldly, upright colonists had suffered greatly from exposure at close quarters to the "loose doctrines and licentious practices" of the British regulars alongside whom they fought. The British army had contained "many infidels," and "all infidels," Dwight insisted, "wish to make proselytes." Unaccustomed to any sort of religious skepticism, the innocent Americans were defenseless against the jaded British. Moreover, "the contagion spread" when the American soldiers returned home and communicated their dangerous new ideas in every town and village.[60]

New England was spared the worst effects of this plague, a blessing Dwight attributed to the "very extensive and happy revival of religion" there in the years just before the war. He credited the Great Awakening with having "retarded essentially the progress" of the infidel British "evil." Only a strong and vital faith had saved the colonies from ruin. But this was merely one in a series of onslaughts that each time grew in strength. Whatever damage New England's religion had sustained during the Seven Years' War, it "suffered far more" during the American Revolution. "All the evils which flowed from the former were multiplied in the latter." Once more the problem was the harmful influence on New Englanders of

"the foreigners with whom they had interacted." By this
Dwight no longer had in mind the redcoats but two other
groups of strangers. First there were the "multitudes of their
countrymen from the other colonies," spiritual inferiors who
corrupted New Englanders when "united with them in military life." Dwight, who had been a chaplain in Connecticut
in 1777 before becoming a schoolmaster, recalled with bitter sarcasm the army's role as a "school for moral improvement." Even those who stayed at home were not safe, since
they soon showed themselves "susceptible . . . to receive from
the scholars whatever they had gained from their instructors"
in irreligion.[61]

The regrettable necessity of intercourse with other colonists had exposed New England to profanity, greed, and imper-
tinent "ambition" on the part of the lower orders. Still, these
paled beside the moral harm occasioned by contact with a second group of strangers: the French. Dwight explicitly identified the French Alliance as the chief culprit in the religious
declension that had accompanied the Revolution. On the contribution of the alliance to the success of American arms he
was silent. Accusing the French of having attempted to extort
the cession of Newport, Rhode Island, he denounced "the in-
sidiousness of the proposal" as proof of France's disposition
"to rule and ride over us according to their pleasure." But it
was the moral effects of the alliance, rather than the military or
political, that preoccupied Dwight. He was no longer willing,
as he had been in 1781, to grant that the alliance had in some
ways benefited New England by providing an opening to the
wider world. By 1816 he saw only the damage it had done,
damage whose source lay in the fact that the French were
"even more dissolute characters" than Englishmen or Virginians. Worse than Anglicans, worse even than pious Catholics,
they were devotees of "loose and undefined atheism," "disciples of Voltaire, Rousseau, d'Alembert, and Diderot."[62]

Like Stiles, Dwight claimed to prefer a French Catholic to
a French atheist, though given the pointed anti-Catholic tone

throughout the *Travels*, one has to wonder how much he meant this. In any case, and in contrast to Stiles, he saw atheism as the more authentic national characteristic. Whereas Stiles had rested his apology for the alliance on the assertion that French Catholicism was compatible with republicanism, Dwight took up the other strain of wartime reasoning and turned it to his own purpose. Sounding like John Adams or the tourist William Greene, he said the French only pretended to be Catholic. Adams had embraced the idea as a way of minimizing the danger to New England's religion. Dwight, writing much later, had the luxury of attacking the alliance rather than defending it. It had exposed New England to evil forces of nearly overwhelming power. Already weakened by contact with other outsiders, the inhabitants were at a disadvantage as soon as they encountered their *"très chers et tres grands amis et alliés."* New Englanders were not sophisticated enough to cope with those who, although they might have lost their faith, had been "too long accustomed to the business of making proselytes" not to retain the necessary predatory skills. Dwight's sense of the fragility of virtue permeated his description of the alliance as an encounter with dangerous men who "despised" God and brazenly denied every article of Christian faith, from the existence of future rewards and punishments to the very idea of moral obligation. "The Frenchman, when you express your belief of these doctrines, looks at you with a stare made up of pity, surprise, and contempt, as an ignorant rustic entering for the first time, or not having entered at all, the world's great metropolis of science and improvement." And "having himself been born and educated a citizen" thereof, he "pities you for your own weakness, is astonished at your ignorance, and is irresistibly compelled to despise the clownishness of your moral sentiments." [63]

This searing encapsulation of the French perspective on the alliance put the problem squarely. What horrified Dwight was the suspicion that a certain number of Americans had themselves been "irresistibly compelled" to entertain the French

point of view. While "not corrupted with a hopeless putrid-
ity," even "New England men" had "exhibited unequivocal
proofs of disease and decay" after prolonged acquaintance
with French ideas. The urgent need, then, was to pull up the
drawbridge and defend whatever remained of true religion.
Thanks to its peculiar Calvinist heritage, New England had
"stood the shock of this war of moral elements . . . more firmly
than could rationally have been expected." If there were
"breaches" in the "walls," these had not been fatal. "The fortress, though partially undermined, was still defensible, and
invited both the labor and the expense necessary to repair it."
Dwight was confident that he understood what kind of labor
and expense the necessary repairs entailed, and by the time
he composed this section of the *Travels* he was satisfied that
the repairs were complete. They had begun at the proper
place, with a shoring up of the twin foundations of government and religion. A strong national government had eventually emerged in the Federal Constitution of 1787, one that
could curb the "avarice" and moral banditry of the promoters
of "paper currency." At the same time, the framers of the Constitution had wisely left undisturbed the state provisions in
Connecticut and Massachusetts for the public support of Protestant worship. In both cases "men of wisdom and worth" had
managed to preserve their "habitual influence" despite the
chaotic aftermath of independence.[64]

No sooner was this accomplished than there came the third
assault on the city on a hill in Dwight's lifetime. This time it
took the hideous shape of the philosophical excretions of the
French Revolution. These had taken some time to come to
light, Dwight admitted. At first many Americans fell under the
spell of its "enchantment," and "most eyes were disabled from
seeing clearly the nature of the purposes" of the new regime.
The awful truth, which members of the New England clergy
were the first to discern, was that "France during the Revolution exhibited . . . the strongest resemblance to Hell which the
human eye in this world had ever been permitted to behold."

In comparison to the Jacobins with whom Stiles felt such empathy, Louis XVI had been "the meekest and mildest monarch" in French history. The victims of the Terror, "entombed in prisons or made the food of the guillotine," were no weeds in the garden of liberty but the wisest and worthiest French citizens.[65]

Why, then, had so many Americans been blind to these facts? The problem, as before, was the seductive power of new ideas. The young, with their "strong passions and feeble principles," were especially vulnerable to the carnal lure of French thinking. Predisposed to "sensuality and ambition," they were so "delighted with the prospect of unrestrained gratification" that they leaped to subscribe to the permissive "new doctrines." Worse yet, they dressed up their libertinism in the language of learning and had the effrontery to pretend that they were advancing into "the light of wisdom" while their critics lagged behind "in a general darkness." Rejecting revelation in favor of a spurious science, they even claimed that mankind, instead of being created by God, "sprang like a mushroom out of the earth by a chemical process." A century later, American Protestants who championed revelation as a guide to the origin of the species would decry the growing influence of German ideas through the "higher criticism" of the Bible. Timothy Dwight, though he counted German and British writers among those who had "vomited" the "dregs of infidelity" on America, never lost sight of the primary culpability of the French.[66]

Dwight was equally clear about the nature of the crime itself, which had been to tear America loose from its philosophical moorings at a crucial juncture, casting the infant nation adrift on a sea of doubt. The harm had begun during the War of Independence, when men whose upbringing had taught them "just and exact views of what was right" fell away "from such views by an imperceptible declension." The generation then rising suffered the effects of this decline, since "virtues mathematically defined and perfectly known in a sound state of society, were now to a great extent seen only in a fluctuating light." It was precisely this crisis of moral epistemology that the French then seized upon and made worse. Their pernicious doctrines were actually designed to confuse. "Were they delivered in language capable of being understood, their authors would be considered the Newtons and Aristotles of folly." But meaninglessness was itself a French stratagem, according to Dwight. "He who cannot convince may perplex. He who cannot inform may beguile. He who cannot guide may entice. He who cannot explain may overbear. He who can do all of these may, and often will, persuade." [67]

Dwight thus enunciated a theory of moral knowledge at once more traditional and—to our ear—more postmodern than Thomas Jefferson's confident belief in the transcendental power of truth to prevail over error. Dwight understood arguments over meaning to be contests of power: he found it "no enigma" that "philosophical sinners should wish to reign and riot." He took it for granted that the ability to persuade "the ignorant, unthinking, and vulgar" conferred power on the persuader. Quite consistently, then, he had no truck with extravagant claims that religious toleration was a virtue in itself. On the contrary, when explaining how New England had survived even this fiercest attack on its faith, he pointed not just to the faith but to the legal arrangements that buttressed it. "Without the influence of religion," he wrote in defense of Connecticut's tax support for Protestant ministers, "political freedom cannot be enjoyed." It was the reflection of this fact in wise "New England institutions" that had made that region stronger than any other in first resisting and then expunging French influence.[68]

Dwight died in 1817, a year after composing his letters on the religion of New England. The following year, with the advent of the state constitution of 1818, the Connecticut establishment died as well. Though he would have been disappointed had he lived to see it, Dwight would not have despaired. He believed that New England's salvation had another, firmer foundation than the public financing of ministers' salaries, and that was the rebirth of "vital Christianity" itself. One of his main aims and proudest accomplishments during his long tenure at Yale was the reinvigoration of evangelical religion among the students. He presided over four revivals in twenty-two years, the first in 1802. Whatever the shortcomings of his own times when measured against the righteousness of the Puritans, Dwight saw in these revivals and in the new missions to Asia a shining future for the work of redemption.[69]

Timothy Dwight lived long enough to portray his rival and predecessor, Ezra Stiles, as someone who had never fully grasped the extent of the danger emanating from France. Furthermore, he lived to see the rise of the Second Great Awakening and to see in it a counterrevolution that would win back what had been lost in the upheavals in America and France. He enjoyed a feeling of vindication through the return of the New England clergy to something like the prestige they had so rudely lost. A Federalist to the end, he had his doubts about the ability of men like himself to exercise political influence commensurate with their virtue in a country that insisted on electing presidents from Virginia. Still, he died secure in the belief that New Englanders had triumphed over repeated challenges to their moral leadership of the United States, and indeed the world. John Leland, who outlived Dwight by another fifteen years, had another sort of satisfaction. He loathed the Federalist Party and the Massachusetts and Connecticut establishments as much as Dwight valued them, and he witnessed the collapse of both.

Stiles, Dwight, and Leland were all Calvinists. Stiles, the only one of them to live his entire life in the eighteenth century, had an eighteenth-century millennialist's confidence in history as the working out of the divine will. When he took his last look in the mid-1790s, he had little difficulty incorporating into his providential vision the rapprochement between New England and France. He managed this by understanding the American Revolution, the French Alliance, and the French Revolution as parts of a worldwide movement that would defeat tyranny, redeem mankind, and inaugurate an age of civil and religious liberty. He did not live long enough to see this holistic construct disintegrate and the French Revolution become an ideological dividing line among Americans.[70] By taking sides in this great rift of party politics, the Federalist Timothy Dwight and the Democratic-Republican John Leland became men of the nineteenth century. Leland, who had been present at the battle of Yorktown, concluded from his wartime experiences that Catholics and other non-Protestants had a natural right not just to toleration but to liberty. It seems doubtful that his view of the absolute need to "exclude religious opinions from the list of objects of legislation" has ever enjoyed the support of a majority of Americans, but it has been a persistent influence in American thought since Leland and his hero, Thomas Jefferson, put it forward. It was less the force of argument than the weight of numbers that effected the transition from toleration to liberty for American Catholics. Just as old-line Congregationalists in Massachusetts lost their taste for establishments when they began losing parish elections to Unitarians, so it was the growing electoral strength of Catholic immigrants that converted Protestants in general to a keener appreciation of Jefferson's "wall of separation" between church and state.[71] By that point, after the Civil War, the combination of Protestant disestablishment and a burgeoning Catholic presence convinced the heirs of Timothy Dwight that the Baptists had after all had a point about the perils of consorting too closely with civil power.

But all this lay in the future. This book has examined the impact of New England's first encounter with Catholicism, a Catholicism that was foreign, spoke French, and had its nearest outpost in Quebec. The coming of the Revolution drastically altered the terms of relations between the colonial neighbors when cooperation gave the lie to the traditional hostility so recently reaffirmed in protest against the Quebec Act. To nearly everyone's surprise and the disappointment of not a few defenders of either faith, the Revolutionary encounter with Catholicism was by and large amicable. In the context of the Quebec Expedition, the root cause of this was the dismayed reaction of the French Canadian peasantry to the pro-British behavior of their priests and seigneurs after 1763. No longer convinced of the legitimacy of their putative leaders, the habitants were amenable to the American offers of alliance and even political union. The American invaders, when they came, were greeted as liberators. The unexpectedly warm reception was both a blessing and a challenge to the Yankee troops. In one sense, it saved their lives as they staggered out of the Maine woods. At the same time, it confronted them with their own alienation from their Calvinist ministers. Traditional anti-Catholicism, however comfortably worn at home, was of little use to an American soldier in Quebec. To the distress of men like Judah Champion, they quickly shrugged it off.

That is not to say that New England anti-Catholicism melted away at the behest of George Washington or in response to Quebecois hospitality, or even out of gratitude for French help. So simple a conclusion does violence to the subtlety of the change. The softening of Protestant prejudice did not extend to a willingness to accept Catholicism as a Christian denomination entitled to the same treatment in law and custom as the Baptists or Episcopalians. That came much later, and in response to different forces. Yet it is implausible to deny that the more limited principle of tolerating the presence of Catholics and permitting their public worship had a certain legitimacy conferred on it by the mere fact of the Canadian and French alliances. The informal partnership in Quebec, as its clerical detractors on both sides complained, abruptly cast in doubt the previously sacrosanct notion that Protestant and Catholic interests were inimical in principle. Once rendered obsolete, that idea needed to be replaced—but with what? When they looked at Catholics, New Englanders were no longer sure what they saw.

The formal alliance with France intensified to the breaking point this pressure on the familiar architecture of the Protestant world. The promulgation of the alliance presented New England's religious leaders with a Hobson's choice, since whoever opposed the accommodation to Catholics on principle risked being branded an enemy of his country. Despite a certain amount of hemming and hawing, not one minister changed his political position on these grounds. The very fact underscored the essentially political nature of the Standing Order's behavior, since when unexpected developments drove a wedge between Calvinism and patriotism, they all lined up on the same side.

This called for explanation, and not all explanations were equally flattering. Indeed, any account of the pragmatic religious politics of the New England clergy, whether put forward by themselves or attributed to them by others, tended to subvert their authority. Seen from outside, the Congregationalist establishments had forfeited a certain amount of prestige in their willingness to hurry along behind public sentiments they had long presumed to lead. Declarations on the duty to shun Catholics could never again carry quite the weight they once had. At the same time, internal differences of opinion over how to respond to events reflected the perceived need to come up with a conceptualization of "popery" that could be squared with the facts on the ground. One way was to reimagine Catholicism as something less powerful and hence less dangerous than previously supposed. This was the central theme of the apologetic Revolutionary propaganda that asserted the previously unthinkable compatibility of Catholicism and Republicanism. Less charitably, new images of Catholicism were also brought to bear after the war as sticks with which to beat one's opponents in the Universalist controversy. Chauncy and the other liberals, called papists for repudiating an exclusivist idea of Protestantism, called their critics papists for clinging to it.

Timothy Dwight, who deplored the new thinking and traced it to France, convinced himself that the lasting effects of Franco-American intimacy had been few. He did a fair job of convincing posterity as well. If V. S. Parrington took issue by raising up Dwight's liberal opponents to pride of place in Revolutionary lore, who now reads Parrington?[72] Dwight's rendition of that lore—one that stressed the evangelical contribution and suppressed the engagement with Catholicism to the point of invisibility—thrives once again. An understanding of the Revolution which incorporates that engagement brings us face to face with what Dwight managed to avoid: a recognition of the pragmatic character of Revolutionary history and its implications.

The alternatives to providential history are daunting, and it is easy to see why Dwight evaded them. But in averting his eyes from what he considered the more tawdry aspects of his tale, he discouraged his readers from facing up to some bracing facts about their nation's origins. There are worse secrets, after all, than moral ordinariness. If the Catholic alliances represent America's original sin, to say so is only to grant that politics involves a mixture of idealism and self-interest. There is nothing un-American about admitting this. The notion of exceptionalism—applied to Americans, New Englanders, Protestants, or anyone—always begs the question of special pleading. And indeed, the evidence does not urge us to ascribe to the American Revolutionaries quite so zealous a commitment to principle or so magnanimous a spirit of brotherhood as we might wish to grant them. Either quality, militant faith or forbearing tolerance, holds the promise of escape from the dissatisfying verdict of ordinariness. Yet as Richard Rorty has argued, it is as fruitless as it is tempting to try to justify our present civic arrangements by projecting ahistorical ideals, be they secular or sectarian, onto the past. If we are willing instead to accept the sheer contingency of "our upbringing, our historical situation," we will gain access to a past that is no less instructive for being less therapeutic.[73] The religious history of the Revolution is one of contingent events. The Patriots' foreign sponsors happened to be Catholic. However uninviting this may be as a point of departure, it is from here that we begin disentangling the skein of faith and citizenship in the American republic.

# *Notes*

## LIST OF ABBREVIATIONS

*BQ*  F. C. Würtele, ed., *Blockade of Quebec in 1775–1776 by the American Revolutionists*, Literary and Historical Society of Quebec, *Historical Documents*, 7th ser. (Quebec City, 1905).

*BTW*  Ægidius Fauteux, ed., "Journal tenu par Mess. François Baby, Gab. Taschereau et Jenkin Williams . . . ," *Rapport de l'Archiviste de la Province de Québec* 1927–28.

CCP  Continental Congress Papers, National Archives, Washington, D.C.

*DCB*  Frances Halpenny et al., ed., *Dictionary of Canadian Biography* (12 vols., Toronto, 1983).

HHL  Henry E. Huntington Library, San Marino, Calif.

*ICA*  Hospice Verreau, ed., *Invasion du Canada par les Américains* (Montreal, 1873).

*JCC*  W. C. Ford, ed., *Journals of the Continental Congress* (34 vols., Washington, D.C., 1904–37).

MHS  Massachusetts Historical Society, Boston.

*MQ*  Kenneth Roberts, *March to Quebec* (New York, 1938).

NAC  National Archives of Canada.

PAC  Public Archives of Canada, *Report concerning Canadian Archives for the Year 1904* (Ottawa, 1905), app. 1, "Documents Relating to the War of 1775–76."

*WAL*  W. C. Ford, ed., *Warren-Adams Letters*, Massachusetts Historical Society, *Collections*, vols. 72 (1917), 73 (1925).

# INTRODUCTION

1. Kramnick and Moore, *Godless Constitution*; Levy, *Establishment Clause*; Thomas Curry, *First Freedoms*; Carter, *Culture of Disbelief*.

2. Heimert, *Religion and the American Mind*, vii-viii, 15–16, 449–53. Heimert had in mind particularly Parrington, *Colonial Mind, 1620–1800*.

3. Labaree, "Classrooms," 489; Gerstle, "Protean Character of American Liberalism," 1073; Philip Gleason, "American Identity and Americanization," in Petersen, Novak, and Gleason, *Concepts of Ethnicity*, 133–35.

4. Nash, *Urban Crucible*; Bonomi, *Under the Cope of Heaven*.

5. The Reverend Pat Robertson, while among the most influential of these polemicists, moves outside the orbit of academic discourse. For an expression of evangelical concern that stays within it, see Marsden, *Soul of the American University*.

6. See the works cited in note 1, above.

7. Gaustad, *Faith of Our Fathers*; Peterson and Vaughan, *Virginia Statute for Religious Freedom*; Hoffman and Albert, *Religion in a Revolutionary Age*.

8. A notable recent exception is Cogliano, *"No King, No Popery."* See also Stinchcombe, *American Revolution and the French Alliance*.

# 1. THE CATHOLIC QUESTION

1. The setting of Spring's sermon is vividly described in Royster, *A Revolutionary People at War*, 23–24.

2. Heimert, *Religion and the American Mind*, 483.

3. Winthrop, *History of New England* 1:98–99. See also the account of the English Reformation in Bradford, *Of Plymouth Plantation*, chap. 1.

4. Massachusetts Act against Jesuits, 1647, in Hazard, *Historical Collections* 1:550.

5. Eccles, *France in America*, especially chap. 4; Mayhew, *Sermon Preach'd in the Audience of William Shirley*, 38.

6. Bloch, *Visionary Republic*; Thomas M. Brown, "The Images of the Beast: Anti-Papal Rhetoric in Colonial America," in Curry and Brown, *Conspiracy*, 1–20.

7. Joseph Lathrop, "On 'Revelation.'" "In this interpretation," he added, "most Protestant writers are agreed."

8. *Canada Subjected: A New Song*, broadside, in Walett, *Patriots, Loyalists, and Printers*, 11.

9. *South End Forever, North End Forever: Extraordinary Verses on Pope-Night*, broadside. Cf. Revelation 13:18: "Let him that hath understanding count the number of the beast: for it is the number of a man; and his number is Six hundred threescore and six."

10. John Lathrop, *Errors of Popery*, 17–22; see also Gavin, *Master Key to Popery*. The latter, a classic exposé of the church purportedly written by a defrocked Spanish priest, was popular in New England long after its publication in Dublin and London.

11. Cooper, *Man of Sin*, 66; Locke, *Letter concerning Toleration*; Benjamin Gale, *Reply to a Pamphlet*, quoted in Thomas Curry, *First Freedoms*, 103; [John Adams], "Novanglus," Jan. 23, 1775, *Novanglus and Massachusettensis*, 13.

12. Bridenbaugh, *Mitre and Sceptre*; Bloch, *Visionary Republic*. Patricia Bonomi maintains, *contra* Alan Heimert, that "rational-minded liberals of the educated elite" took the lead in such attacks joined by "New Light Congregationalists, Baptists, and other evangelicals" (Bonomi, *Under the Cope of Heaven*, 208).

13. The text of the act is reprinted in Shortt and Doughty, *Constitutional History of Canada* 1:570–76. On its significance, see Metzger, *Quebec Act*; Ellis, *Catholics in Colonial America*; Coffin, *Province of Quebec*; Ammerman, *In the Common Cause*.

14. Barber, *History of My Own Times* 1:5, 17. Born in Simsbury, Connecticut, in 1756, Barber became an Anglican minister in Claremont, New Hampshire, and later a Roman Catholic.

15. Jones, *Defensive War*, 19; Ezra Stiles to Richard Price, April 10, 1775, quoted in Morgan, *Gentle Puritan*, 266. See also Bloch, *Visionary Republic*, 58–59; Heimert, *Religion and the American Mind*, 387–91.

16. Heimert, *Religion and the American Mind*, 387; Low, *An Astronomical Diary: or, Almanack for 1775*; "Letter from a Clergyman to his Friend in England," Aug. 2, 1775, Force, *American Archives* 3:10; Shebbeare, *An Answer to the Queries*, 30–31.

17. [Leonard], *Massachusettensis*, 74. The entire debate is reprinted in [Adams and Leonard], *Novanglus and Massachusettensis*. The discussion here refers to Adams's "Novanglus" pamphlet of Feb. 27, 1775.

18. Arnold, *Address to the Inhabitants of America*, Oct. 7, 1780. See also his *Proclamation* of Oct. 20, 1780.

19. Heimert, *Religion and the American Mind*, 484–86.

20. Bonomi, "Religious Dissent and the Case for American Exceptionalism," in Hoffman and Albert, *Religion in a Revolution-*

*ary Age*, 50, 33. None of the chapters in this collection addresses the problem of the Catholic alliances. Weber, *Rhetoric and History in Revolutionary New England*, also omits any discussion of Catholicism and anti-Catholicism. On Weber's argument in relation to Heimert and Bonomi as well as to Bloch, see Gura, "Role of the 'Black Regiment.'"

21. Hatch, *Sacred Cause of Liberty*; Hatch, *Democratization of American Christianity*; Bloch, *Visionary Republic*, 148.

22. Stinchcombe, *American Revolution and the French Alliance*; Dull, *Diplomatic History of the American Revolution*; Alden, *History of the American Revolution*; Jensen, *Founding of a Nation*; Countryman, *American Revolution*.

23. Noll, *Christians in the American Revolution*; Marini, *Radical Sects of Revolutionary New England*; Hoffman and Albert, *Religion in a Revolutionary Age*.

24. Royster, *A Revolutionary People at War*, viii, 22–24, 157. For evidence of irreligion in the ranks, see Beebe, "Journal of a Physician in the Expedition against Canada," 27, 28, 33–34.

25. Bonomi, *Under the Cope of Heaven*, 221.

26. Heimert, *Religion and the American Mind*, 490, 492, 497.

27. Avery, *Lord Is to Be Praised*, 14, 33.

28. For the Calvinist critique of Universalism, see Buckminster, *Brief Paraphrase upon Romans X*. For the liberal critique of Puritanism, see Mercy Otis Warren, *History of the American Revolution*, 11–12, 337.

29. Franchot, *Roads to Rome*.


## 2. THE ENCOUNTER IN QUEBEC

1. Briand, "Mandement pour la visite des paroisses . . . ," May 22, 1775, NAC microfilm, reel M-298.

2. Exceptions are Lanctot, *Canada et la révolution américaine*, and Eccles, *France in America*. See also Justin Smith, *Our Struggle for the Fourteenth Colony*.

3. Simon Sanguinet, "Le témoin oculaire de la guerre des Bastonnois en Canada dans les années 1775 et 1776," *ICA*, 36; *JCC* 2:109–10.

4. Claude-Nicolas-Guillaume de Lorimier, "Mes services pendant la guerre américaine de 1775," *ICA*, 246–47.

5. See any of the journals reprinted in *MQ*.

6. Jean-Baptiste Badeaux, "Journal commencé à Trois-

Rivières, le 18 May, l'an 1775," Nov. 17, 1775, *ICA*, 176; Amable Berthelot, "Extraits d'un Mémoire de M. Amable Berthelot sur l'invasion du Canada en 1775," Nov. 17–19, 1775, ibid., 234.

7. Thomas Ainslie, *BQ*, 18; Isaac Senter, *MQ*, 227; Simon Sanguinet, "Siège . . . de Québec," *ICA*, 115–16. Except in cases where the English version is in general use, such as the St. Lawrence River, I have retained the French spelling of all place-names.

8. "Journal" [copied and elaborated from Ainslie's], *BQ*, 97; Howe to Secretary of State, Dec. 3, 1775, PAC, 355. Ainslie wrote to a friend in Boston: "We must fall in a few days. . . . God forgive those who have so cruelly abandoned us" (Thomas Ainslie to Sylvester Gardiner, Nov. 1775, Gardiner Correspondence, 2:89, MHS).

9. Ainslie, April 21, 1776, *BQ*, 75.

10. Arnold to Wooster, Jan. 2, 1776, Simon Fobes, *MQ*, 105, 593; "Journal," Jan. 7, 1776, Ainslie, Feb. 16, 1776, *BQ*, 108, 43.

11. Arnold to Wooster, Jan. 2, 1776, to Congress [citing letter from Clinton], Jan. 12, 1776, to John Hancock, Feb. 12, 1776, *MQ*, 105, 113, 121.

12. "Journal," April 6, 9, 1776, *BQ*, 137–38, 140; Badeaux, March 21, 30, 1776, *ICA*, 192, 195; "Petition of Capts. Olivier and Leibert of Hazen's Regiment," Feb. 6, 1784, CCP, M247, reel 55, no. 42, 6:85.

13. Senter, *MQ*, 238.

14. Ainslie, May 6, 1776, *BQ*, 82–83; Sanguinet, "Siège," Badeaux, May 11, 1776, *ICA*, 127, 210; Senter, *MQ*, 240.

15. M[oses] H[azen] to Carroll Commission in Montreal, May 24, 1776, NAC microfilm; Sanguinet, "Témoin," *ICA*, 134.

16. PAC, 376 (rain); Badeaux, *ICA*, 207 (snow); Melvin, *MQ*, 452 (corn).

17. *BTW*, Nouvelle Beauce, parish of Sainte-Marie, 471. Carleton's order of March 29, 1777, permitted the rehabilitation as militiamen of those who agreed to "make submission to the militia captain, in the presence of the most notable members of the parish at the church door on a Sunday or other feast day" (Sanguinet, "Témoin," *ICA*, 137).

18. Saint-Antoine (Rousseau), Ile d'Orléans (Buché), *BTW*, 467, 442. Similar scenes occurred at Saint-Jean and Becancour (ibid., 444, 460).

19. On the sectarian overtones of the nearly constant cross-border raids and kidnappings, see Demos, *Unredeemed Captive*.

20. For the new tone, see the "Letter to the Inhabitants of

the Province of Quebec," *JCC* 1:105–13. See also Zwierlin, "End of No-Popery."

21. Briand, "Mandement aux sujets rebels," 1776, in Têtu and Gagnon, *Mandements* 2:275–76; Sanguinet, "Témoin," *ICA*, 18–19.

22. Briand, "Circulaire à Messieurs les curés à l'occasion des rumeurs de guerre," 1793, NAC microfilm, reel M-298; Briand, "Lettre Circulaire," 1768, in Têtu and Gagnon, *Mandements* 2:214.

23. Quebec Act, in Shortt and Doughty, *Constitutional History of Canada* 1:570–76. The religious clauses are on p. 572.

24. "Lettre de Mgr. Briand à un personnage ecclésiastique [perhaps the papal nuncio] en France," March 10, 1775, facsimile in Caron, "Inventaire," 112.

25. Ibid.

26. Briand to Montgolfier, Oct. 9, 1775, quoted in Lanctot, *Canada et la revolution américaine*, 101; Briand to Maisonbasse, Oct. 25, 1775, Caron, "Inventaire," 112.

27. *DCB*, s.v. "Montgolfier, Etienne."

28. Arnold to Congress, Jan. 24, 1776, *MQ*, 118; "Journal," *BQ*, 84.

29. Lorimier, "Mes services," Veuve Benoist to François Baby, Sept. 7, 1775, *ICA*, 259, 312; Têtu and Gagnon, *Mandements* 2:266, 281–83; Badeaux, April 9, 1776, *ICA*, 199; Ainslie, April 6, 1776, *BQ*, 67; Lorimier, "Mes services," *ICA*, 269, 281; *Authentic Narrative of the Facts Relating to the Cedars*, 29–30.

30. Briand, "Lettre pastorale aux habitants de Saint-François-du-Sud," 1776, Caron, "Inventaire," 113; Briand, "Mandement aux sujets rebels," in Têtu and Gagnon, *Mandements* 2:277.

31. *BTW*, Saint-Antoine, 468; Briand to Lagroix, Oct. 1, 1775, Maisonbasse to Briand, Oct. 22, 1775, Lanctot, *Canada et la révolution américaine*, 100; *BTW*, Cap la Madelaine, 459. A parenthetical aside in an enduringly popular historical novel captures in apocryphal form this sentiment of the habitants in 1775. "It is reported that one of these rebels lay on his deathbed and the priest came to encourage him to admit his error. The dying man raised himself halfway, gave the priest an angry look, and said, 'You smell English!'" (Aubert de Gaspé, *Les anciens canadiens*, 319n).

32. *BTW*, Saint-Laurent Ile d'Orléans, Saint-Pierre, 445–46, 447. Similar cases were noted in Sainte-Famille, Saint-François, and Saint-Feréol (ibid., 443, 483, 440).

33. *BTW*, Sainte-Marie de la Nouvelle Beauce, 470.

34. Briand to Montgolfier, Nov. 5, 1775, Caron, "Inven-

taire," 112; Briand to Maisonbasse, Oct. 25, 1775, Lanctot, *Canada et la révolution américaine*, 101.

35. *BTW*, Champlain, 458.

36. Washington to Schuyler, Sept. 8, 1775, "Instructions to Arnold," Sept. 14, 1775, "To the Inhabitants of Canada," Sept. 7, 1775, orderly book, Nov. 5, 1775, Fitzpatrick, *Writings of Washington* 3:485, 495–96, 480, 4:64–65.

37. "Narrative of Ethan Allen," Force, *American Archives* 3:799–801n; Abner Stocking, Nov. 4, 1775, *MQ*, 557.

38. Caleb Haskell, Nov. 3, 1775, Isaac Senter, Nov. 4, 5, 1775, John Henry, Nov. 10, 1775, Senter, Nov. 5, 1775, ibid., 478, 222, 348, 222.

39. Simon Fobes, ibid., 586. Fobes would benefit from Chaudière River hospitality a second time. After being taken prisoner at Quebec City, he escaped from a British ship in the St. Lawrence and was sheltered and helped on his way by friendly habitants in August 1776. He eventually reached Boston by retracing the route he had taken with Arnold the previous year (ibid., 603–8).

40. *BTW*, 471, 478–80, Fauteux, "Suite du Journal," 139; *DCB*, s.v. "Gosselin, Clement."

41. Amable Berthelot, Oct. 15, 1775, Badeaux, Nov. 2, 1775, *ICA*, 166, 230, 174.

42. Montgomery to Washington, Nov. 3, 1775, *Almon's Remembrancer*, 1776, 2:126.

43. Sanguinet, "Témoin," *ICA*, 46; MacLean to Barrington, Nov. 20, 1775, PAC, 386; "Journal," Dec. 2, 1775, *BQ*, 95. Carleton, it may be noted, arrived the same day and immediately began such expulsions without provoking a mutiny.

44. Arnold to Montgomery, Nov. 20, 1775, *MQ*, 92.

45. Badeaux, Nov. 20, 1775, *ICA*, 179.

46. Isaac Senter, Dec. 31, 1775, Arnold to Congress, Jan. 11, 1776, *MQ*, 235, 112.

47. Ainslie, Feb. 28, 1776, *BQ*, 48; Sanguinet, "Témoin," Badeaux, April 10, 1776, *ICA*, 125, 195–96.

48. Trying to set up forward communications with Quebec City as he struggled up through Maine, Arnold insisted that he "must have John Hall, as he speaks French," to "get . . . intelligence" (Arnold to Steel, Oct. 13, 1775, *MQ*, 71). See also Senter, Oct. 7, 1775, ibid., 203.

49. Samuel Mott to Governor Trumbull, Oct. 6, 1775, Force, *American Archives* 3:974.

50. Ainslie, Dec. 2, 1775, *BQ*, 19.

51. John Henry, Nov. 5, 1775, *MQ*, 346; *DCB*, s.v. "Arnold, Benedict." Washington and Montgomery expressed misgivings about Wooster in their letters of Oct. 6 and Nov. 13, 1775, respectively (Force, *American Archives* 3:976, 1603).

52. "Second Book of Minutes of the Court of Inquiry of Damages Occasioned by the Rebels," Verreau Collection, NAC.

53. *DCB*, s.v. "Glapion, Augustin-Louis de," and "Floquet, Pierre-René."

54. Sanguinet, "Témoin," *ICA*, 95; *BTW*, Saint-Pierre, 463; Lorimier, "Mes services," *ICA*, 266; *DCB*, s.v. "Huet de La Valinière, Pierre."

55. Pelissier to the President of Congress, Jan. 8, 1776, Force, *American Archives* 4:599; Badeaux, March 18, 1776, *ICA*, 191.

56. Badeaux, Feb. 29, 1776, *ICA*, 186; Stocking, Oct. 2, 1775, Simeon Thayer, Oct. 2, 1775, *MQ*, 549, 251. For a discussion of similar encounters in an earlier period, see Cogliano, "*Nil Desperandum Christo Duce.*"

57. James Melvin, Jan. 18, 1776, *MQ*, 443–44.

58. July 27, 1776, ibid., 452–53.

59. Simon Fobes, ibid., 584, 613.

60. Haskell, March 17, 1776, Meigs, Dec. 4, 1775, Dearborn, Nov. 21, 1775, Thayer, Nov. 7, 1775, ibid., 492, 185, 143, 262.

61. Colquhoun, "An Account and Transaction of a Voyage to Quebec," NAC.

62. Fobes, [July 1776], *MQ*, 599–600.

63. Badeaux, April 19, 1776, *ICA*, 202.

64. Sanguinet, "Témoin," ibid., 18.

65. Sanguinet, "Lettre aux citoyens de Montréal," March 1776, ibid., 103–5.

66. Sanguinet, "Témoin," ibid., 31, 34.

67. Carleton, Order of March 29, 1777, in Sanguinet, "Témoin," ibid., 142.

68. Badeaux, Oct. 15, 20, 24, 1775, Comte Dupré to François Baby, Oct. 21, 1775, ibid., 172–73, 319.

69. Sanguinet, "Témoin," ibid., 105. After the battle of the Cedars two months later, Lorimier refused to grant war rights to French Canadian officers taken prisoner with the Americans (Lorimier, "Mes services," ibid., 282).

70. Badeaux, April 3, 1776, ibid., 197; Briand, "Mandement aux sujets rebels," in Têtu and Gagnon, *Mandements* 2:277–78.

71. Badeaux, Nov. 20, 1775, May 13, 1776, *ICA*, 179, 212.

72. *BTW*, Rivière-Ouelle, 498.

73. The transgressive behavior of several women earned them the sobriquet of "Queen of Hungary," an allusion to the empress Maria Theresa meant to mock their pretensions to power (*BTW*, 447, 480).

74. Badeaux, Oct. 10–12, Oct. 8, 1775, *ICA*, 170–71, 169; *BTW*, Saint-Thomas, 488.

75. Mme DeMuy-DeLisle to Charlotte DeMuy, [ca. 1777], Verreau Collection, NAC.

76. Tryon to Dartmouth, Sept. 8, 1775, PAC, 373; Ainslie, March 8, 1776, *BQ*, 55. Ainslie dismissed John Thomas as "formerly an apothecary now a General" and noted that Benedict Arnold had also been an apothecary and Remember Baker a millwright. He wrote of Montgomery, "If he gives commissions to such men his army will not be formidable" (ibid., 76, 20).

77. Gordon, *History* 2:250–51.

78. *BTW*, Rivière Basticant, Lobinière, 457, 465.

79. Ibid., Pointe Levy, Saint-Pierre-les-Becquets, Saint-Jean de l'Echaillon, Sainte-Croix, 474, 463, 464, 466.

80. Ibid., Nouvelle Beauce, Sainte-Anne, 470–71, 454–55.

81. Ibid., Saint-Pierre Ile d'Orléans, Nouvelle Beauce, Saint-Pierre-les-Becquets, 447, 471, 463.

82. Badeaux, Feb. 29, 1776, *ICA*, 186–87.

83. *BTW*, Saint-Augustin, 449. The commissioners resorted to the same policy in Pointe Levy, 473.

84. Ibid., Basticant, 456. Compare the cases of Pierre Frigon and Alexis Marchand.

85. Ibid., Saint-Pierre du Sud, Pointe Levy, 486, 474.

86. Ibid., Champlain, Saint-Augustin, 458, 449.

87. Some members of the bourgeoisie felt the same way. See Valentin Jautard, "Lettre à M. Richard Montgomery," *ICA*, 86; *DCB*, s.v. "Jautard, Valentin."

88. On the repeated proposals for Quebec to send delegates to the Continental Congress, see John Hancock to Philip Schuyler, Oct. 11, 1775, in Burnett, *Letters of Members of the Continental Congress* 1:227; Montgomery to Schuyler, Nov. 13, 1775, Force, *American Archives* 3:1603; Arnold to Congress, Jan. 11, 1776, *MQ*, 110.

89. "To the Inhabitants of Canada," Fitzpatrick, *Writings of Washington* 3:479.

90. Senter, Nov. 1, 1775, *MQ*, 219. The next day his party met up with "three horned cattle, two horses, eighteen Canadians and one American" (Nov. 2, ibid.).

91. Senter, Nov. 1, 1775, ibid.

## 3. CONQUERED INTO LIBERTY

1. Shortt and Doughty, *Constitutional History of Canada* 1:572.

2. Ibid., 570–76.

3. "To the People of Great Britain," *JCC* 1:83, 88.

4. "To the Inhabitants of the Province of Quebec," ibid., 112, 110, 108–9.

5. "The Association," ibid., 76.

6. New York Provincial Congress, *Résolution*, May 25, 1775, *A messieurs les habitans de la province de Québec*, June 2, 1775, PAC, 382, 383. Such sentiments did not stop New York Whigs from hounding John McKenna, a Roman Catholic priest, out of the colony. In early 1776 he retired to the Jesuit residence in Montreal, where he dined with Moses Hazen when the latter came to see Pierre-René Floquet, the pro-American priest (*DCB*, s.v. "Floquet, Pierre-René").

7. "To the Oppressed Inhabitants of Canada," *New York Gazetteer*, June 22, 1775. The address is attributed to James Price; see *JCC* 1:66–68.

8. Zwierlin, "End of No-Popery," 364–65; "Declaration of Causes of Taking up Arms," July 6, 1775, *JCC* 2:145.

9. Dalrymple, *Address of the People of Great-Britain*, 1–2.

10. [Chandler], *What Think Ye of the Congress Now?*, 14–15; [Leonard], "Massachusettensis," no. 16, March 27, 1775, *Massachusettensis*, 108; Oliver, *Origin and Progress*, 135–36.

11. The phrase appears in the title of an earlier pamphlet, *Friendly Address to All Reasonable Americans*, also attributed to Chandler.

12. [Samuel Johnson], *Hypocrisy Unmasked*, 15–16. The pamphlet Johnson refers to is the Continental Congress's *Extracts from the Votes and Proceedings*.

13. [Johnson], *Hypocrisy Unmasked*, 17–18.

14. Ibid., 3–4.

15. Paul Wentworth to William Eden, Dec. 17, 1777, Stevens, *Facsimiles*, no. 231. Recounting a conversation with Silas Deane, Wentworth said that "the invasion of Canada lost twice in the Congress; and carried by one Voice at last—then only to seize the warlike stores and evacuate it."

16. "Is it possible to get in Boston Silver and Gold for the service in Canada? Our Affairs have been ruined there for Want of it

and can never be retrieved without it" (John Adams to James Warren, May 18, 1776, *WAL* 1:249).

17. Samuel Adams to James Warren, Nov. 4, 1775, John Adams to James Warren, May 18, 1776, ibid., 169, 248.

18. "In war the laws are silent" (extract of a letter, Aug. 31, 1775, "from a gentleman at Ticonderoga to a friend in New York," *Pennsylvania Ledger*, Sept. 16, 1775).

19. Champion, *Christian and Civil Liberty*, 20–21.

20. [John Murray], *Bath-Kol: A Voice from the Wilderness*, 71. This tract is attributed to John Murray of Newburyport (1742–1793), also known as "Damnation Murray" to distinguish him from John "Salvation" Murray of Gloucester (1741–1815), the radical Universalist. On the two Murrays, see Griffin, *Old Brick*.

21. Maccarty, *Praise to God*, 22–23.

22. Like hypocrisy, moral realism is the tribute vice pays to virtue. By denying the applicability of moral rules in situations where much is at stake, the realist implicitly concedes that we prefer to act morally even at such times. See Walzer, *Just and Unjust Wars*.

23. "To the Inhabitants of Great Britain," July 8, 1775, *JCC* 2:167. The Reverend William Gordon, an English dissenting minister who lived in Roxbury during the Revolution and was a partisan thereof, chided the Patriots for fanning such fears (Gordon, *History* 2:157).

24. John Adams to James Warren, Feb. 18, 1776, *WAL* 1:208.

25. "To the Inhabitants of the Province of Quebec," *JCC* 1:112–13.

26. John Adams to James Warren, Oct. 8, 1775, *WAL* 1:131; John Hancock to Philip Schuyler, Oct. 11, 1775, Burnett, *Letters of Members of the Continental Congress* 1:227.

27. Montgomery to Schuyler, Nov. 13, 1775, Force, *American Archives* 3:1603; Arnold to Congress, Jan. 11, 1776, *MQ*, 110.

28. "To the Inhabitants of the Province of Canada," Jan. 24, 1776, *JCC* 4:85–86.

29. Sanguinet, "Témoin," *ICA*, 21.

30. Jautard, "Lettre à M. Richard Montgomery," ibid., 86.

31. Pelissier to the President of Congress, Jan. 8, 1776, Force, *American Archives* 4:596–97. Pelissier managed the forge at St.-Maurice, near Trois-Rivières.

32. D'Estaing, *Déclaration*, Oct. 28, 1778.

33. Cooper, "The Political State of Canada," Samuel Cooper Papers, HHL.

34. Baron de Kalb to the comte de Broglie, Nov. 7, 1778, Stevens, *Facsimiles*, no. 1987. De Kalb's fear was that with complete victory, including the conquest of Canada, the Americans would cease to fear Britain and revert to "their ancient habits" of hostility to France.

35. M. Garnier to the comte de Vergennes, Aug. 16, 1776, ibid., no. 891.

36. Lord North to William Eden, April 23, 1778, William Smith to William Eden, Jan. 21, 1781, ibid., nos. 447, 747.

37. [John Adams], "Novanglus," March 6, 1775, *Novanglus and Massachusettensis*, 92; John Adams to Jedidiah Morse, Dec. 2, 1815, quoted in Morse, *Annals of the American Revolution*, 200.

38. John Lathrop, *Discourse Preached in Thanksgiving*, 14; [John Adams], "Novanglus," Feb. 6, 1775, *Novanglus and Massachusettensis*, 33.

39. Urquhart and Buckley, *Historical Statistics of Canada*, 54.

40. Allen to Trumbull, Aug. 3, 1775, Force, *American Archives* 3:17. Washington's correspondence during the fall of 1775 reveals a similar tendency to view the Mohawks as much more formidable than the Canadians, whether as allies or as enemies (Fitzpatrick, *Writings of Washington* 3:303, 373, 397–98, 437, 526).

41. *DCB*, s.v. "Carleton, Guy"; *ICA*, 200, 61.

42. Montreal Committee of Correspondence to Massachusetts Committee of Correspondence, April 8, 1775, in Ketchum, *Shurtleff Manuscript*, app. 3, 58.

43. Henry Dearborn, Nov. 5, 1775, May 17, 1776, Abner Stocking, Nov. 3, 1775, Arnold to Congress, Jan. 11, 1776, *MQ*, 140, 161, 557, 110.

44. Richard Montgomery, "Letter to the Citizens of the City of Quebec," Dec. 6, 1775, in Sanguinet, "Témoin," *ICA*, 115.

45. John Henry, Nov. 6, Dec. 24, 1775, *MQ*, 346, 372.

46. *America Invincible* 2:28.

47. "To the Inhabitants of the Province of Quebec," *JCC* 1:106–8.

48. John Adams to James Warren, Oct. 8, 1775, *WAL* 1:131. Warren replied, "I am sensible of the importance of the question you propose about the government of Canada. It is indeed a curious problem, and I am glad it is in such good hands." He meant the hands of Congress, not of the Canadians (Warren to Adams, Oct. 20, 1775, ibid., 155).

49. "To the Inhabitants," *JCC* 1:111.

50. D'Estaing, *Déclaration*.

51. If the Canadians could be schooled in republicanism, one might even imagine lifting them out of their Catholicism. One of Montgomery's New York officers thought the Canadians could be "bro't to proper Discipline" and made into real soldiers if marched down into the Protestant colonies where "they would not dread the Anathemas of the Church" (Ritzema, "Journal," Feb. 16, 1776, 106).

52. Cooper, "Political State of Canada," 5–9.

53. *New York Gazetteer*, July 15, 1775. In the event, the distribution of passports to Anglo-Canadian merchants for up-country fur trading was one of the Carroll Commission's few accomplishments (Sanguinet, "Témoin," *ICA*, 106).

54. On the question of such a transethnic notion of American identity in the Revolutionary period, see Gleason, "American Identity and Americanization," in Petersen, Novak, and Gleason, *Concepts of Ethnicity*, 58–68.

55. Otis, *Vindication of the Conduct of the House*, 15, 20–21.

## 4. ASTRIDE THE TIGER

1. Dalrymple, *Address of the People of Great-Britain*, 52.

2. Samuel Johnson, *Patriot*, 10–13.

3. Ibid., 9, 11.

4. [Samuel Johnson], *Hypocrisy Unmasked*, 4, 9, 11, 19, 22.

5. Shebbeare, *An Answer to the Queries*, 8–9, 121, 178, 120, 123.

6. Ibid., 137, 141, 177–78.

7. [Tucker], *Present Posture of Affairs*, 8.

8. Bob Jingle [pseud.], *Association Versified*, 1:8.

9. [Leonard], *Massachusettensis*, 73–74. Peter Oliver made the same objection to anti-Quebec Act hysteria in his "Address to the Soldiers of Massachusetts Bay," Jan. 11, 1776, in Oliver, *Origin and Progress*, 165–66. See also [Leonard], *Massachusettensis*, 35: "Persecution has the same effect in politics, that it has in religion; it confirms the sectary."

10. [Leonard], *Massachusettensis*, 24, 37.

11. Sir William Meredith, *Letter to the Earl of Chatham on the Quebec Bill*, 24–25, quoted in [Towers], *Letter to Dr. Samuel Johnson*, 25.

12. [Towers], *Letter to Dr. Samuel Johnson*, 25–26. It was a

shrewd question, as later events were to prove. The habitants did resent the reimposition of tithes, and their clergy had good reason to fear a free market, so to speak, in clerical support.

13. Ibid., 26, 30, 3, 51.

14. John Erskine, *Spirit of Popery*, 31, 21–22, 37–40. On Erskine and Bellamy, see Dexter, *Biographical Sketches* 1:524.

15. [Erskine], *Present Contentions*, 52, 45.

16. Galloway, *Candid Examination*, 57, 59–60.

17. [Chandler], *What Think Ye of the Congress Now?*, 4; [Chandler], *Friendly Address to All Reasonable Americans*, 21, 23.

18. [Gray], *Two Congresses Cut Up*, 7–8.

19. "St. George's Day," [*Loyal and Humorous Songs*], 31–33. An asterisk in the original identifies "pimps" as "Congress."

20. [Gibbon], *Mémoire justificatif*, 30–31; [Inglis], *Letters of Papinian*, 8.

21. Tucker, *Cui Bono?*, 21, 24.

22. Camillo Querno [John André], "The American Times," in *Cow-Chace*, 54, 47, 64.

23. [Inglis], *Letters of Papinian*, 2, 22, 14. As Inglis told the story, Borgia joined forces with Louis XII in an unsuccessful effort against Milan. Later, when he had disgraced himself (and accidentally killed his father) in a plot to assassinate nine cardinals, he applied to his former patron for protection. Louis "not only refused to assist him, but also confiscated his Dukedom, and withdrew his pension. Despised and detested by all, he dragged on a miserable life of dependence, and was finally killed at the battle of Viana" (ibid., 26).

24. Ibid., 68–73.

25. *Independent Ledger*, Oct. 26, 1778, July 1, 1782.

26. Baxter, "Tyrannicide Proved Lawful," in Phelps, *History of Newgate*, 72, 75; *Pennsylvania Ledger*, May 13, 1778; [Inglis], *Letters of Papinian*, 72. For Congress's attendance at mass in Philadelphia on July 4, 1779, see *Connecticut Journal*, July 28, 1779.

27. Andrew Elliott, "Narrative of the Capture and Execution of Major John André," Oct. 4–5, 1780, Stevens, *Facsimiles*, no. 739.

28. Arnold, *Address to the Inhabitants of America*, Oct. 7, 1780; Arnold, *Proclamation*, Oct. 20, 1780. Miralles died at Washington's camp at Morristown, New Jersey, on April 28, 1780. His funeral was held at St. Mary's, with the chaplain of the French minister officiating.

29. Mercy Otis Warren to John Adams, Oct. 15, 1778, *WAL*

2:55; Elbridge Gerry to James Warren, May 26, 1778, in Gardiner, *Warren-Gerry Correspondence*, 121.

30. [West], *Bickerstaff's Boston Almanack, for 1775.*

31. This summary of the course of the alliance is drawn from Stinchcombe, *American Revolution and the French Alliance*, and Dull, *Diplomatic History of the American Revolution.*

32. Sainneville arrived on May 5 in the frigate *Nymphe*, and d'Estaing's larger fleet in July. See Fitz-Henry Smith, "The French at Boston during the Revolution," 13–14.

33. [Breck], *Recollections of Samuel Breck*, 24; Robin, *New Travels*, 20; James Warren to Elbridge Gerry, March 24, 1777, *Warren-Gerry Correspondence*, 55; Samuel Adams to James Warren, July 15, 1778, *WAL* 2:34.

34. Fitz-Henry Smith, "Memorial to the Chevalier de St.-Sauveur," 23n.

35. Robin, *New Travels*, 13.

36. Deux-Ponts, *My Campaigns in America*, 15.

37. William Heath to George Washington, July 12, 1780, quoted in ibid., 91n.

38. Ibid., 15. Beaumarchais, the playwright and main French agent for the alliance during its clandestine phase, slyly adduced "the cold reception some of the French officers received in America" before the signing of the treaty as "proof that they were not sent by his Majesty." See his *Observations on the Justificative Memorial*, 49.

39. *Essex Journal*, Jan. 12, 1776; James Warren to John Adams, July 10, Aug. 11, 1776, Feb. 22, 1777, *WAL* 1:259, 269, 295.

40. Mercy Otis Warren to John Adams, Oct. 15, 1778, *WAL* 2:55; Abigail Adams to John Adams, Oct. 25, 1778, quoted in Butterfield, Friedlaender, and Kline, *Book of Abigail and John*, 225.

41. *Gazette Françoise*, Dec. 8, 1780 (Jastram), Jan. 1, 1781, Supplement (Lemonier). Jastram held classes at Eleazar Trevett's house when his private lessons were oversubscribed.

42. Robin, *New Travels*, 24; Vicomte de Noailles to Mary Robinson, June 30, 1781, quoted in Forbes and Cadman, *France and New England* 2:34.

43. Gordon, *History* 4:128; Robin, *New Travels*, 20.

44. Robin, *New Travels*, 19–21.

45. Ibid., 21, 19.

46. *Herald of Freedom*, Sept. 18, 1788; chevalier de Fleury, "Sommaire de l'Etat politique et militaire de l'amérique," Nov. 16, 1779, Stevens, *Facsimiles*, no. 1616.

47. Greene, "Diary," July 23, 1778, 133.

48. April 7, 17, June 18, 1778, ibid., 88, 91, 125–26.

49. April 23, July 11, June 5–6, 18, 1778, ibid., 97, 130–31, 122, 126.

50. April 27, 22, July 9, Aug. 15, 1778, ibid., 98, 96, 129, 134.

51. Sept. 5, July 13, 1778, ibid., 137, 132.

52. Paul Wentworth attributed this opinion to Benjamin Franklin in the fall of 1777 (Stevens, *Facsimiles*, no. 277).

53. John Adams to James Warren, May 3, 1777, to Mercy Otis Warren, Jan. 8, 1776, *WAL* 1:322, 202. It was this sort of expression Warren had in mind when she accused Adams, in her *History of the American Revolution*, of having subsequently retreated from a solidly antimonarchical position. See his testy response in a letter of July 20, 1807, *Warren Papers*, 332.

54. Arthur Lee to James Warren, Dec. 12, 1782, *WAL* 2:184; Samuel Adams to Elbridge Gerry, Nov. 27, 1780, in Austin, *Life of Gerry*, 362; John Adams to James Warren, Dec. 15, 1782, James Warren to John Adams, Oct. 7, 1782, *WAL* 2:187, 178.

55. James Warren to Samuel Adams, May 10, 1778, *WAL* 2:9; chevalier de Fleury, "Sommaire de l'Etat politique et militaire de l'amérique," Nov. 16, 1779, Stevens, *Facsimiles*, no. 1616.

56. *DCB*, s.v. "Hazen, Moses."

57. Lafayette to Vergennes, June 1, 1779, Stevens, *Facsimiles*, no. 1605. Lafayette referred to a letter from the president of Congress of Jan. 1, 1779.

58. George Washington to Henry Laurens, Nov. 14, 1778, Fitzpatrick, *Writings of Washington* 13:254–55. See also his formal letter to Congress of Nov. 11, ibid., 223–44.

59. "Protest of the General Officers of the Army in Rhode Island," Aug. 22, 1778, Sullivan Papers, 7:65–66, MHS. According to an American officer who afterwards went over to the British, d'Estaing had offended "even the Whigg Party of the Militia" while still at Newport. He "insisted on his Authority in the Island, with Intimations of the Cession of it to his Master" ("Notes of Information from Simon Philips," Stevens, *Facsimiles*, no. 530).

60. Gordon, *History* 3:197.

61. Ibid., 200. On d'Estaing's concern that he might not find enough food in Boston to supply his men, see ibid., 199.

62. Comte de Breugnon to Minister of the Marine, Oct. 10, 1778, Stevens, *Facsimiles*, no. 1974; Fitz-Henry Smith, "Memorial to the Chevalier de Saint-Sauveur," 34.

63. *Independent Ledger*, Sept. 14, 1778; General Court of Massachusetts Bay, vote of Sept. 16, 1778, reprinted in Fitz-Henry

Smith, "Memorial to the Chevalier de Saint-Sauveur," 36. The project was somehow forgotten, and the "monumental Stone" not installed in the yard of King's Chapel until 1917.

64. D'Estaing to Artemus Ward, President of the Massachusetts Council, Sept. 19, 1778, Ward Papers, MHS, P-209, reel 3.

65. Gordon, *History* 3:210; Fitz-Henry Smith, "Memorial to the Chevalier de Saint-Sauveur," 37.

66. James Warren to John Adams, Oct. 7, 1778, *WAL* 2:51; George Washington to William Heath, Sept. 22, 1778, *Heath Papers*, MHS, *Collections*, 5th ser., 4 (1878): 95; Gordon, *History* 3:164.

67. *Massachusetts Spy*, Sept. 30, 1779; Suffolk County Massachusetts Supreme Judicial Court, docket book, 1767–83, reel 5, Feb. 20, 1781. The other members of the jury were James Goodridge, Thomas Holland, Josiah Eliot, Thomas Nolen, Nathaniel Weld, Ebenezer Oliver, Archibald McNeill, Asa Stoddard, Samuel Downes, Norton Brailsford, and Uriah Oakes. I am indebted to Francis Cogliano for this reference.

68. See the Samuel Cooper Papers, HHL, especially his correspondence with La Luzerne and Louis Dominique Ethis de Corny.

69. La Luzerne to Cooper, Nov. 1, 1779, ibid.

70. *New York Gazette*, July 15, 1780, quoted in La Luzerne to Cooper, [July 1780], Cooper Papers, HHL.

71. Ibid.

72. Ibid.

## 5. THE GREATEST PRINCE ON EARTH

1. U.S. Continental Congress, *Observations on the American Revolution*, 72, 97; Samuel Cooper to Benjamin Franklin, May 13, 1778, Stevens, *Facsimiles*, no. 826; Gordon, *History* 3:81–82.

2. "To the Inhabitants of the United States," May 8, 1778, *JCC* 11:478.

3. "In Congress, May 6, 1778, Extract from the Minutes," *Exeter Journal or New-Hampshire Gazette*, June 2, 1778. The same issue reprinted Articles 6 through 29 of the treaty of alliance.

4. [André], "The American Times," in *Cow-Chace* 1:32.

5. Tulley, *An Almanack for 1695*. The "Account" ran to six pages. The calendar section noted only two historical anniversaries, King William's birthday on Nov. 4 and the Powder Plot on Nov. 5.

6. "Character of the French Nation," *New American Magazine*, Dec. 1759, 742.

7. See John Thayer's bitter complaint to Jeremy Belknap

(Thayer to Belknap, [ca. 1792], Belknap Papers, MHS), in which he takes Belknap to task for repeating this slur in his *History of New Hampshire*.

8. "The Impartial Politician," *New American Magazine*, Feb. 1759, 365.

9. Greene, "Diary"; [Daboll], *Freebetter's Connecticut Almanac for 1774*; "Why a Gardener Is the Most Extraordinary Man in the World—Addressed to a LADY," in Low, *An Astronomical Diary: or Almanack, for 1779*; Abigail Adams to Mercy Otis Warren, Sept. 5, 1784, *WAL* 2:242–43.

10. [Daboll], *Freebetter's Connecticut Almanack for 1774*.

11. Of more than a dozen New England almanacs for 1778 in the collection of the American Antiquarian Society, only one has a standard "Powder Plot 1605" entry on Nov. 5, Strong's *Connecticut Almanack for 1778*.

12. [West], *New-England Almanack for 1780*.

13. [West], *Bickerstaff's Boston Almanack for 1786*. In contrast, the Tory editor Samuel Stearns pointedly referred to Charles I as "Martyrd" rather than "Beheaded" on Jan. 30 and gave birth and other anniversary dates for King George, Queen Charlotte, and the Prince of Wales (Samuel Stearns [William Slygood, pseud.], *Universal Kalendar for 1784*).

14. "The Character of the French," in [Gleason], *Thomas's Massachusetts, New-Hampshire, and Connecticut Almanac for 1780*.

15. "Anecdote, from the French, of Marshall Montluc," in [West], *Bickerstaff's Boston Almanack for 1778*; "A Remarkable Anecdote of Humanity and True Heroism," in [West], *North-American Calendar for 1781*.

16. Strong, *An Astronomical Ephemeris, or Almanack for 1783*; "The Character of the French," in [Gleason], *Thomas's Massachusetts, New-Hampshire, and Connecticut Almanack for 1780*.

17. *Massachusetts Spy*, Sept. 23, 1779. See also *Continental Journal*, Sept. 9, 1779, and *New-Hampshire Gazette*, Sept. 21, 1779.

18. *Connecticut Courant*, Aug. 10, 1779; *Continental Journal*, Aug. 19, 1779.

19. *Massachusetts Spy*, Sept. 2, 1779. This sense of the alliance as a chance to garner greater respect for American cultural sophistication is clear in Samuel Cooper's correspondence with La Luzerne and especially with Louis Dominique Ethis de Corny. See, for example, Corny to Cooper, Sept. 27, 1780, Cooper Papers, HHL.

20. *Massachusetts Spy*, Sept. 16, 1779.

21. Ibid., Oct. 7, 1779.

22. Gordon, *History* 4:14.

23. *Massachusetts Spy*, July 6, 1780, Sept. 14, 1780, Dec. 19, 1782; Paine and Pope, *Paine Ancestry*, 25, 29.

24. *Massachusetts Spy*, June 11, 20, 13, 1782.

25. *Independent Ledger*, June 17, 1782. See also *Boston Gazette* of the same date.

26. *Independent Ledger*, June 17, 1782.

27. "An Address to the Inhabitants of the United States of America" and "State of New Hampshire. In the House of Representatives, June 17, 1779," *New-Hampshire Gazette*, July 6, 1779.

28. Charles Inglis attributed the editorship of this pamphlet to John Jay; it is the main target of his attacks in *Letters of Papinian*.

29. U.S. Continental Congress, *Observations on the American Revolution*, 2–3.

30. Ibid., 4.

31. *Pennsylvania Ledger*, May 13, 1778.

32. Greene, "Diary," May 10, 1778, 104. Franklin was "still so fond of the fair sex, that one was not enough for him but he must have one on each side, and all the ladies both old and young were ready to eat him up." Even so, Greene admitted, "I think him an honor to his country." He also approved of John Adams, despite an opposite objection to "the natural restraint which was always in his behaviour" (ibid., May 9, 1778, 103).

33. Ibid., May 10, 1778, 104–5.

34. Ibid., June 5–6, May 10, June 18, 27, 1778, 122, 105, 125–26, 127–28.

35. Ibid., June 18, 1778, 126.

36. John Adams to James Warren, Aug. 4, 1778, *WAL* 2:39–40.

37. Tappan, *Discourse Delivered at the 3rd Parish in Newbury*, 12; [Dwight], *Sermon Preached at Northampton*, 30.

38. *New-Hampshire Gazette*, June 23, 1778. On the Huguenots, see also Hannah Adams, *Alphabetical Compendium*, app., xxx. For the text of the treaty of alliance, which contains no such clause, see Parry, *Consolidated Treaty Series* 46:449–55.

39. Hannah Adams, *Alphabetical Compendium*, app., xxxii. See also Tappan, *Discourse Delivered at the 3rd Parish in Newbury*, 12. Joseph issued an edict in 1781 establishing the official toleration of all Christian sects and earlier suppressed hundreds of monasteries and convents.

40. Hannah Adams, *Alphabetical Compendium*, app., xxix–xxx; Cooper, *Man of Sin*, 46. For the Tory position before 1778, that

the pope did not in fact wield such influence, see [Barry], *General Attacked by a Subaltern*, 9.

41. Stiles, *United States Elevated to Glory*, 17–18, 53. Stiles pointed out encouragingly that the "re-establishment of the edict of nantz would honor the grand monarch by doing public justice to a large body of his best and most loyal subjects."

42. Gordon, *History* 4:243–44; see also *Massachusetts Spy*, July 18, 1782.

43. Tappan, *Discourse Delivered at the 3rd Parish in Newbury*, 12; Gordon, *History* 4:15. Gordon's account is copied from newspapers of the time.

44. "A Judgment of Don Pedro, King of Portugal, in a Case of Murder," in Low, *An Astronomical Diary: or, Almanack, for 1778*.

45. [Dwight], *Sermon Preached at Northampton*, 29; Hannah Adams, *Alphabetical Compendium*, app., xxxii–xxxiii, xxxvii.

46. For a typical expression of this belief, see *Scots Anticipation*, 16.

47. Dana, *Sermon Preached before the General Assembly*, 15.

48. Ibid.; Stiles, *United States Elevated to Glory*, 55.

49. Belknap to Reverend Louis de Rousselet, [after 1789], Belknap Papers, MHS; Mercy Otis Warren, *History of the American Revolution*, 682.

50. *Pennsylvania Ledger*, May 13, 1778.

51. [Samuel Johnson], *Hypocrisy Unmasked*, 10–11, 23n.

52. "A Description of the Antient Tories," in [Daboll], *New-England Almanack for 1777*.

53. On the Spanish Inquisition, see the extract from Gavin, *Master-Key to Popery*, in Low, *Astronomical Diary; or Almanack, for 1776*.

54. "The Providential Escape of the Protestants in Ireland from Queen Mary's Persecution," in [West], *Bickerstaff's New-England Almanack, for 1778*.

55. [Gleason], *Thomas's Massachusetts, New-Hampshire, and Connecticut Almanack for 1780*. The articles are on consecutive pages, and the titles of both appear in an advertisement for the almanac printed in the *Massachusetts Spy*, Oct. 28, 1779.

56. Champion, *Christian and Civil Liberty*, 18.

57. Charles Lee, "Strictures on a Pamphlet, Entitled 'A Friendly Address to All Reasonable Americans,' Addressed to the People of America," in [Barry], *General Attacked By a Subaltern*, 20. Of Chandler, author of the *Friendly Address to All Reasonable Ameri-*

*cans,* Lee remarked that "the moment a head begins to itch for a mitre, it loses the faculty of reasoning" (ibid., 16).

58. "The Last Will and Testament of Old England," *Connecticut Journal,* Aug. 4, 1779. The author was Thomas Waring, a Nova Scotia refugee.

59. Ambrose Searle to the Earl of Dartmouth, Nov. 8, 1776, Stevens, *Facsimiles,* no. 2045.

60. John Adams to William Tudor, Sept. 18, 1818, *Novanglus and Massachusettensis,* 308–9. The reference is to the practice of anointing bishops. Even at this late date, force of habit led Adams to see in the British impressment of American seamen the "miserable remnants of priestcraft and despotism" (ibid., 309).

61. Continental Congress, *Observations on the American Revolution,* 110; "To the Inhabitants of the United States," *JCC* 11:479.

62. "The Politicians," in [Daboll], *New-England Almanack for 1777.* The "Description of the Antient Tories" appeared in the same edition.

63. Gordon, "Doctrine of Transubstantiation," 13, 18; Tappan, *Discourse Delivered at the 3rd Parish in Newbury,* 12; John Lathrop, *Errors of Popery,* 17.

64. *Massachusetts Spy,* Oct. 19, 1780; "Satire," *Massachusetts Spy,* Nov. 9, 1780. On Arnold's effigy, see Shaw, *American Patriots and the Rituals of Revolution,* 221.

65. *Massachusetts Spy,* Dec. 6, 1780.

66. In the words of the Reverend Charles Inglis, a Tory: "To speak against Popery . . . would draw as severe persecution from many of the most zealous abettors of Congress, as to speak against Congress itself. They will not permit a word to be said to the disadvantage of Popery. In very many districts of the continent—and in some of New England—where Popery was formerly detested, and scarcely a Papist was to be seen, numbers of Popish books are now dispersed, and read with avidity" ([Inglis], *Letters of Papinian,* 70).

67. Strong, *Stafford's Almanack for 1781.*

68. John Adams to Mercy Otis Warren, April 16, 1776, *WAL* 1:222–23. "This Same Spirit of Commerce," he added, "is as rampant in New England as in any Part of the World. Trade is as well understood and as passionately loved there as any where."

69. "To the People of the United States of America," in *Observations on the American Revolution,* 77–78, 122.

70. John Adams, *Twenty-Six Letters,* 18, 49. Not only did the

French buy large quantities of supplies for their campaigns in America, they sold many of them back at low prices when they left. On the buyer's market for horses in Boston at the time of the French evacuation, see Samuel Pierce's diary entry for Dec. 8, 1782, in Dorchester Antiquarian and Historical Society, *History of the Town of Dorchester, Massachusetts*, 370.

71. James Warren to John Adams, Oct. 12, 1780, *WAL* 2: 140–41.

72. James Warren to Samuel Adams, May 10, 1778, ibid., 9.

73. Louis, comte de Barras, to Merchants of Boston, July 21, 1781, John Hancock to the Gentlemen Merchants of Boston, Oct. 14, 1781, Ezekiel Price Papers, MHS, reel P-43.

74. William Phillips, Chairman for the Merchants of Boston, to the marquis de Vaudreuil, Aug. 20, 1782, Vaudreuil to the Boston Merchants, Aug. 22, 1782, ibid.

75. Advertisements for freight or passage to and from France were common in Boston newspapers by 1782. See, among many other instances, the *Continental Journal*, Dec. 5, Dec. 12, 1782. For anticommercial Congregationalist breast-beating, see "An Address from the General Association of the State of Connecticut, Convened in Haddam, June 15, 1779," ibid., July 7, 1779.

76. *New-Haven Gazette*, Aug. 23, 1787, 212. The article is probably reprinted from a Boston paper.

77. Morse, *American Geography*, vii. Zimmermann's volume was published in London in 1787.

78. Morse, *American Geography*, 496–97.

79. Ibid., 86.

80. Ibid., 537.


## 6. ROMANISTS IN DISGUISE

1. Isaiah 8:12, in Devotion, *Duty and Interest*, 7.

2. Ibid., 8n, 13. Judah Champion had raised a similar objection to the invasion of Quebec from the same platform a year before. See his election sermon, *Christian and Civil Liberty*.

3. Howard, *Sermon Preached before the Honorable Council*, 47.

4. Dana, *Sermon Preached before the General Assembly*, 10. Dana was considerably more voluble on the subject of the "boundless ambition, pride, avarice and the intolerant spirit of persecution in the Romish clergy" (ibid., 44).

5. Cumings, *Sermon Preached before His Honor Thomas Cushing*, 31; Belknap, *Election Sermon*, 41. See also John Lathrop, *Discourse Preached on March the Fifth*, 17.

6. Matthew 15:6, in Wigglesworth, *Authority of Tradition*, 5.

7. Gordon, "Doctrine of Transubstantiation."

8. John Eliot to Jeremy Belknap, Sept. 5, 1781, *Belknap Papers*, 215.

9. Gordon, "Doctrine of Transubstantiation," 28.

10. Stiles, *United States Elevated to Glory*, 44, 40, 36; Dana, *Sermon Preached before the General Assembly*, 8.

11. "The Honest Politician," *Massachusetts Spy*, Oct. 7, 1779.

12. "A Breviate of Scriptural Prophecies," *United States Magazine* 1 (1779): 305. The reference is to verse 15: "And the serpent cast out of his mouth water as a flood after the woman, that he might cause her to be carried away of the flood." See also verses 16–17.

13. 2 Chronicles 36:22–23; Ezra 1:1–3, 6:2–5.

14. Payson, *Sermon Preached before the Honorable Council*, 30–31.

15. Clark, *Sermon Preached before His Excellency John Hancock*, 47–49 and note. Clark directed his readers to the promises recorded in Isaiah 44:28, 45:1–5, 13 and Jeremiah 29:10, 30:18–21.

16. Tappan, *Discourse Delivered at the 3rd Parish in Newbury*, 7, 14. The psalm served as Tappan's text. For another comparison to Cyrus, see John Murray, *Nehemiah*, 16, 50.

17. [Inglis], *Letters of Papinian*, 58.

18. For a discussion that ranges well beyond the intra-Congregationalist and Protestant-Catholic relations considered here, see Marini, *Radical Sects of Revolutionary New England*.

19. Belknap to the Town of Wakefield, June 30, 1783, *Belknap Papers*, 255–56. On the history of Universalism, see Robinson, *Unitarians and the Universalists*; Wright, *Beginnings of Unitarianism in America*.

20. *DAB*, s.v. "Murray, John"; *Salem Gazette*, Feb. 14, 1775; George Washington, General Orders, Sept. 17, 1775, Fitzpatrick, *Writings of Washington* 3:497.

21. Eliot, *Heralds of a Liberal Faith* 1:21. On Chauncy's ideas and career, see Griffin, *Old Brick*.

22. Chauncy, *All Nations Blessed in Christ*.

23. T. W. [Charles Chauncy], *Salvation for All Men*; Chauncy, *Mystery Hid from Ages*.

24. [Chauncy], *Salvation for All Men*, ii–iii.

25. John Eliot to Jeremy Belknap, Sept. 30, 1782, *Belknap Papers*, 236.

26. Griffin, *Old Brick*, 173–74.

27. Eliot to Belknap, Sept. 30, 1782, *Belknap Papers*, 236–37.

28. "A Treaty on Orthodoxy," in *Three Curious Pieces*, 19.

29. [Dwight], *Sermon Preached at Northampton*, 10, 26, 8.

30. Ibid., 8–9.

31. The ordination took place in New Braintree in October 1778. The text from Romans is, "For Christ is the end of the law for righteousness to every one that believeth." See Foster, *Defense of Religious Liberty*.

32. Foster, ordination sermon, Oct. 29, 1778, cited in Buckminster, *Brief Paraphrase upon Romans X*, 11–12.

33. Buckminster, *Brief Paraphrase upon Romans X*, 26, 43.

34. Ezra Stiles to——, Dec. 24, 1777, in Eddy, *Universalism in America* 1:162–65.

35. Murray held that the Parable of the Tares in Matthew 13 implied the final punishment of the sins themselves, not those who had committed them.

36. Chauncy, *Salvation for All Men*, ii–iii. On the Universalists' response to the charge that they encouraged libertinism, see Robinson, *Unitarians and the Universalists*, 53, 56–57.

37. "Address of the Late Rev. Mr. Chandler," in John Cleaveland, *An Attempt to Nip in the Bud*, 46.

38. Stephen Johnson, *Everlasting Punishment*, iii, 325. See the similar pronouncements on pp. 336, 342.

39. Buckminster, *Brief Paraphrase upon Romans X*, 66.

40. Margaret Mascarene Hutchinson to Margaret Holyoke Mascarene, April 16, 1785, Mascarene Family Papers, MHS, reel P-44.

41. Ibid., Aug. 16, 1785.

42. Ibid.

43. This had taken place the previous November, in 1788. See Merritt, "Sketches of the Three Earliest Roman Catholic Priests in Boston," 174–75.

44. Margaret Hutchinson to Margaret Mascarene, April 25, 1789, Mascarene Family Papers, MHS.

45. See Edmund Morgan's biography of Stiles, *Gentle Puritan*.

46. Stiles, *United States Elevated to Glory*, 76. On the following page Stiles cites Dr. Middleton's conclusion that "the speci-

fical worship, with a change of name only, is paid at rome to the modern canonized saints, as to the deified heroes of the antient romans and greeks."

47. Ibid., 54.

48. Ibid., 53–54. See also John Lathrop, *Discourse on the Peace*, 33n.

49. John Lathrop, *Errors of Popery*, 30.

50. Willard, "Persecution Opposite to the Genius of the Gospel," 47.

51. Gatchel, *Signs of the Times*, 6; [Dwight], *Sermon Preached at Northampton*, 29–30; Christopher Ebeling to Jeremy Belknap, April 28, 1798, *Belknap Papers*, 626.

52. Gordon, "Doctrine of Transubstantiation," 8; John Lathrop, *Errors of Popery*, 7, 22, 29.

53. Zabdiel Adams, *Sermon Preached before His Excellency, John Hancock*, 41–42; John Lathrop, *Errors of Popery*, 7.

54. Stiles, *United States Elevated to Glory*, 55–56; Belknap to Louis de Rousselet, ca. 1790, Belknap Papers, MHS, reel 6.

55. Willard, "Persecution Opposite to the Spirit of the Gospel," 19. George Washington expressed the same feeling on several occasions. See the glowing account of his liberality in the *Gazette Françoise*, Dec. 30, 1780. See also his farewell message to the thirteen state governors and his address to the American Catholics, Fitzpatrick, *Writings of Washington* 26:485, 31:22n.

56. Willard, "Persecution," 1, 5.

57. Ibid., 44, 45, 52–54.

58. Ibid., 13, 49.

59. *New Jersey Gazette*, Dec. 5, 1777.

60. *Massachusetts Spy*, Aug. 31, 1780.

61. Ibid., Sept. 7, 14, 1780; *Gazette Françoise*, Nov. 30, 1780.

62. Cooper to La Luzerne, Aug. 17, 1780, Samuel Cooper Papers, HHL. I am indebted to Francis Cogliano for this reference.

63. John Adams to Mercy Otis Warren, June 23, 1780, *WAL* 2:133.

64. *Massachusetts Spy*, Sept. 28, 1780.

65. John Adams to James Warren, Aug. 4, 1778, *WAL* 2:40.

66. Mercy Otis Warren, *History of the American Revolution*, 337. The quoted passage appears in Warren's discussion of the Gordon Riots. On Warren, see Zagarri, *Woman's Dilemma*.

67. Mercy Otis Warren, *History of the American Revolution*, 11. For a similar view from the pulpit, see Zabdiel Adams, *Sermon Preached before His Excellency*, 41–42.

68. Mercy Otis Warren, *History of the American Revolution*, 11–12.

69. Hannah Adams, *Summary History of New-England*, 94, 102–3. On later attempts to deal with Calvin's troublesome legacy, see Davis, "Images of Intolerance."

70. Morse, *American Geography*, 146. On Morse, see Phillips, *Jedidiah Morse*; Wright, "The Controversial Career of Jedidiah Morse," in *Unitarian Controversy*, 59–82.

71. Morse, *American Geography*, 146–47. For Hannah Adams's assessment of this risk, see *Summary History of New-England*, 12.

72. Morse, *American Geography*, 146.


## 7. COMING TO TERMS

1. *Herald of Freedom*, Oct. 30, 1788.

2. Belknap to Ebenezer Hazard, Dec. 7, 1780, *Belknap Papers*, 240–41.

3. John Lathrop, *Errors of Popery*, 30. The lecture was given until 1910. See Ray, *American Opinion of Roman Catholicism*, 380n.

4. "Bob Short's Reasons for Being a Papist," *Massachusetts Centinel*, Oct. 1, 1788. The same item appeared in the *Massachusetts Magazine*, July 1793, 391, and the *New-Hampshire Magazine*, Sept. 1793, 256.

5. *Courier de Boston*, April 23, 1789.

6. François de la E——[pseud.] to Pierre Dubois, *Herald of Freedom*, Dec. 22, 1788.

7. The deceased was Breckvelt de Larive, the treasurer of Guadeloupe. Articles on the affair appeared in the *Boston Gazette*, Nov. 8, 1790, *Independent Chronicle*, Nov. 11, 1790, and *Columbian Centinel*, Nov. 10, 24, Dec. 1, and esp. Dec. 4, 1790.

8. Belknap to Ebenezer Hazard, Dec. 7, 1790, *Correspondence between Belknap and Hazard, Part 2*, 240–41.

9. John Eliot, June 6, 1791, quoted in Merritt, "Sketches of the Three Earliest Roman Catholic Priests in Boston," 206. Two nights later, Eliot "dined with Bp. Carroll at Dr. Parkers."

10. Pierre Dubois to François de la E——, *Herald of Freedom*, Oct. 2, 1788.

11. Locke, *Letter concerning Toleration*, 89–91.

12. Handlin and Handlin, *Popular Sources of Political Authority*, 853, 491, 419. See also the petitions of Holden and Northbridge, ibid., 738, 847.

13. Ibid., 711–12, 686, 738. Article 4 is reprinted on p. 443.

14. Ibid., 660–61.

15. Compare the explanations in ibid.; Levy, *Establishment Clause*; Thomas Curry, *First Freedoms*; Carter, *Culture of Disbelief*. The last two authors are especially attentive to the role of anti-Catholic ideology as against sheer numbers. See ibid., 298n.

16. Levy, *Establishment Clause*, 34. For a different interpretation of events in 1820, see John T. Noonan, "A Quota of Imps," in Peterson and Vaughan, *Virginia Statute for Religious Freedom*.

17. Quoted by Noonan, "Quota of Imps," in Peterson and Vaughan, *Virginia Statute for Religious Freedom*, 181–82.

18. The story of the gradual disestablishment in Massachusetts is well told in Noonan, ibid., and Wright, "The Dedham Case Revisited," in *Unitarian Controversy*, 111–35. See also Levy, *Establishment Clause*.

19. Carter, *Culture of Disbelief*, 96.

20. John Adams to Mercy Otis Warren, July 20, 1807, *Warren Papers*, 350.

21. Stiles, *History of Three of the Judges of Charles I*, 338.

22. Ibid., 112.

23. Ibid., 108–10. Goffe, who had been a general in Cromwell's army, did emerge from hiding on one memorable occasion to direct the defense of the Hadley church when Indians attacked during a service at the time of King Philip's War in 1675. Since his presence was kept secret from the townspeople until Russell's death in 1692, this apparition spawned rumors that a ghost had saved the town.

24. Ibid., 244. Stiles admitted that he wrote "more from the result and recollection of former reading, than from recent reviews of the histories."

25. Ibid., 247. Stiles had used the same phrase to describe the late Pope Clement XIV in his Connecticut election sermon of 1783, *United States Elevated to Glory*, 36.

26. Stiles, *History of Three of the Judges of Charles I*, 244, 252, 256.

27. Ibid., 245, 255.

28. Ibid., 253. This was a dig at the hardline anti-Universalists. After quoting from a biographical account of Cromwell's policies of religious toleration, Stiles remarked, "Ideas, how just, liberal and noble! how becoming the dignity and benevolence of the head and father of a republic!" (ibid., 255).

29. Ibid., 245, 246.

30. Ibid., 242–43.

31. Ibid., 242, 244. Stiles listed Hollis, Hale, Barnet, and Locke as his main influences in this regard.

32. Ibid.

33. Ibid., 318, 337, 319.

34. Ibid., 318, 337, 319, 321. Stiles went on to explain that "whether this was owing to his contemplation of the abstract principles of government, . . . to his view of the comparatively happy government of England in his vicinity, or to the principles of the American revolution, or to all these collectively, so it was, that he wished . . . to govern with lenity and wisdom." This is the same image of Louis as a frustrated reformer that Jedidiah Morse had offered in his 1789 edition of the *American Geography*.

35. Stiles, *History of Three of the Judges of Charles I*, 321, 315.

36. Ibid., 308, 314.

37. Ibid., 335.

38. Quoted in Morgan, *Gentle Puritan*, 456.

39. Stiles to Jacob Richardson, July 9, 1794, in ibid., 456–57.

40. The Quebec Expedition and the French Alliance proved awkward topics for historians of the Revolution right from the start. On Quebec, see Williams, *History of the American Revolution*, 32; Gordon, *History* 1:407; Mercy Otis Warren, *History of the American Revolution*, 82–83; Hannah Adams, *Summary History of New-England*, 283; Pitkin, *History of the United States* 1:293. On the French Alliance, see Williams, *History of the American Revolution*, 15; Lendrum, *History of the American Revolution* 2:191; Hannah Adams, *Summary History of New-England*, 398; Gordon, *History* 2:240–43; Belknap, *History of New Hampshire* 2:403; Holmes, *American Annals* 1:344.

41. Morgan, *Gentle Puritan*, 346–47.

42. Dwight, *Travels in New England and New York* 1:72–73, 256–57.

43. Nash, "American Clergy and the French Revolution"; May, *Enlightenment in America*, 252–77.

44. Leland, *Writings*, 73. Compare the French Protestant Pierre Bayle, *Philosophical Commentary on the Words of Jesus Christ, "Compel Them to Come In"* (1687).

45. Leland, "The Yankee Spy," 1794, *Writings*, 220.

46. Ibid., 223. This discussion follows Thomas Curry, *First Freedoms*.

47. Leland, "The Rights of Conscience Inalienable," 1791, *Writings*, 187.

48. Leland, "Yankee Spy," ibid., 226

49. Leland, "A Blow at the Root," 1801, ibid., 253. For Leland's opinion of Jefferson and Madison, see ibid., 255.

50. Leland, "Address to the Massachusetts House of Representatives," 1811, ibid., 357.

51. Leland, "Oration . . . on the Celebration of Independence," 1802, ibid., 259.

52. Dwight, *Travels in New England and New York* 4:51, 1:307, 2:314.

53. Ibid., 2:342–43, 4:169, 1:105, 109, 2:42.

54. Ibid., 2:42, 1:105. Dwight repeats the charge of conversion by kidnapping on 2:57.

55. Ibid., 1:251, 3:375–76.

56. Ibid., 1:214n. These remarks of Dwight's shed an interesting light on the praise a reviewer bestowed on the *Travels* for its "truly catholic liberality of sentiments" regarding religion. The review, quoted in Barbara Solomon's introduction to the *Travels*, appeared in the *Christian Spectator*, no. 4 (1822), 145–51.

57. Dwight, *Travels in New England and New York* 1:214n.

58. The letters on this topic, completed in 1816, are in vol. 4 of ibid. For their date, see 4:275n.

59. Ibid., 4:177.

60. Ibid., 258–59.

61. Ibid., 259, 261.

62. Ibid., 4:261, 3:30, 4:259. Compare his *Sermon Preached at Northampton*.

63. Dwight, *Travels in New England and New York* 4:260–61.

64. Ibid., 260, 263–64.

65. Ibid., 264, 267–68, 273.

66. Ibid., 266–67; Marsden, *Fundamentalism and American Culture*, 148–50.

67. Dwight, *Travels in New England and New York* 4:266.

68. Ibid., 266, 269, 271–72. Underscoring the role of the Protestant quasi-establishments, Dwight pointedly excluded Rhode Island from such praise. Just to look at that state and compare it to Connecticut would convince "a sober man . . . , whatever may have been his original position . . . , that a legislature is bound to establish the public worship of God" (ibid., 291).

69. Ibid., 274–75; Solomon, introduction, ibid., 1:xlii.

70. Elkins and McKitrick, *Age of Federalism*, chap. 8.

71. See Cushing Strout's discussion of Senator James Blaine's promotion of a new constitutional amendment in 1876 (Strout,

"Jeffersonian Religious Liberty and American Pluralism," in Peterson and Vaughan, *Virginia Statute for Religious Freedom*, 215).

72. Parrington, *Colonial Mind, 1620–1800*.

73. Rorty, "The Priority of Democracy to Philosophy," in Peterson and Vaughan, *Virginia Statute*, 267.

# Bibliography

## MANUSCRIPTS

Harvard University Archives, Cambridge, Mass.
  Gordon, William. "The Doctrine of Transubstantiation Considered and Refuted in a Discourse Preached at the Dudleian Lecture, Cambridge, September 5, 1781." Manuscript sermon.
  Willard, Joseph. "Persecution Opposite to the Genius of the Gospel." Dudleian Lecture, Sept. 7, 1785. Manuscript sermon.
Henry E. Huntington Library, San Marino, Calif.
  Brock Collection
  Cooper, Samuel, Papers
Massachusetts Historical Society, Boston
  Belknap, Jeremy, Papers
  Caryl, Benjamin, Papers
  Coffin Collection
  Gardiner Correspondence
  Gerry-Knight Papers
  Heath, William, Papers
  Lathrop, Joseph. "On 'Revelation,'" c. 1760. Manuscript sermon.
  Mascarene Family Papers
  Miscellaneous manuscripts
  Pickering Papers
  Price, Ezekiel, Papers
  Smith, Justin H., Transcripts
  Sullivan Papers
  Ward, Artemus, Papers
National Archives, Washington, D.C.
  Continental Congress Papers. Microfilm.

National Archives of Canada, Ottawa
  [Briand, Jean-Olivier, et al.]. "Mandements [des] Mgrs. Briand, d'Esgly, Hubert, Denaut, Plessis, [et] Panet, 1762–1833." Microfilm, reel M-298.
  Colquhoun, Alexander. "An Account and Transaction of a Voyage to Quebec . . . on Board of a Man-of-War in . . . 1777."
  H[azen], M[oses]. Letter to Charles Carroll, et al., May 24, 1776, La Prairie. Microfilm, reel A-652.
  Verreau Collection
Suffolk County Supreme Judicial Court, Boston
  Docket book, 1767–83


## NEWSPAPERS AND ALMANACS

*Almon's Remembrancer.* London.
*Columbian Centinel.* Boston.
*Connecticut Courant.* Hartford.
*Connecticut Journal.* New Haven.
*Continental Journal and Weekly Advertiser.* Boston.
*Courier de Boston.*
[Daboll, Nathan], ed. *Freebetter's Connecticut Almanack.* New London, 1771–73.
[——]. *Freebetter's New-England Almanack.* New London, Conn., 1772–91.
*Essex Journal.* Boston.
*Exeter Journal or New Hampshire Gazette.* Exeter.
*Gazette Françoise.* Newport, R.I.
George, Daniel, ed. *Almanack.* Newburyport, Mass., and Boston, 1782–86.
——. *George's Cambridge Almanack, or The Essex Calendar.* Salem, Mass., 1774–75.
[Gleason, Ezra], ed. *Thomas's Almanack.* Boston, 1779–81.
*Herald of Freedom.* Boston.
*Independent Chronicle.* Boston.
*Independent Ledger and American Advertiser.* Boston.
Low, Nathaniel, ed. *An Astronomical Diary: or, Almanack.* Boston, 1774–82.
*Massachusetts Centinel.* Boston.
*Massachusetts Gazette and Boston Weekly News-Letter.*
*Massachusetts Magazine.* Boston.
*Massachusetts Spy or American Oracle of Liberty.* Worcester, Mass.

*New American Magazine*. Woodbridge, N.J.
*New Hampshire Gazette, or State Journal, and General Advertiser*. Portsmouth.
*New Hampshire Magazine*. Concord.
*New Haven Gazette and the Connecticut Magazine*.
*New Jersey Gazette*. Burlington and Trenton.
*New York Gazetteer*. New York City.
*Pennsylvania Packet*. Philadelphia.
Slygood, William [Samuel Stearns], ed. *The Universal Kalendar*. New York, 1782–83.
Stearns, Samuel, ed. *The North American's Almanack*. Worcester, Mass., 1774–76.
Strong, Nehemiah, ed. *An Astronomical Ephemeris, Kalendar, or Almanack*. New Haven, 1775–88.
——. *The Connecticut Almanack*. Hartford, 1777–84.
——. *Stafford's Almanack*. New Haven, 1780.
Tulley, John, ed. *An Almanack for 1695*. Boston.
*United States Magazine*. Philadelphia.
[West, Benjamin], ed. *Bickerstaff's Boston Almanack*. Boston, 1774–85.
[——]. *Bickerstaff's New-England Almanack*. Providence, R.I., and Norwich, Conn., 1774–82.
[——]. *The North-American Calendar*. Providence, 1780.
*Worcester Magazine*. Worcester, Mass.

## BOOKS AND OTHER PRINTED SEPARATES

Adams, Hannah. *An Alphabetical Compendium of the Various Sects Which Have Appeared in the World*. Boston, 1784. Evans no. 18319.
——. *A Summary History of New-England, from the First Settlement at Plymouth, to the Acceptance of the Federal Constitution*. Dedham, Mass., 1799. Evans no. 35075.
Adams, John. *Twenty-Six Letters, upon Interesting Subjects, respecting the Revolution of America*. [New York, 1789]. Evans no. 21624.
[Adams, John, and Daniel Leonard]. *Novanglus and Massachusettensis*. Boston, 1819.
Adams, Thomas R. *The American Controversy*. 2 vols. Providence, 1980.
Adams, Zabdiel. *Brotherly Love and Compassion*. Worcester, Mass., 1778. Evans no. 15716.

——. *The Grounds of Confidence and Success in War, Represented.* Boston, 1775. Evans no. 13788.

——. *A Sermon Preached before His Excellency John Hancock.* [Boston, 1782]. Evans no. 17450.

*Address to the Soldiers.* Salem, [1775]. Broadside, Massachusetts Historical Society.

*Advices from St. John's.* [Cambridge, Mass.] Nov. 15, 1775. Broadside. Evans no. 42762.

Akers, Charles. *The Divine Politician: Samuel Cooper and the American Revolution in Boston.* Boston, 1982.

Alden, John. *A History of the American Revolution.* New York, 1969.

*America Invincible: An Heroic Poem.* Danvers, Mass., 1779. Evans no. 16185.

Ammerman, David. *In the Common Cause: American Response to the Coercive Acts of 1774.* Charlottesville, Va., 1974.

[André, John]. *Cow-Chace, in Three Cantos.* New York, 1780. Evans no. 16697.

Annan, Robert. *Brief Animadversions on the Doctrine of Universal Salvation.* Philadelphia, 1787. Evans no. 20203.

Arnold, Benedict. *Proclamation.* [New York], Oct. 20, 1780. Evans no. 16789.

——. *To the Inhabitants of America.* [New York], Oct. 7, 1780. Evans no. 16701.

Aubert de Gaspé, Philippe. *Les anciens canadiens.* 1864; rept., Montreal, 1967.

Austin, James T. *The Life of Elbridge Gerry.* 1828–29, rept., New York, 1970.

*Authentic Narrative of the Facts Relating to the Exchange of Prisoners at the Cedars.* London, 1777.

Avery, David. *The Lord Is to Be Praised.* Norwich, Conn., 1778. Evans no. 15726.

Bailyn, Bernard, ed. *The Debates on the Constitution.* 2 vols. New York, 1993.

Barber, Daniel. *The History of My Own Times.* 2 pts. Washington, D.C., 1827–28.

[Barry, Henry]. *The General Attacked by a Subaltern: or, The Strictures on the Friendly Address Examined.* New York, [1775]. Evans no. 13824.

[Beaumarchais, Pierre]. *Observations on the Justificative Memorial.* Philadelphia, 1781. Evans no. 17093.

Belknap, Jeremy. *An Election Sermon, Preached at Portsmouth.* Portsmouth, N.H., 1785. Evans no. 18927.

——. *History of New Hampshire.* 3 vols. Boston, 1792. Evans nos. 24087–88.

[Belknap, Jeremy, and Ebenezer Hazard]. *Correspondence between Jeremy Belknap and Ebenzer Hazard: Part 2.* Massachusetts Historical Society, *Collections*, 5th ser., 3 (1877).

*Belknap Papers.* Massachusetts Historical Society, *Collections*, 6th ser., 4 (1891).

Bemis, Samuel Flagg. *The Diplomacy of the American Revolution.* Bloomington, Ind., 1957.

Ben Saddi, Nathan [Robert Dodsley]. *The Chronicle of the Kings of England.* 1740; rept., Norwich, Conn., 1773. Evans no. 12755.

Billings, William. *The New-England Psalm-Singer.* Boston, [1770]. Evans no. 11572.

Billington, Ray. *The Protestant Crusade: A Study of the Origins of American Nativism.* New York, 1952.

Bloch, Ruth. *Visionary Republic: Millennial Themes in American Thought, 1756–1800.* Cambridge, Mass., 1985.

Bonomi, Patricia. *Under the Cope of Heaven: Religion, Society, and Politics in Colonial America.* New York, 1986.

Brackenridge, H[ugh] H[enry]. *Gazette Publications.* Carlisle, Pa., 1806.

Bradford, William. *Of Plymouth Plantation.* New York, 1981.

[Breck, Samuel]. *Recollections of Samuel Breck.* Philadelphia, 1877.

Bridenbaugh, Carl. *Mitre and Sceptre: Transatlantic Faiths, Ideas, Personalities, and Politics.* New York, 1962.

Buckminster, Joseph [1720–1792]. *A Brief Paraphrase upon Romans X.* Worcester, Mass., 1779. Evans no. 16215.

Burnett, Edmund C., ed. *Letters of Members of the Continental Congress.* 8 vols. Washington, D.C., 1921–36.

Bushman, Richard. *From Puritan to Yankee: Character and the Social Order in Connecticut, 1690–1765.* Cambridge, Mass., 1967.

Butler, John. *Index, The Papers of the Continental Congress, 1774–1789.* 5 vols. Washington, D.C., 1978.

Butler, Jon. *Awash in a Sea of Faith: Christianizing the American People.* Cambridge, Mass., 1990.

——. *The Huguenots in America.* Cambridge, Mass., 1983.

Butterfield, L. H., Marc Friedlaender, and Mary-Jo Kline, eds. *The Book of Abigail and John: Selected Letters of the Adams Family, 1762–1784.* Cambridge, Mass., 1975.

*Calendrier français, pour l'année commune 1781.* Newport, [1780]. Evans no. 17110.

Carroll, Charles. *Journal of Charles Carroll of Carrollton, during His Visit to Canada in 1776.* Ed. Brantz Mayer et al. Baltimore, 1876.

Carter, Stephen L. *The Culture of Disbelief: How American Law and Politics Trivialize Religious Devotion.* New York, 1993.

Champion, Judah. *Christian and Civil Liberty and Freedom Considered.* Hartford, 1776. Evans no. 14675.

[Chandler, Thomas]. *The Friendly Address to All Reasonable Americans.* New York, 1774. Evans no. 13226.

[————]. *What Think Ye of the Congress Now?* New York, 1775. Evans no. 13866.

Chauncy, Charles. *All Nations Blessed in Christ.* Boston, 1762. Evans no. 9088.

————. *The Mystery Hid from Ages: or, The Salvation of All Men.* London, 1784.

[————]. *Salvation for All Men, Illustrated and Vindicated as a Scriptural Doctrine.* Boston, 1782. Evans no. 17489.

Clark, Jonas. *A Sermon Preached before His Excellency John Hancock, Esq.* Boston, 1781. Evans no. 17114.

Clarke, Samuel. *The American Wonder: or, The New-England Vision of the Night.* Salem, Mass., 1776. Evans no. 14681.

Cleaveland, John. *An Attempt to Nip in the Bud the Unscriptural Doctrine of Universal Salvation.* Salem, Mass., 1776. Evans no. 14684.

————. *An Essay to Defend Some of the Most Important Principles in the Protestant Reformed System of Christianity.* Boston, 1763. Evans no. 9364.

————. *A Reply to Dr. Mayhew's Letter of Reproof.* Boston, 1765. Evans no. 9932.

Coffin, Victor. *The Province of Quebec and the Early American Revolution.* Univ. of Wisconsin, *Bulletin,*Economics, Political Science, and History Series, 1:3 (1896).

Cogliano, Francis. *"No King! No Popery!": Anti-Catholicism in Revolutionary New England.* Westport, Conn., 1995.

Cohen, Lester. *The Revolutionary Histories: Contemporary Narratives of the American Revolution.* Ithaca, N.Y., 1980.

*A Collection of the Acts Passed in the Parliament of Great Britain and of Other Public Acts Relative to Canada.* Quebec City, 1824.

*Considerations on the French and American War.* London, [1779].

Cooper, Samuel. *A Discourse on the Man of Sin.* Boston, 1774. Evans no. 13227.

Countryman, Edward. *The American Revolution.* New York, 1985.

Cumings, Henry. *A Sermon Preached before His Honor Thomas Cushing, Esq.* Boston, 1783. Evans no. 17899.

Curry, Richard, and Thomas Brown, eds. *Conspiracy: The Fear of Subversion in American History.* New York, 1972.

Curry, Thomas. *The First Freedoms: Church and State in America to the Passage of the First Amendment.* New York, 1986.

[Dalrymple, Sir John]. *The Address of the People of Great-Britain to the Inhabitants of America.* London, 1775.

Dana, James. *A Sermon Preached before the General Assembly of the State of Connecticut.* Hartford, 1779. Evans no. 16252.

Davidson, Philip. *Propaganda and the American Revolution, 1763–1783.* Chapel Hill, N.C., 1941.

Demos, John. *The Unredeemed Captive: A Family Story from Early America.* New York, 1994.

Devotion, John. *The Duty and Interest of a People.* Hartford, 1777. Evans no. 15285.

Deux Ponts, Guillaume, comte de. *Mes campagnes d'Amérique.* Ed. Samuel Abbott Green. Boston, 1868.

Dexter, Franklin Bowditch. *Biographical Sketches of the Graduates of Yale College.* 6 vols. New York, 1896.

Dorchester Antiquarian and Historical Society. *History of the Town of Dorchester, Massachusetts.* Boston, 1859.

Drayton, John. *Memoirs of the American Revolution.* 2 vols. Charleston, S.C., 1821.

Dull, Jonathan. *A Diplomatic History of the American Revolution.* New Haven, 1985.

[Dwight, Timothy]. *A Sermon, Preached at Northampton . . . Occasioned by the Capture of the British Army, under the Command of Earl Cornwallis.* Hartford, [1781]. Evans no. 17144.

——. *Travels in New England and New York.* 4 vols. 1822; rept., with an introduction by Barbara Solomon, Cambridge, Mass., 1969.

Eccles, W. J. *France in America.* New York, 1972.

[Eckley, Joseph]. *Divine Glory, Brought to View, in the Condemnation of the Ungodly.* Boston, 1782. Evans no. 17524.

Eddy, Richard. *Universalism in America.* 2 vols. Boston, 1891.

Eden, William. *Four Letters to the Earl of Carlisle.* London, 1779.

Edwards, Jonathan. *The Salvation of All Men Strictly Examined: and, The Endless Punishment of Those Who Die Impenitent, Argued.* New Haven, 1790. Evans no. 22478.

Eliot, Samuel, ed. *Heralds of a Liberal Faith.* 3 vols. Boston, 1910.

Elkins, Stanley, and Eric McKitrick. *The Age of Federalism*. New York, 1993.

Ellis, John Tracy. *Catholics in Colonial America*. Baltimore, 1965.

Erskine, John. *Considerations on the Spirit of Popery, and the Intended Bill for the Relief of Papists in Scotland*. Edinburgh, 1778.

[——]. *Reflections on the Rise, Progress, and Probable Consequences of the Present Contentions with the Colonies*. Edinburgh, [1776].

Estaing, Charles Hector, comte d'. *Déclaration adressée au nom du roi à tous les anciens françois de l'Amérique septentrionale*. Boston, Oct. 28, 1778. Broadside. Evans no. 43452.

Everest, Allan. *Moses Hazen and the Canadian Refugees in the American Revolution*. Syracuse, N.Y., 1976.

Fitzpatrick, John, ed. *Writings of George Washington from the Original Manuscript Sources, 1745–1799*. 39 vols. Washington, D.C., 1931–44.

Forbes, Allan, and Paul Cadman. *France and New England*. 3 vols. Boston, 1925–29.

Force, Peter, ed. *American Archives*. 4th ser. Washington, D.C., 1837–46.

Ford, W. C., ed. *Journals of the Continental Congress*. 34 vols. Washington, D.C., 1904–37.

——. *Writings of George Washington*. 14 vols. New York, 1889–93.

Foster, Isaac. *A Defense of Religious Liberty*. Worcester, Mass., 1780. Evans no. 16775.

Fraser, Antonia. *Cromwell: The Lord Protector*. New York, 1973.

Franchot, Jenny. *Roads to Rome: The Protestant Encounter with Catholicism, 1830–1860*. Berkeley, Calif., 1994.

Galloway, Joseph. *A Candid Examination of the Mutual Claims of Great-Britain and the Colonies*. [1775]; rept., London, [1780].

——. *Historical and Political Reflections on the Rise and Progress of the American Rebellion*. London, 1780.

[——]. *A Reply to An Address to the Author of a Pamphlet, Entitled, A Candid Examination of the Mutual Claims. . . .* New York, 1775. Evans no. 14060.

Gardiner, C. Harvey, ed. *A Study in Dissent: The Warren-Gerry Correspondence, 1776–1792*. Carbondale, Ill., 1968.

Gatchel, Samuel. *Signs of the Times*. Danvers, Mass., 1781. Evans no. 17169.

Gaustad, Edwin S. *Faith of Our Fathers: Religion and the New Nation*. San Francisco, 1987.

Gavin, Antonio. *The Great Red Dragon: or, The Master-Key to Popery*. 1724; rept., Newport, R.I., 1773. Evans no. 12784.

[Gibbon, Edward]. *Memoire justificatif pour servir de réponse à l'exposé, &c., de la cour de France*. London, 1779.

Gordon, William. *The Doctrine of Final Universal Salvation Examined and Shewn to Be Unscriptural*. Boston, 1783. Evans no. 17959.

——. *The History of the Rise, Progress, and Establishment, of the Independence of the United States of America*. 4 vols. London, 1788.

——. *A Sermon Preached before the Honorable House of Representatives*. Watertown, Mass., 1775. Evans no. 14073.

[Gray, Harrison]. *The Two Congresses Cut Up*. 1774; rept., New York, [1775]. Evans no. 13698.

[Green, Jacob]. *Observations on the Reconciliation*. New York, 1776. Evans no. 14790.

Griffin, Edward. *Old Brick: Charles Chauncy of Boston, 1705–1787*. Minneapolis, 1980.

Halpenny, Frances G., et al., eds. *Dictionary of Canadian Biography*. 12 vols. Toronto, 1983.

Handlin, Oscar and Mary, eds. *The Popular Sources of Political Authority: Documents on the Massachusetts Constitution of 1780*. Cambridge, Mass., 1966.

Hatch, Nathan O. *The Democratization of American Christianity*. New Haven, 1989.

——. *The Sacred Cause of Liberty: Republican Thought and the Millennium in Revolutionary New England*. New Haven, 1977.

Hazard, Ebenezer. *Historical Collections . . . for an History of the United States of America*. 2 vols. Philadelphia, 1792.

Headley, Joel T. *The Chaplains and Clergy of the Revolution*. Springfield, Mass., 1861.

Heimert, Alan. *Religion and the American Mind: From the Great Awakening to the Revolution*. Cambridge, Mass., 1966.

Hoffman, Ronald, and Peter J. Albert, eds. *Religion in a Revolutionary Age*. Charlottesville, Va., 1994.

Holmes, Abiel. *American Annals*. 2 vols. Cambridge, Mass., 1805.

Howard, Simeon. *A Sermon Preached before the Honorable Council*. Boston, 1780. Evans no. 16800.

Huntington, Joseph. *Calvinism Improved; or, The Gospel Illustrated as a System of Real Grace, Issuing in the Salvation of All Men*. New London, Conn., 1796. Evans no. 30609.

[Inglis, Charles]. *Letters of Papinian*. New York, 1779. Evans no. 16311.

Jensen, Merrill. *The Founding of a Nation: A History of the American Revolution, 1763–1776*. New York, 1968.

Jingle, Bob [pseud.]. *The Association, &c., of the Delegates . . . Versified.* [New York], 1774. Evans no. 13355.

[Johnson, Samuel]. *Hypocrisy Unmasked; or, A Short Inquiry into the Religious Complaints of Our American Colonies.* 3d ed. London, 1776.

———. *The Patriot.* 2d ed. London, 1774.

Johnson, Stephen. *The Everlasting Punishment of the Ungodly, Illustrated.* New London, Conn., 1786. Evans no. 19737.

Jones, David. *Defensive War in a Just Cause Sinless.* Philadelphia, 1775. Evans no. 14133.

Jones, Michael Wynn. *Cartoon History of the American Revolution.* New York, [1975].

Ketchum, Silas, ed. *The Shurtleff Manuscript, no. 153: A Diary of the Invasion of Canada, 1775.* New Hampshire Antiquarian Society, *Collections* 2 (1876).

Keteltas, Abraham. *God Arising and Pleading.* Newburyport, Mass., 1777. Evans no. 15378.

Kingston, John. *The Life of General George Washington.* Baltimore, 1813.

Kling, David. *A Field of Divine Wonders: The New Divinity and Village Revivals in Northwestern Connecticut, 1792–1822.* University Park, Pa., 1993.

Koch, Adrienne, and William Peden, eds. *The Selected Writings of John and John Quincy Adams.* New York, 1946.

Kramnick, Isaac, and R. Laurence Moore. *The Godless Constitution: The Case against Religious Correctness.* New York, 1996.

Kuklick, Bruce. *Churchmen and Philosophers from Jonathan Edwards to John Dewey.* New Haven, 1985.

Lanctot, Gustave. *Canada et la revolution américaine.* Montreal, 1965; rept., trans. Margaret M. Cameron, Cambridge, Mass., 1967.

Langdon, Samuel. *The Republic of the Israelites an Example to the American States.* Exeter, N.H., 1788. Evans no. 21192.

Lathrop, John. *A Discourse on the Errors of Popery.* Boston, 1793. Evans no. 25703.

———. *A Discourse on the Peace.* Boston, 1784. Evans no. 18551.

———. *A Discourse Preached . . . in Thanksgiving.* Boston, 1774. Evans no. 13370.

———. *A Discourse Preached on March the Fifth, 1778.* Boston, 1778. Evans no. 15866.

Leland, John. *Writings of John Leland.* Ed. L. F. Greene. 1845, rept., New York, 1969.

Lendrum, John. *A Concise and Impartial History of the American Revolution.* 2 vols. Boston, 1795. Evans no. 28963.

[Leonard, Daniel]. *Massachusettensis.* [Boston, 1775]. Evans no. 14157.

*A Letter to the Author of Divine Glory Brought to View, in the Condemnation and Punishment of the Ungodly.* [Boston, 1783]. Evans no. 19420.

*A Letter to the People of Great Britain from the Delagates of the American Congress in Philadelphia.* London, [1774].

Levy, Leonard. *The Establishment Clause: Religion and the First Amendment.* New York, 1986.

Locke, John. *A Letter concerning Toleration.* Ed. M. Montuori. The Hague, 1963.

[*Loyal and Humorous Songs*]. New York, 1779. Evans no. 16326.

Maccarty, Thaddeus. *Praise to God.* Worcester, Mass., [1776]. Evans no. 14830.

M'Culloch, John. *A Concise History of the United States.* 4th ed. Philadelphia, 1813.

Marini, Stephen. *Radical Sects of Revolutionary New England.* Cambridge, Mass., 1982.

Marsden, George M. *Fundamentalism and American Culture: The Shaping of Twentieth-Century Evangelicalism, 1870–1925.* New York, 1982.

———. *The Soul of the American University: From Protestant Establishment to Established Nonbelief.* New York, 1994.

Mather, Samuel. *All Men Will Not Be Saved Forever.* Boston, 1783. Evans no. 18031.

May, Henry. *The Enlightenment in America.* New York, 1976.

Mayhew, Jonathan. *A Letter of Reproof to Mr. John Cleaveland, of Ipswich.* Boston, 1764. Evans no. 9737.

———. *Popish Idolatry.* Boston, 1765. Evans no. 10068.

———. *A Sermon Preach'd in the Audience of His Excellency William Shirley, Esq.* Boston, 1754. Evans no. 7256.

*At a Meeting of the True Sons of Liberty, in New York, July 27, 1774.* [New York, 1774]. Broadside. Evans no. 13126.

Metzger, Charles. *Catholics and the American Revolution: A Study in Religious Climate.* Chicago, 1962.

———. *The Quebec Act: A Primary Cause of the American Revolution.* New York, 1935.

Middlekauff, Robert. *The Glorious Cause: The American Revolution, 1763–1789.* New York, 1982.

[Miles, William Augustus]. *Observations on the Answer of the King of Great Britain to the Manifesto, &c., of the Court of Versailles. By an Independent Whig.* London, 1779.

Miller, Perry. *Orthodoxy in Massachusetts.* Cambridge, Mass., 1933.

Moore, Frank. *Diary of the American Revolution.* 2 vols. New York, [1859].

Morgan, Edmund S. *The Gentle Puritan: A Life of Ezra Stiles.* New Haven, 1962.

——. *Visible Saints: The History of a Puritan Idea.* New York, 1963.

Morse, Jedidiah. *The American Geography; or, A View of the Present Situation of the United States of America.* Elizabethtown, N.J., [1789]. Evans no. 21978.

——. *Annals of the American Revolution.* 1824; rept., Port Washington, N.Y., 1968.

[Murray, John]. *Bath-Kol: A Voice from the Wilderness.* Boston, 1783. Evans no. 18040.

[——]. *Nehemiah: or, The Struggle for Liberty Never in Vain.* Newbury, Mass., 1779. Evans no. 16379.

Murray, John. *Universalism Vindicated.* Charlestown, Mass., [1798]. Evans no. 34161.

Nash, Gary. *Urban Crucible: Social Change, Political Consciousness, and the Origins of the American Revolution.* Cambridge, Mass., 1979.

Noll, Mark. *Christians in the American Revolution.* Washington, D.C., 1977.

Oliver, Peter. *Origin and Progress of the American Rebellion.* 1781; rept., ed. Douglass Adair and John Schutz, San Marino, Calif., 1961.

Otis, James. *A Vindication of the Conduct of the House.* Boston, 1762. Evans no. 9225.

Paine, Sarah Cushing, comp., and Charles Henry Pope, ed. *Paine Ancestry.* Boston, 1912.

Parrington, Vernon S. *The Colonial Mind, 1620–1800.* New York, 1927.

Parry, Clive, ed. *Consolidated Treaty Series.* New York, 1969.

Payson, Philips. *A Sermon Preached before the Honorable Council of Boston.* Boston, 1778. Evans no. 15956.

Petersen, William, Michael Novak, and Philip Gleason. *Concepts of Ethnicity.* Cambridge, Mass., 1982.

Peterson, Merrill, and Robert Vaughan, eds. *The Virginia Statute for Religious Freedom.* New York, 1988.

Phelps, Richard. *A History of Newgate of Connecticut.* Albany, N.Y., 1860.

Phillips, Joseph. *Jedidiah Morse and New England Congregationalism*. New Brunswick, N.J., 1983.

Pitkin, Timothy. *A Political and Civil History of the United States of America, from the Year 1763 to . . . 1797.* 2 vols. New Haven, 1828.

Public Archives of Canada. *Report concerning Canadian Archives for the Year 1904.* Appendix 1, "War of 1775–76." Ottawa, 1905.

Ray, Mary Augustina. *American Opinion of Roman Catholicism in the Eighteenth Century.* New York, 1936.

Roberts, Kenneth. *Arundel.* Garden City, N.Y., 1938.

——. *March to Quebec.* New York, 1938.

Robin, Claude. *New Travels through North America.* Trans. Philip Freneau. Philadelphia, 1783. Evans no. 18167.

Robinson, David. *The Unitarians and the Universalists.* Westport, Conn., 1985.

Royster, Charles. *A Revolutionary People at War: The Continental Army and American Character, 1775–1783.* Chapel Hill, N.C., 1979.

Scales, William. *The Confusion of Babel Discovered.* America, 1780. Evans no. 16989.

——. *Priestcraft Exposed from Its Foundation: or, Religious Freedom Defended.* Danvers, Mass., 1781. Evans no. 44057.

*Scots Anticipation: or, A Summary of a Debate Relating to Popery.* Edinburgh, 1779.

[Scott, John]. *Remarks on* The Patriot: *Including Some Hints respecting the Americans.* London, 1775.

*Secret Journals of the Continental Congress.* 4 vols. Boston, 1820–21.

Shaffer, Arthur. *The Politics of History: Writing the History of the American Revolution, 1783–1815.* Chicago, 1975.

Shaw, Peter. *American Patriots and the Rituals of Revolution.* Cambridge, Mass., 1981.

Shebbeare, J[ohn]. *An Answer to the Queries, Contained in a Letter to Dr. Shebbeare, Printed in the* Public Ledger. Dublin, 1775.

Shipton, Clifford K., ed. *Sibley's Harvard Graduates.* Vol. 4. Cambridge, Mass., 1933.

Shipton, Clifford K., and James E. Mooney, eds. *National Index of American Imprints through 1800: The Short-Title Evans.* 2 vols. Worcester, Mass., 1969.

Shortt, Adam, and Arthur G. Doughty, eds. *Documents Relating to the Constitutional History of Canada, 1759–1791.* 4 vols. Ottawa, 1918.

Smith, Justin H. *Our Struggle for the Fourteenth Colony.* 2 vols. New York, 1907.

[Smith, William]. *The Candid Retrospect; or The American War Examined by Whig Principles.* New York, 1780. Evans no. 16729.

*South End Forever, North End Forever:Extraordinary Verses on Pope-Night.* Boston, [1768]. Broadside. Evans no. 41883.

Sprague, William. *Annals of the American Pulpit.* 9 vols. New York, 1857–69.

Stevens, Benjamin. *Facsimiles of Manuscripts in European Archives Relating to America, 1773–1783.* 25 vols., London, 1889–98.

Stiles, Ezra. *History of Three of the Judges of Charles I.* Hartford, 1794. Evans no. 27743.

———. *The United States Elevated to Glory and Honor.* New Haven, 1783. Evans no. 18198.

Stillman, Samuel. *A Sermon Preached before the Honorable Council.* Boston, 1779. Evans no. 16537.

Stinchcombe, William. *The American Revolution and the French Alliance.* Syracuse, N.Y., 1969.

Tappan, David. *A Discourse Delivered at the 3rd Parish in Newbury.* Salem, Mass., 1783. Evans no. 18203.

Têtu, H., and Gagnon, C.-O., eds. *Mandements, lettres pastorales, et circulaires des évêques de Québec.* 2 vols. Quebec City, 1888.

*Three Curious Pieces: Being a Ready Way to Unpopularity: or, Truth a General Enemy.* Boston, 1782. Evans no. 17447.

[Towers, Joseph]. *A Letter to Dr. Samuel Johnson.* London, 1775.

Trumbull, Benjamin. *A Complete History of Connecticut, Civil and Ecclesiastical.* 2 vols. New Haven, 1818.

———. *A General History of the United States of America.* Boston, 1810.

Tucker, Josiah. *Cui Bono?* Glo[u]cester, [Eng.], 1781.

[———]. *Thoughts on the Present Posture of Affairs, July 24, 1779.* N.p., n.d.

Tuckerman, Bayard. *Life of General Philip Schuyler.* New York, 1903.

United States Continental Congress, 1774. *Extracts from the Votes and Proceedings of the American Continental Congress.* Philadelphia, 1774. Evans no. 13726.

United States Continental Congress, 1779. *Observations on the American Revolution.* Philadelphia, [1779]. Evans no. 16625.

Urquhart, M. C., and K. A. H. Buckley. *Historical Statistics of Canada.* Cambridge, Eng., 1965.

Verreau, Hospice, ed. *Invasion du Canada par les Américains.* Montreal, 1873.

Walett, Francis G. *Patriots, Loyalists, and Printers.* Worcester, Mass., 1976.

Walzer, Michael. *Just and Unjust Wars.* New York, 1977.

Warren, Mercy Otis. *History of the Rise, Progress, and Termination of the American Revolution*. 3 vols. 1805; rept. (3 vols. in 1), ed. Lester Cohen, Indianapolis, 1988.

*Warren-Adams Letters*. Ed. W. C. Ford. Vols. 1 and 2. Massachusetts Historical Society, *Collections* 72 (1917) and 73 (1925).

*Warren Papers*. Massachusetts Historical Society, *Collections*, 5th ser., 4 (1878).

Weber, Donald. *Rhetoric and History in Revolutionary New England*. New York, 1988.

West, Samuel. *Greatness the Result of Goodness: A Sermon, Occasioned by the Death of George Washington*. Boston, [1800]. Evans no. 39070.

Whitney, Peter. *Weeping and Mourning at the Death of Eminent Persons a National Duty*. Brookfield, Mass., 1800. Evans no. 39095.

Wigglesworth, Edward. *The Authority of Tradition*. Boston, 1778. Evans no. 16171.

Williams, Samuel. *A Discourse on the Love of Our Country*. Salem, Mass., 1775. Evans no. 14627.

——. *A History of the American Revolution*. 2d ed. Stonington, Conn., 1826.

Winthrop, John. *The History of New England from 1630 to 1649*. 2 vols. Boston, 1825.

Withington, Ann Fairfax. *Toward a More Perfect Union: Virtue and the Formation of American Republics*. New York, 1991.

Woodward, Samuel. *The Help of the Lord, in Signal Deliverances and Special Salvations*. Boston, 1779. Evans no. 16885.

Wright, Conrad. *The Beginnings of Unitarianism in America*. Boston, 1955.

——. *The Unitarian Controversy: Essays on American Unitarian History*. Boston, 1994.

Würtele, F. C., ed. *Blockade of Quebec in 1775–1776 by the American Revolutionists*. Literary and Historical Society of Quebec, *Historical Documents*. 7th ser. Quebec City, 1905.

Zagarri, Rosemarie. *A Woman's Dilemma: Mercy Otis Warren and the American Revolution*. Wheeling, Ill., 1996.

## ARTICLES

Bailyn, Bernard. "Religion and Revolution: Three Biographical Studies." *Perspectives in American History* 4 (1970): 85–172.

Beebe, Dr. Lewis. "Journal of a Physician in the Expedition against

Canada." Ed. Frederick Kirkland. *Pennsylvania Magazine of History and Biography* 59 (1935): 321–61.

Caron, Ivanhoë, ed. "Inventaire de la correspondance de Mgr. Jean-Olivier Briand, évêque de Québec, 1741 à 1794." *Rapport de l'Archiviste de la Province de Québec*, 1929–30: 45–136.

Coffin, Victor. "The Quebec Act and the American Revolution." American Historical Association, *Annual Report*. Washington, D.C., 1895.

Cogliano, Francis. "*Nil Desperandum Christo Duce*: The New England Crusade against Louisbourg, 1745," *Essex Institute Historical Collections* 128:3 (1992): 180–207.

Davis, Thomas J. "Images of Intolerance: John Calvin in Nineteenth-Century History Textbooks." *Church History* 65:2 (1996): 234–48.

Fauteux, Ægidius, ed. "Journal tenu par Mess. François Baby, Gab. Taschereau et Jenkin Williams. . . ." *Rapport de l'Archiviste de la Province de Québec*, 1927–28: 431–99.

——, ed. "Suite du Journal de la tournée faite par Messieurs Baby, Taschereau, et Williams, 1776 et 1777." *Rapport de l'Archiviste de la Province de Québec*, 1929–30: 137–40.

Gerstle, Gary. "The Protean Character of American Liberalism." *American Historical Review* 99:4 (1994): 1043–73.

Gordon, William. "Letters of William Gordon." *MHS Proceedings* 63 (1929–30): 303–613.

Greene, William. "Diary of William Greene." *MHS Proceedings* 54 (1920–21): 84–138.

Gura, Philip F. "The Role of the 'Black Regiment': Religion and the American Revolution." *New England Quarterly* 41:3 (1988): 439–54.

Labaree, Benjamin Woods. "Classrooms." *William and Mary Quarterly*, 3d ser., 52:3 (1995): 488–93.

Maier, Pauline. "The Pope at Harvard: The Dudleian Lectures, Anti-Catholicism, and the Politics of Protestantism." *MHS Proceedings* 97 (1986): 16–41.

Merritt, Percival. "Sketches of the Three Earliest Roman Catholic Priests in Boston." *Colonial Society of Massachusetts Transactions* 25 (1922–24): 173–228.

Nash, Gary. "The American Clergy and the French Revolution." *William and Mary Quarterly*, 3d ser., 22:3 (1965): 392–412.

[Ritzema, Rudolphus]. "Journal of Colonel Rudolphus Ritzema, of the 1st N.Y. Regiment, August 8, 1775, to March 30, 1776." *Magazine of American History* 1 (1877): 98–107.

Smith, Fitz-Henry, Jr. "The French at Boston during the Revolution." *Bostonian Society Publications* 10 (1913): 9–75.

——. "The Memorial to the Chevalier de Saint-Sauveur." *Bostonian Society Proceedings*, 1918: 31–58.

Upham, William P., ed. "Extracts from Letters Written at the Time of the Occupation of Boston by the British, 1775–6." *Historical Collections of the Essex Institute* 13:3 (1876): 153–236.

Zwierlin, F. J. "The End of No-Popery in the Continental Congress." *Thought* 11:3 (1936): 357–77.

# Index

Adams, Abigail, 104, 122
Adams, Hannah, 134, 136,
184–85
Adams, John: on French Alliance, 109, 110, 126, 133–
34, 196; on Quebec Act, 77,
78; on Quebec expedition,
69, 72, 73, 81; on religion,
11, 13–14, 133–34, 182,
183; on trade, 146, 147
Adams, Samuel, 69, 109–10
Adams, Rev. Zabdiel, 177
Allen, Ethan, 24, 25, 39, 79
Almanacs: and Guy Fawkes,
123, 143; portrayal, of
British in, 140–41; —, of
French, 99, 120, 121–22;
and Quebec Act, 13
*American Geography* (Morse),
150–52
Anglican Church. *See* England,
Church of
Anti-Catholicism: in anti-British
propaganda, 140, 141, 142,
143, 144; diminution of, 175,
189, 190; expressions of, by
John Adams, 13–14; —, by
American Tories, 89–90,
92–93, 94–96, 97; —, by

British, 47, 64, 90–92, 96,
181–82; —, by Timothy
Dwight, 207–8; —, by Wil-
liam Greene, 106–7; and
French Alliance, 20, 106,
137, 139; historians' treatment of, 16, 17; as New England tradition, 1, 4, 7, 8–14,
121; and papacy, 135; persistence of, 192, 194, 205, 219;
and Universalist controversy,
163, 169, 170, 171, 172, 175.
*See also* Dudleian Lectures
Antichrist, 9, 16, 160, 188
Arnold, Benedict: and Quebec
expedition, military aspects,
24, 25–26, 27–28, 29, 30; —,
political aspects, 41, 74, 79;
—, religious aspects, 6, 46;
and treason, 14, 97–98,
144–45
Association, Continental, 64,
89, 93, 149
Avery, Rev. David, 19–20

Baby, François, 31–32, 36–37,
51, 53, 55
Badeaux, Jean-Baptiste, 41, 47,
50, 51, 79

271